THE

DORSET

YEAR BOOK

FOR 2019

ONE HUNDRED AND TENTH YEAR OF ISSUE

First published in Great Britain in 2018 by The Society of Dorset Men

A CIP catalogue record for this book is available from the British Library.

Paperback ISBN 978-0-9926594-79

Price £8.00

Edited by Selwyn Williams

Printed and bound in Great Britain by
Print Team (Dorset) Limited
www.printteam.co.uk

Cover photo: Hell Lane, a holloway near North Chideock and Symondsbury - *Mark Godden*
See Hell Lane poem on Page 6

THE SOCIETY OF DORSET MEN

FOUNDED JULY 7th, 1904

'A Silver Tower Dorset Red Banner Bears'

President:
LORD FELLOWES OF WEST STAFFORD, DL

Deputy Presidents:
SIR ANTHONY JOLLIFFE, GBE, DL, D.Sc, D.Mus
DR. PAUL ATTERBURY, B.A. FRSA

Past Presidents:
SIR FREDERICK TREVES, BART, GCVO, CB, LLD, 1904 - 1907
THOMAS HARDY, OM, LITT.D, JP, 1907 - 1909
COLONEL JOHN MOUNT BATTEN, CB, 1909 - 1911
COLONEL SIR ROBERT WILLIAMS, BART, VD, 1911 - 1913
SIR STEPHEN COLLINS, JP, 1913 - 1915
JOHN CASTLEMAN SWINBURNE-HANHAM, JP, 1915 - 1919
THE RIGHT HON. The EARL of SHAFTESBURY, KP, PC, GCVO, 1919 - 1922, 1924 - 1925
CAPTAIN THE RIGHT HON. F. E. GUEST, CBE, DSO, 1922 - 1924
CAPTAIN ANGUS V. HAMBRO, DL, JP, 1925-33, 1936 - 1944
LIEUT.-COL. SIR PHILIP COLFOX, BART, MC, 1933 - 1936
H.E. THE RIGHT HON. LORD LLEWELLIN, CBE, MC, TD, DL, 1944 - 1957
BRIGADIER G. M. B. PORTMAN, CB, TD, DL, 1957 - 1961
ROBERT TOM WARREN, 1962 - 1963
COLONEL SIR RICHARD GLYN, BART, OBE, TD, DL, 1964 - 1969
SIMON WINGFIELD DIGBY, MA, TD, DL, 1970 - 1984
SIR ANTHONY JOLLIFFE, GBE, DL, D.Sc, D.Mus, 1984 - 2011

Past Hon. Secretaries:	Past Hon. Editors:
WILLIAM WATKINS, JP, 1904 - 1925	SIR NEWMAN FLOWER, 1914 - 1920
H. LL. WATKINS, 1925 - 1937	STANLEY L. GALPIN, 1920 - 1932
S . H. J. DUNN, 1937 - 1940	H. LL. WATKINS, 1935 - 1937
E. G. GALE, 1940 - 1941	ASHLEY C. ROGERS, 1937 - 1950
HARRY J. HARVEY, 1941 - 1942	FRANK C. H. DENNETT, 1951 - 1960
F. C. H. DENNETT, AACCA, FRES, 1942 - 1961	N. J. ('NAT') BYLES, 1961 - 1978
W. T. G. PERROTT, MIWO, 1961 - 1969	FRED LANGFORD, 1979 - 1994
J. C. R. PREWER, 1969 - 1979	GEORGE LANNING, 1995 - 2000
G. E. HINE, FRICS, 1979 - 2004	PETER PITMAN, 2001 - 2013
	TREVOR VACHER-DEAN, 2014 - 2015

INDEX *(Advertisers in Italics)*

Hell Lane

Fran Gardner

Grey day !

Festooned

In multi-shades

Of green.

Lichens, moss

Ferns.

Glow in

Faint light.

Shadows cast

On rocky sides.

Where names

Carved over

Years.

Stand in

Stark relief.

Gradually eroding,

As weather

Takes its

Toll.

A magical place.

Oozing history

From every

Pore and

Crevice.

James Albert Brown 1854 - 1911

Susan E. Dean (nee Brown)

The name James Albert Brown would not be instantly recognisable to the majority of Dorset inhabitants or even frequent visitors. Many more of us would have heard of 'Dancing Ledge', a long time attraction for lovers of sea and coast.

James, my great-grandfather was responsible for the creation of the pool at Dancing Ledge for Thomas Pellatt, the owner of Durnford House School. In the photograph of James (left) his damaged left eye is noticeable, caused by a mistimed explosion several years before his work for Mr. Pellatt. The Kelly's Directory of Dorset printed in 1895 is the first to mention Thomas Pellatt being resident at Durnford House, Langton Matravers. Chris Jesty in his 'Guide to the Isle of Purbeck' quotes that the pool was excavated in 1893.

James was christened at St. George's church Langton Matravers on 25th July 1854. His parents Timothy and Mary Ellen nee Chinchen had married at the same church on 22nd November 1853. James was the couple's first of eight children, four boys and four girls. James and his brother Timothy were the only sons who survived beyond childhood. All four sisters reached adulthood, Alice and Eleanor marrying young men from local families.

On 22nd December 1882 James Albert married his first cousin, Emily Mary Smith Brown at Wareham Register Office. He would have paid the marriage shilling when the Ancient Order of the Purbeck Marblers and Stonecutters met on the following Shrove Tuesday at Corfe Castle.

The Electoral Register of 1888 listed an Albert Brown, living at Langton Matravers and owning a dwelling at Acton, in Langton Parish. Kelly's Directory for Dorsetshire between 1890 and 1907 lists James Albert Brown as stone merchant, Purbeck Stone Works, Langton Matravers.

Shortly after the pool was excavated a metal grill was secured over the top of the pool to prevent its use by anyone other than the pupils of Durnford House School. Postcards of that time show what an oversized and ugly addition it seems to a very natural scene. The Kelly's Directory of 1895 lists John Bower, blacksmith, and perhaps he was behind the making and fixing of the metal grill for Thomas Pellatt. As can be seen from the postcard below, nature had the last word, the grill and most of its fixings were ripped away by a storm.

Dancing Ledge, Langton.

How James created the pool at Dancing Ledge is an interesting question. The tides and weather generally would have played a huge part in the timing.

Holes would be created at various depths in the rock to place the gelignite for a succession of small explosions to loosen the rock into smaller pieces for easier removal. After the area was cleared, James would have used a hammer and chisel to make the sides of the pool smoother; as the day wore on, he would be standing in deep water as the pool began to fill on the incoming tide.

James and Emily May had four children listed on census night 1891: Albert Samuel, my grandfather, born 1884; Grace Mansel born 1886, Sidney born 1888 and Florence Emily born 1890. Although damaged, the photograph [right] taken by W. Pouncy at Swanage shows a smartly dressed and well behaved family group. This kind of portrait sitting was expensive and it would appear

to have been taken around 1894. Was this one of the luxuries James purchased after his profitable excavation of the pool at Dancing Ledge?

"An Early Morning Dip"

James Albert Brown was buried in St. George's churchyard on 24th November 1911.

Common Rights by Devina Symes

Thinking back to those days beyond the track,
We had such freedom on the common land.
Where often 'mid the gorse, a piebald horse
Was seen drinking from the lake close at hand.

Everything was used, and nothing was abused,
Dried ferns were made into animal bedding,
Furze became a pyre, and used to light the fire,
Many folks dwelt there after their wedding.

Ancient common rights eased the labourer's plight,
Which lasted down the ages for many a century,
Ponies, donkeys, sows; horses, goats and cows,
All thrived on the Common, rent free.

Spring water was put on eyes that erupted in styes,
And before too long the redness would go,
Gypsies passing through, camped for a night or two,
Curing chilblains with spit and a cross on the toe.

Way back then, the common was alive with men,
And a host of wildlife thrived 'mid the heather.
Then came a new dawn, their rights were withdrawn,
And the old way of life gone for ever.

(Winfrith common changed when the UKAEA came in the 1950s)

Allan T. P. Cooper (1928-2017)

by his nephew, Paul Martyn Cooper

Allan moved to Wimborne Saint Giles in 1956 – with his wife and young son – to take up a teaching post in the village school. He would continue to live there, in the same house, for the rest of his life. But it was a Hampshire village that was the initial focal point of Allan's life. Allan was born on the 17th December 1928 at Sarisbury Green near the Hamble River in Hampshire and at the age of four he went with his loving parents Frank and Mary and baby brother Michael to live at a house about a mile away called 1, Sunnyside, overlooking the village green.

Here he knew the warmth and security of hearth and home, the companionship of a large extended family and friends around the Green, and on its east side at St Paul's church he was nourished in the Christian faith which would bring him joy, encouragement and consolation.

Allan's father, Frank, served in the Royal Navy from the time he left the Royal Hospital School, Greenwich in March 1918. Long periods of absence at sea for Frank, including during peace time, meant that family time together was especially precious and the family particularly enjoyed cycling along the river and nearby coast. It came as a devastating blow to Mary, Allan and Michael when Frank was killed on active service on the Russian convoy in Arctic waters in September 1942. Throughout their lives they would all cherish and revere Frank's memory. Mary continued to live at the house on the Green during a long widowhood – a stalwart of the village and the church, and a devoted grandmother.

Perhaps the example of his father's outstanding service influenced Allan in his career choices, or vocations, as a school teacher and then as a nurse. He took pride in obtaining the SRN qualification following three years training (1976-79) at the then Salisbury District Hospital. Certainly Allan was able to touch many lives for the good. His former pupil, Dr Steve Wharton, Senior Lecturer in French at Bath University, has written, "Allan was an inspirational teacher who enabled his pupils to realize their potential".

When I think of Allan I need to use the slightly old fashioned term 'school master' – as he retained that style and tone, a school master's enquiring mind and interest in others, and a schoolmaster's sociability and jocularity. I can imagine that Allan's piercing look, when directed at the school boys and girls in his charge, would have been enough to maintain order in class !

I got to know Allan better, and to understand him better, in the last thirty years or so. Allan created a home and garden which reflected aspects of his character and interests in a rather extraordinary way. Drawing near to the house dense planting meant that it remained somewhat hidden from view, perhaps a little off-putting. But it was the case that Allan had a fondness for nurturing trees from his youth, at times having used his mother's garden for tree growing experiments. Allan happily created a small scale sanctuary for wildlife welcoming and feeding foxes, the occasional pheasant which had hopped across from the Shaftesbury estate, a stray cat seeking a new home and perhaps a hedgehog, such as Thomas Hardy described in his poem Afterwards, which would travel "furtively over the lawn, One may say, He strove that such innocent creatures should come to no harm".

I made periodic visits to Saint Giles and I recall with pleasure Allan's welcome and hospitality, his keenness to share news of his daughters in France and Switzerland, including showing photos of his grandchildren and latterly his great-grandchildren.

Allan spent time and effort in building up a multi subject library – essentially a writer's reference collection – but ultimately the sheer volume of books overwhelmed any classified arrangement. Here he wrote the many articles he published about local history – in Fareham past and present with regard to Hampshire but particularly in The Dorset Year Book. Indeed, he was made a member of the Society of Dorset Men in recognition of 55 years of contributing to the yearbook. Wimborne Saint Giles church, its monuments and the lives of Shaftesbury family members from history were favourite subjects for him to write on.(*)

He maintained an extensive correspondence with family and old friends, including from college days at Trenton, New Jersey at the beginning of the 1950s. Trenton always provoked special memories for Allan – the scene, one felt, of his salad days. But he told me that he had become homesick by the end of his scholarship and in the time afterwards he was always very home oriented.

It is appropriate to close with a verse from Thomas Hardy. Born in the year that Hardy died, Allan would go on to form an abiding love for his adopted county of Dorset and he found beauty and solace in Hardy's writing.

From I Am the One,

I hear above: "We stars must lend
No fierce regard
To his gaze, so hard
Bent on us thus, -
Must scathe him not. He is one with us
Beginning and end."

(*) DYB 1972-1973,   "Wimborne Saint Giles, a guide to the parish church : A Ninian Comper restoration"
                  page 49-58

A T P Cooper
(Allan) of Wimborne St Giles who died on 24 Dec 2017

Martyn Cubitt

I first met Allan when we moved next door to him in the village over 20 years ago. We got a cheerful hello, a warm welcome, lots of useful information and an offer of help in any way he could; an offer that he made good countless times over the coming years.

As we set about getting our house and garden into shape over the coming months we shared countless cups of tea with Allan and not only learned a lot about him but also about the village, what happened here, who did what and who had done what. This was liberally laced with all sorts of other historical facts and stories about the school, the church, St Giles House, the local great families, the war, Sarisbury Green where he grew up, Lawrence of Arabia, teaching, nursing and plastic surgery – to only scratch the surface of where his conversation ranged.

Having clearly been adopted by Allan we were introduced gleefully to all and sundry on every possible occasion, which certainly helped us to get to know people and to feel at home so much so that we soon found that we had been quietly volunteered for practically everything. Our friendship grew, helped by sharing a love of books but my avid and rather excessive accumulation of books paled into insignificance compared to Allan's. He had them everywhere and he continued to gather them until he could no longer physically do it.

To Allan books were a real gateway to knowledge and understanding and fed his inquiring mind. An avid writer as well as reader, he corresponded widely and was not beyond writing in person to the author of this book or that offering usually a favourable critique and not infrequently an interesting anecdote or fact pertinent to the subject. So one found in his rather rambling archive, a filing system does not describe it, letters from the likes of A L Rowse the historian and Sir John Betjeman and on his shelves or in the middle of a pile of books might be found volumes personally inscribed to him from a remarkable range of people.

Allan was in fact a man of letters, having had learned papers published in a number of journals which betrayed both a fascination with history and an appetite for research which was always meticulous. With such an interest and ability it was no surprise to learn that he had come to the village in 1956 to take up a post as junior master at St Giles School, then taking pupils up to the age of 14. Talking to his former pupils, and there are many, they all remember him and although it is clear that he was one of the old school as far as classroom discipline was concerned, there is no doubt that his main desire was to see all his charges do well and get on in life. An accomplished pianist he shared in the school's music activities and I remember being serenaded through the party wall of our house on many an occasion by delightful recitals. In teaching he was ahead of his time in many ways and is still remembered for instigating an exchange of pupils audio diaries with schools in Canada and Africa which he, meticulously of course, produced using a reel to reel recorder when such instruments were rare – no blogs or social media in those days. After twenty years at the school he retired from teaching for a number of personal reasons.

He decided to train as a nurse and persuaded the authorities that despite his age, and being a man, less usual in nursing in those days, that they should take him on. After completing his training he worked with vulnerable teenagers in West London while waiting for the results of his finals. Then, as a newly qualified SRN he started nursing at Salisbury General Hospital where he continued mainly in the Plastic Surgery Department until he retired.

He was a devout man and attended services at St Giles, then high church, soon after arriving. He became a committed member of the church council and a Sanctuary Server. In 1976 our local parishes were reorganised and amalgamated and St Giles moved to its broad church pattern of services that we still have, while retaining one High Mass on the first Sunday. The Rev Robert Prance remembers that Allan's support for the changes helped him greatly in what could have been a very difficult time. Allan attended church until he was no longer able. I can picture him each high mass with his incense burner, robed and with a ruff like a mischievous choirboy. His long attendance at church council meetings must be a record, his interventions were enthusiastic, animated, frequently interesting although some times on a totally unrelated subject. The meetings now are not the same without him although noticeably shorter.

Among the many products of his historical research are the history of the church and the chronicle of the great restoration after the fire of 1908 which he also had printed. He also participated in the writing of a history of the village itself. He contributed numerous articles to the Dorset Yearbook on a range of subjects many linked to Dorset and St Giles history. The Society of Dorset Menvisited him a couple of years ago to present him with the parchment warrant of an Honorary Man of Dorset, which he greatly enjoyed.

At home he was an accomplished cook and housekeeper and a keen but not ostentatious gardener. He was green before it became fashionable and a self appointed guardian of wildlife and trees, both of which in due course came to fill his garden. He rescued abandoned cats, and some that hadn't been abandoned, and he was the self appointed guardian of all moles in the school playing field, which I, as a school governor, with the aid of our excellent mole catcher, Lewis Burroughs was doing my best to deport. He certainly lived life fully and believed in doing things, he fixed gates and stiles, he cleaned headstones in the cemetery, and we learn from a 1970s newspaper cutting, while chairman of the Parish Council and its successor Knowlton Parish Council, he was the driving force in getting a conservation area established here.

Allan's presence out and about in the village was as tangible as the Church clock or the village sign. He was there to be seen and to talk to, though often this carried a time penalty. He was remarkably hardy and braved all weathers, always with a cheerful countenance and a hearty greeting for all he met. Many of us will remember him walking Bottlebush Lane for the weekly Salisbury bus, a good mile and a half, and returning laden with shopping, and, yes, books. In more recent years when the bus called here he could be seen again in all weathers on the seat under St Giles waiting for the bus. Once on the bus he was familiar with all the regular users and presided over each journey rather like a scoutmaster on an educational outing.

Although always outgoing and enthusiastic, Allan remained a very private man. Always willing to tell you the facts of his life but never disclosing the emotions that they aroused in him. I know a lot about him but at the same time very little. He never complained or fretted at adverse circumstances and either accepted them or tried to do something positive about them. A complex man we cannot explain him, let us just remember him as we each saw him, part of the spirit of Wimborne St Giles, a good friend, a good neighbour, Allan Cooper.

The Plum Tree

(With acknowledgement to F.W.J)

Do'ee mind wold Varmer Dan
'Ee wor woonce a labouring chap
Till 'ee got our Susan Ann
By vallin' in 'er lap

Well ! this yer tree, it were a plum
Vunny things they be
Cos' this yer branch, en went an' broke
'An zet poor Susan vree

Tis loike this yer it comes about
Wold Dan wor spreadin' muck
When zuddenly 'ee 'eard a zhout
Dan'l yere Oi be stuck !

Both went down wi' a vearsome crash
But Dan'l - lucky chap
'Ee cum down last an' landed clear
Right in our Susan's lap

Twas vrom the top of a girt big tree
Young Susan, wor 'er zeen
Wi' dress all broke and feace all rid
An uppity zort a' queen

Susan made out zhe were bad
An' zaid "Please carry Oi"
Zo feelin' nice while in 'is arms
Thought zhe -' Ee'l marry I

What be up to? Dan'l cried
But Susan wi' a frown
Said " Doant 'ee look up. Dan'l dear
Oi be up an' caint get down

Zo Dan'l vound that vrom that day
'Ee never were alone
'Cos Susan went an' badgered 'ee
Until 'ee wor 'er own

Zo Dan'l looked - an scratched his head
An 'ee went white skeered
Zaw Susan hanging be 'er dress
She'll vall ! 'ee zaid Im veared

Now Dan'l zez "Jest listen y'ere
They Plum trees, doant'ee zee
Baint t' zame as Oaks or Ash
But what a plum wor zhe!

Zo off 'ee goes - a ladder gets
To rest agin a branch
On which t' belt o' Susan's dress
'Ad caught be lucky chance

Zo doant'ee climb nar Plum tree now
Dratted things they be
These might not vind a Susan there
But Wopsies - zertainly.

Good timing

Found in "Dorset Up Along and Down Along 1935"

FARMER: Well me bwoy, what do 'ee want then?

A FARM LAD: A place, plaze, zur!

FARMER: What have 'e left down therevor?

FARM LAD: Wael , 'twas jist like this , zur - Vust the woold zow died,we salted she in, an ate she: then the woold cow died, we salted she in and ate she: then the woold 'ooman died, they zent I vor the salt, and I comed on .

Keeping the oldest profession alive on Portland

Mark Godden

Despite rumours to the contrary, I like to speculate that quarrying is in fact the oldest profession. The exploitation of Dorset's rich and varied mineral wealth is at least as old as farming and fishing within the county.

In the past, transporting building stones over any distance would have been onerous, and hence parochial buildings were traditionally constructed using locally sourced rocks, often extracted from nearby quarries or 'borrow-pits'. This is one of the reasons why many older buildings in Dorset's villages and hamlets mirror their underlying geology and tend to look like comfortable extensions of the ground upon which they are founded. Consequently, villages in different parts of Dorset, which overlie different rock types, often exhibit quite different styles of vernacular architecture. The same principle holds true on the Isle of Portland where, for 'time-out-of-mind', buildings were invariably constructed using Portland stone. There is an important distinction however, for the last three hundred years, the white oolitic limestone quarried on Portland has influenced the visage of architecture across a very much wider sphere, literally covering the four corners of the Earth.
Portland limestone was originally dubbed 'superior oolite' by Victorian geologists, unfortunately this was because of its stratigraphic position in relation to the slightly older and hence more deeply buried inferior and great oolites – not it's superior quality!

Portland stone was laid down at the very end of the Jurassic period (around 145 million years ago) in a warm sub-tropical corner of the Tethys Ocean, an ocean which has now been tectonically squeezed out of existence. The freestone beds on Portland were largely spared the crushing tectonic forces which tightly buckled and fractured so many of the other, more unfortunate rocks that are exposed along Dorset's Jurassic Coast. Portland Stone (or at least the Portland Stone from Portland) has survived its 145-million-year journey through geological time, remaining reasonably unmolested by earth movements, so that Portland's quarrymen are now able to extract large blocks of building stone (dimension stone) with no tectonically induced flaws. The Portland Stone found around Swanage and on the Ridgeway to the north of Weymouth is often not so lucky, this stone has been more tectonized and therefore tends to be more fractured. Portland Stone is composed almost entirely of billions of minute calcareous spheres called ooliths. The calcium carbonate which forms the ooliths was chemically precipitated from sea water and it is this that gives Portland stone its famously desirable white colour. Portland stone is strong enough to resist the attack of rain and frost but not so strong that it can't be readily cut and shaped by stonemasons.

When Sir Christopher Wren came to Portland to find a stone type suitable for the re-building of St Paul's Cathedral after the original one burnt down in London's great fire of 1666; the stone was easily sourced. Geologically recent land-slips had placed huge quantities of good building stone onto the beaches between Balaclava Bay and Church Ope Cove, on the island's north-east coast. It would have been relatively simple for the quarrymen of the time to square these blocks and then move them onto barges for transportation along

England's south coast and up the river Thames into the heart of London.

All the above elements came together in the late 17th Century to effectively kick-start Portland's stone industry which is still going strong today.

Over three hundred years of continuous opencast quarrying has left its mark upon Portland's landscape. The Island is littered with holes from which stone was once extracted. Fortunately, many of these former quarries have returned to nature and become legally protected homes to numerous rare types of plant and animal. The Demographic of Portland's populace has similarly changed quite radically over the last 100 years. Where once almost every resident either worked (or was closely linked to others who worked) in the stone industry, this is not true today. Environmental disturbances caused by opencast quarrying which would have once been tolerated as an economic imperative are no longer viewed quite so stoically. The size of Portland's population has also increased, which has yielded a proportional increase in the pressure on land use. Potential quarrying land has now become very scarce on Portland.

For all these reasons, in the late 1990's Albion Stone, a company employing 70 people on Portland, began to consider underground mining as a more environmentally acceptable and hence sustainable way of extracting stone from areas on Portland where opencast quarrying would be completely impractical.

With no historical precedents to follow, Albion Stone began the first underground mining of Portland Stone ever to take place on the island in 2002. Following a very complex planning process, a trial mine was established in the south-west corner of Bowers Quarry and within this mine, safe and successful working methods began to be refined. The trial mine was eventually rolled out (along with all the lessons learned during its development) into other more productive underground mining operations.

Jordans Mine, located in the former Jordans Quarry to the north-west of Easton, was begun in 2008 and the nearby

The twin portals at Jordans Mine, this operation was begun in 2008 and has yielded tens of thousands of tonnes of top quality building stone

Bowers Playing Fields Mine was started in Bowers Quarry, a few years after that. Both operations are currently working at full capacity.

Albion Stone has also won planning permission to mine stone from beneath a 60-acre agricultural area which lies between Weston and Southwell known as Stoneshill. Some enabling work has already been done there but no underground mining has yet begun. The reserves of Portland stone still entombed at Stoneshill are expected to yield good stone for many decades into the future.

The availability of sophisticated mining machinery which was being introduced by Fantini, a mining equipment manufacturer based in Italy, at around the same time as the trial mine was being established greatly assisted with the development of a viable mining process on Portland. Albion Stone has worked closely with Fantini, tweaking their standard designs to produce machines that are custom built for working in Portland's geology. These machines are electrically powered, computer controlled and fitted with diamond tipped chain-saw type blades.

called Hydro-Bags, which forcefully inflate when pumped full of water. This powerful – yet gentle procedure ensures that valuable stone is not accidentally damaged during the mining process.

A Basebed face within Jordans Mine, which has been cut using a Fantini mining machine, loosened by Hydro-Bags and is awaiting extraction by forklift.

Large forklift trucks, custom made by Volvo to fit in the mines are used to take the loosened blocks out of the mines where they are either sold to other stone masonry contractors or processed in Albion Stone's own factory which is the largest stone processing works in the UK. This factory supplies bespoke finished stone masonry for either restoration or new-build projects world-wide.

A remotely controlled Fantini mining machine making cuts in a working face within Jordans Mine.

A Volvo fork lift transporting a large block of Basebed out of Bowers Mine

Blocks of dimension stone weighing up-to 20 tonnes can be cut from the ground. These blocks are then displaced using innovative steel envelopes (or pillows)

The layout (in pan-view) of Albion Stone's mining operations is based upon a 6.5m x 6.5m grid. Pillars are a minimum of 6.5m square and roadways are all 6.5m wide. The ratio of mined area to unmined area maintained at a maximum of 3:1 or put another way, a minimum of 25% of the mine's area remains untouched to form the pillars needed to safely support the mine's roof.

Evenly spaced, 2.4m long high tensile steel rock-bolts are also used to systematically reinforce the mine's roof and stabilize pillars as mining advances. The competency of the roof is continuously checked by survey and very little deflection of the roof-beam

Roof bolting operations
taking place in Bowers Mine

has been measured in the last ten years (typically just a few millimetres).

Albion Stone's Jordans and Bowers Basebed, a very fine grained stone, used in many applications where few shell inclusions are desirable.

The mines are force ventilated. Large electrically driven fans deliver a high

volume of fresh air to the deepest parts of the workings via flexible ducting. The purpose of the air is to efficiently flush diesel exhaust fumes out of the mine. Besides a small amount of radon, there are no naturally occurring poisonous or explosive gasses in the rocks on Portland.

Albion Stone's Ostrea Patch Reef Whitbed, this attractive bed of stone contains the trace fossils of oyster patch reef.

Portland stone comes in three main beds. Basebed is the oldest (and deepest) bed. It is typically very homogenous and contains few visible shell fragments. Whitbed which can vary between being shell-free to containing heavy inclusions of shell and other types of fossil.

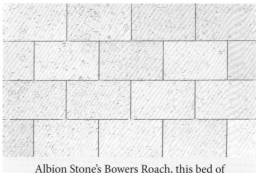

Albion Stone's Bowers Roach, this bed of stone was used to construct the famous Cobb (breakwater) at Lyme Regis.

Roach is the youngest (and upper-most) bed of Portland Stone. Roach is full of high-spired gastropod fossils called Aptyxiella portlandica or more colloquially 'Portland screws' giving Roach its very distinctive appearance.

St James's Market in central London. The Basebed and Whitbed used on this magnificent building was mined and processed by Albion Stone during 2015.

Albion Stone regularly supplies finished Portland stone for export to prestigious building projects around the world but main market for Portland stone still lies within central London. Some of the more notable London projects completed by Albion Stone within the last six years include:

* Wilkins Terrace UCL, London WC1E, completed in 2017.
* The Clarges Estate, Mayfair, London, completed 2017.
* St James's Market, London SW1, completed in 2016.
* The World Conservation and Exhibitions Centre at the British Museum, London, completed in 2014.
* The Bomber Command Memorial in Green Park, London W1, completed in 2012.
* Green Park Tube Station, London W1, completed in 2012.

The work to develop a viable method of mining Portland stone from underground has extended the life of Portland's stone industry well into the foreseeable future. Mining allows this unique building material to be extracted and make its on-going contribution to both historical and contemporary architecture. Furthermore, this work can take place without causing unacceptable environmental disturbances to those living nearby whilst at the same time, providing much needed employment for local people – keeping the oldest profession going for a while longer yet.

Darzet Skiver Cake - *Hayne Russell*

"You puts yer piece o' bacon in a pot an then when he 've a-cooked a bit, put in yer cabbage, then whack up yer dough enough vor the family an' put 'ee in on top. That be yer Skiver Cake, that is, an' good vor 'ee too. But don'ee drow away the water 'tis biled in. Drink that there an' 'twill kip away all manner o' diseases."

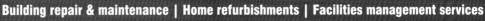

Reflections

Mary Bevan

From Thomas Hardy's Notebooks:
July 1876 "Rowed on the Stour in the evening, the sun setting up the river…Mowers salute us. Rowed among the water-lilies to gather them. Their long, ropey stems."
August 1913 "…visited Blandford with John Lane the publisher…….sent sister Katharine a picture postcard from the Crown Hotel…"

On a balmy August night in 1913, two gentlemen stood in companionable silence on the doorstep of the Crown Hotel in the little Dorsetshire town of Blandford Forum. The two men were both eminent in their respective fields - John Lane, co-founder of the Bodley Head Press, and the author and poet Thomas Hardy.
"I think you said you lodged here once before, did you not, Tom?" enquired Lane.
Hardy reflected. "Oh many years ago – when I was a young man."
"Ah, the years, the years," sighed Lane. "Well, very pleasant, very pleasant. And as excellent a piece of mutton as I've tasted in some time. And now I'm for bed – we've an early start tomorrow."

Hardy contemplated the constellations sprinkling the night sky, "Oh, I fancy I'll stay outside a little while longer. Good night to you, John."

Left alone, he leaned comfortably against the bricks of the old building that gave back the heat of the day. In fact, the mention of an earlier visit here had set off a train of memories. These, and the beauty of the night, now put it into his head to walk the few steps down to the bridge over the River Stour to reflect and remember.

As he neared the bridge, a ribbon of light from a window some distance away picked out the ancient stone parapet with the river flowing darkly and fast beneath it. A clump of water lilies on its surface glowed white in the darkness. And immediately he was travelling back through the years to those summer evenings of early marriage when he and Em had rowed till sunset a few miles upstream at Sturminster Newton. They had gathered armfuls of these lilies, he remembered, their long, ropey stems spattering Em's skirt with water as she laughed while the boat rocked dangerously. How happy they had been then: their 'two-year idyll' he called it, the time before difficulties and disappointments had begun to engulf them. And how hopeful he had been for the future. And now Emma herself was gone – without even a word of farewell to him, her husband, leaving him only the chasm of mutual recrimination that had opened up between them. Oh, the love thing!
As for his young dreams, it was true that he had finally become a celebrated writer - but at what expense? Forced to endure long periods of public and domestic criticism, and with Tess and Jude savaged by his detractors, he had felt forced to abandon novel-writing and had many times even questioned the point of going on at all.

Standing there, caught up in these increasingly dark thoughts, he was reminded of his own creation – Henchard, Mayor of Casterbridge – standing on a bridge over another Dorset river, emptied by misfortune of the will to live, alone and seeking an end of his suffering. Beneath him, he too had heard the dark water suck and sigh as it did now.

With a sudden exclamation he pulled himself away. These were unhealthy indulgencies in melancholy. He was simply exhausted. The whole bad business of Emma's sudden death had brought him down cruelly. He shook his head in agitation and turned quickly towards the lights of the town.

At the hotel he was confronted by an unexpected reception committee in the shape of the landlord and a lanky, embarrassed-looking boy. The landlord was effusive – the family had attended a funeral in Oxford the day before, so he had not been there to welcome his prestigious visitor. It was a singular honour to have such an important guest under his roof; he hoped Mr Hardy had found everything to his liking. And so on.

"May I take the liberty," he gushed, "to introduce to you my son, who I may say devours your books as soon as he can lay hands on them."

Hardy looked at the boy, who seemed to be contemplating his boots. "And which of my pieces have you read?" he asked kindly.

The boy looked up immediately and said, with great intensity, "All of them, sir. They inspire me, sir."

"The fact is, Mr Hardy," his father broke in, "my son has the ambition to become a writer – but I tell him one in a thousand men have the ability to succeed in the profession. Am I not right, sir?" he paused, looking to Hardy for some sign of agreement.

Hardy regarded the young man in silence. In the light of his recent melancholy thoughts on the subject, what could, or should, he tell this boy, who reminded him somewhat of his young self? The direction of the boy's life might hang on his answer.

"I can say only that the decision must be yours and yours alone,' he said at length. 'The life of a writer is hard and lonely. There will be set-backs and rejections: at times you may almost despair. But if you are driven to write because you believe you have something to say that others must hear you will find you have no choice but to do it. I wish you well, young sir, and now if you will excuse me."

Climbing the stairs to his room he found himself in lighter mood: the short encounter seemed to have done him good. All-in-all, had he not won through in life? His works were read and acclaimed and had, perhaps, the power to inspire a new generation of writers. He was blessed with good friends and with Florence, soon to become his wife. And then there was the great outpouring of poetry that had begun in response to Emma's death and his recent pilgrimage to Cornwall to find again the girl with chestnut hair and rose-flushed cheeks he had once fallen in love with. He supposed life could hardly be said to have treated him too badly.

Even now, as he entered his room, a line of poetry on that theme was forming in his head. Seizing the moment, he sat down at the small table, drew out a sheet of paper, and began to write,

"Well world, you have kept faith with me, kept faith with me."

The Dorset Trumps

by John Travell

Going through the old membership lists in the Year Books to check the membership dates for the founder of the RAF, Sir Hugh Trenchard, I found three members with another, now very well-known but not very common, name - Trump. These were: Albert Henry, of the Cross Keys, Bridport; Walter, of the Greyhound, Bridport; and Ernest, who lived in Salisbury.

by immigrants, most Americans have an interest in where their families originally came from. Several former American Presidents, such as John Kennedy and Bill Clinton, have been very pleased to visit the places where the previous generations of their kinsfolk had lived before their parents or grandparents had up-rooted themselves to start a new life in another country. It

With Donald, the President of the United States, about to make an official visit to London, I naturally wondered whether there was any ancestral connection with the Trumps of Dorset. If there was such a link, then it seemed to me that we should pass this information on to him and perhaps invite him to become an Honorary Life Member of this Society, and welcome him to visit his ancestral county. Since the United States, more than any other country, has been built

also occurred to me that, as Albert Henry had by 1930, moved from Bridport to the Rock Hotel in Weymouth, this would be an additional personal reason for the present President of the United States to visit there. It has always seemed to me that Weymouth and Portland ought to be a major place of pilgrimage for any Americans visiting this country, and that big opportunities were missed, particularly in 1994 and again in 2004, when President Reagan and then

President Bush came to the Normandy beaches to mark the anniversaries of the D-Day landings to liberate Europe. Since the vast majority of the American forces – more than half-a-million men – gathered and then left for the beaches of Omaha and Utah from Portland and Weymouth, both these Presidents would surely have welcomed an invitation to lay a wreath at the American Memorial on Weymouth Esplanade, which commemorates this enormous historic event in which these, and other Dorset towns, played such a vital and prominent part.

My son Richard, who is an expert genealogist, tells me that the Dorset Trumps came from Beaminster, where Henry Trump was buried in 1754. Daniel Trump, who was the grandfather of our Dorset Men Trumps, was a sacking weaver in Clapton, Somerset, and was married in South Perrott on 21 October, 1832. Walter was born in 1869, Albert Henry in 1873, and Ernest in 1885. However, although the social background of the President's ancestors is similar to the Trumps of Dorset, his family originated from a small village in Kallstadt in the Palatinate, in the German Rhineland, an area famous for its pork belly delicacy and the birthplace of H.J. Heinz, the inventor of tomato ketchup.

The original German name (Drumph), which in America was simplified to 'Trump', meant a 'drum' or a 'trumpet.' Donald Trump's grandfather moved to America and became a barber in New York. Like the Dorset Trumps he also ran restaurants and hostelries that prospered from serving the prospectors who became wealthy in the gold rush. But, if no personal link can be found between the present President of America and the Trumps of Dorset, I still think that whenever future American Presidents visit this country - and especially when they come to take part in commemorative events to mark the important anniversaries of the D-Day landings - Weymouth and Portland should not be diffident about inviting them to come and pay tribute to all the American troops who gathered and left to fight on the beaches from there.

New Year's Eve 2017

Judi Moore

For nearly a year now we have come
here to the harbour most nights
to see what boats are in, listen
to rigging slapping against masts
admire the touring yachts and greet the local
fishing boats: 'Faith' of Scilly; 'Hannah Beth' of Dartmouth;
'Melwey', named for our river; 'Boy Michael' of Colchester
and all the little Weymouth crab and cockle boats,
named for beloved mothers, wives and daughters
(all martyrs to rust and hard work).

It's nearly midnight. All the parties
are in full swing. Music and laughter bounce
from one side of the harbour to the other,
ricochet around the house-clad hill of Chapelhay,
and the tall brick buildings of Brewers Quay.

And suddenly it's time: the bell
of St Mary's, nestled deep within
the Georgian centre of the town, begins
to ring out the old year, ring in the new.

And after every robust strike,
we hear two echoes, like a descant,
floating o'er the water, as everything does here,
building a bridge between past and future.
Two extra chimes, coming from nowhere,
acknowledged by no-one, resonating,
harmonising, emphasising.

Thirty six ghostly chimes are
an affirmation, at New Year's midnight,
that hammer home how right I was
to up sticks, cats and books, blow in
and anchor on this unknown shore.

The Late Ron Chandler DFM, The Last of The Tail End Charlies

Brian C. Moore

Early in December 1945 a 20 year old RAF Sergeant with one leg missing was escorted into the investiture room of Buckingham Palace where King George VI pinned the Distinguished Flying Medal on to the breast of his best blue. The King thanked the young man for so gallantly serving his country and asked about the action which led to him being so honored.

Sixty years later Ron Chandler, of Sherborne, told me: "I didn't know what to say then and I still don't. However, like I told His Majesty, I was stuck in the rear turret of a Lancaster bomber 15,000 feet up in the night sky over Germany with enemy aircraft attacking from all sides. I had nowhere to go and until my ammunition was gone I simply lined German fighters up in my sights and kept firing. It was what I was trained to do, it is what I did.'

Ron Chandler DFM made his final journey across the Styx in 2016, followed by his wife, June, soon after. For the short time they were apart he would have missed her more than life itself. A few months prior to his death he allowed me to photograph him one last time. I captioned the picture, 'The Last of the Tail End Charlies'

Sergeant Air Gunner Ron Chandler, 1943

A shy and withdrawn man Ron made light of his DFM which is inscribed with the words 'For Courage'. He was adamant that he possessed no more courage than the rest of the crew of the Lancaster bomber or any member of 57 Squadron as they flew toward a ball bearing factory near the town of Schweinfurt on the night of 15 April 1944, intent on disrupting the industrial output of the Third Reich.

He said: "We took off from East Kirby near Boston, Lincolnshire at 20.00 hours - that's 8.00pm. We had a three hour flight ahead of us and a payload of 8,000 to 10,000lbs of conventional bombs. It was our seventh mission out of a possible 30. There were seven in the crew. I was the tail gunner, 'Tail-end Charlie', just like in the film starring Christopher Plummer and Edward Woodward. The film was lifelike – the flying, but not the rest.

"We lumbered down the airstrip in what was the crème-de-la-crème of the RAF bomber force and strained to climb into the night sky as our four Rolls Royce Merlin XX engines, with a combined take-off thrust of 5120 hp, drove us upwards against the awesome pull of gravity. Take off was always a bit stomach-churning when we carried a maximum load, which we invariably did, and being the tail end Charlie I was the last one to view the receding runway as we banked, and climbed to our designated height. There were rare occasions when an aircraft didn't get lift off but I rarely dwelt on that possibility.

"We climbed to around 15,000 feet, switched over to oxygen, took our allocated place in the stacking, and along with countless other squadrons from all over East Anglia headed out over the east coast toward our target. We always flew at night while the Americans in their B17s handled the daylight shift. Two and a half hours into the mission German fighters honed in on the formations and hell came calling. We downed one or two but they came at us in waves and suddenly I saw one coming straight for me. I was firing continuously but his bullets laced into my glass shell and smashed my leg. All I can recall is the pain and the loneliness of being a tail end Charlie. It was like being round the corner and out of sight down a long lonely road.

"I couldn't radio forward as the lines were smashed. I laid there bleeding and prayed the fighter wouldn't come back but he did and I let him have it. I emptied my gun at him, saw a plume of smoke and he disappeared. I was losing a lot of blood but no way was our pilot going to turn back. I was on my own. It is a long way from the pilot's seat to the rear of the plane and I knew that without help I was a goner. But I also knew the ball bearing factory had to be blasted away. I was twenty years old and alone looking out into a freezing night sky 15,000 feet up with little protection from the elements and all I wanted to do was live. It is sixty one years ago and I can remember it like yesterday.

"Twenty minutes or so after the fighter incident I heard the call; 'Bombs away,' we had completed our outward mission. That was the most important part of the operation. As we turned for home one of the crew came back to check on me. His name was Philip Baker a New Zealander. I'd love to meet him again – he saved my life. He put a tourniquet on my thigh to stop the bleeding, dragged me up into the belly of the aircraft and nursed me all the way back to Blighty.

"We were badly shot up but managed to drop into Tangmere on the south coast. Most of the tail had gone and part of the fuselage as well as my gun turret. The Lancaster could fly on half an engine and a bit of a wing we all reckoned. It was the supreme flying machine and lorded it over Bomber Command. I exaggerate - but only just.

"I was operated on at Chichester then sent to RAF Halton. My leg was gone but I had my life thanks to Phil Baker. I was fitted with a new leg at Roehampton in the same hospital that looked after Douglas Bader and thousands of other servicemen.

They gave me the DFM and told me if it hadn't been for me knocking out the fighter we would all have been goners. I didn't deserve it any more than the thousands of other young men who never made it back. Please don't make me out a hero I am far from that."

Ron Chandler was Dorset through and through and any man detecting a slight London lilt to his accent and dared suggest he was a stranger to his adopted county was likely to receive a stern rebuff. Born in Watford in 1925 he and his wife June lived in Dorset so long they all but forgot their birth roots and if it wasn't for family ties Ron claimed he would never have crossed the county border.

He spent many years working for Plessey's at their Templecombe factory and after his retirement in 1990 they lived quietly in the village of Oborne near Sherborne where they created a special English country garden.

Ron and June claimed to owe much to Dorset and over the years endeavored to repay their perceived debt by fostering many of the county's needy children and providing a family environment in their Sherborne home for those less fortunate than themselves.

June said, "There was a desperate need for foster parents and Ron and I decided that we would like to put something back into the community. It was hard at first but gradually we became quite expert at handling homeless young people and found great satisfaction in seeing them grow both physically and in self esteem. Dorset has a fostering and adoption service to be proud of."

Ron had the final word. "The proudest moment in our whole lives came in 1994 when we went to the Devon and Dorset recruit passing out parade in Staffordshire and watched our nineteen year old foster son march past after completing his twelve week training course. He took us to lunch in the soldiers mess and it was like being back with my own mates in 1944. I was as proud then as when I met the King."

Ron Chandler DFM, 11th Feb 2005

Post Script. From Air Chief Marshall Sir Arthur (Bomber) Harris.

"The Lancaster surpassed all other types of heavy bomber. Not only could it take heavier bomb loads, not only was it easier to handle, not only were there fewer accidents with this than with any other type throughout the war, the casualty rate was also considerably below other types. I used the Lancaster alone for those attacks which involved the deepest penetration into Germany and were, consequently, the most dangerous. I would say this to those who placed that shining sword in our hands. Without your genius and efforts we could not have prevailed, for I believe the Lancaster was the greatest single factor in winning the war."

Fifty Years of Writing for the Dorset Year Book

by Devina Symes

One autumn afternoon in 1966, when I was fourteen years of age, without preface I took myself off to the quiet sitting room, sat down by the window and penned my first poem, 'Autumn'.

My grandmother, who worked for the Salvation Army, was so taken with it that she showed it to the Major when she got to work the next day, the result being that he

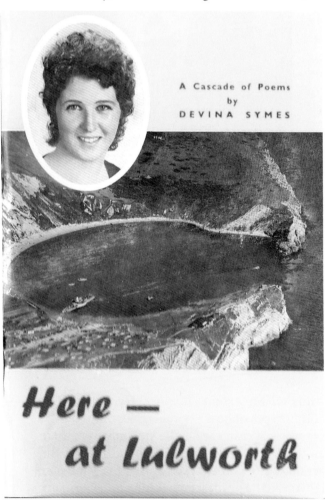

A Cascade of Poems
by
DEVINA SYMES

Here —
at Lulworth

sent it to 'The Young Soldier' magazine, the Salvation Army's magazine for children, and I won first prize, receiving 7 shillings

and 6d, (37 and a half pence today), and I had my poem in print.

Soon after this, my father, Leslie, showed me some Dorset Year Books, and poetry books, and in particular the poetry of William Barnes and Thomas Hardy. I loved them both, particularly the Dorset dialect, which, perhaps because of my deep Dorset roots, struck a chord within me, and I quickly wrote my first dialect poem.

Having had my interest in all things Dorset fired up, my poems continued to flow , and when my father joined the Society of Dorset Men in 1968, we both submitted articles, which were successful, mine being my poem, Autumn, and a very short story about Portland. And so it was from that 1968/69 Dorset Year Book that my submitting articles for the Dorset Year Book began, and has continued until this day.

Over the years I have felt very fortunate in having known many local characters, some of whom were the last of the Victorians, and whose quirkiness and language inspired much of my writing.

When, in the early 1970s, Hugh Simpson, a farmer, poet and neighbour from Lulworth, whom I much admired, published a volume of his poems, he encouraged me to do the same, and my book 'Here at Lulworth' was published in

1975, with 'Here in Dorset' following in 1977, and I am proud to say that many of those poems have appeared on the pages of the Dorset Year Book.

In 1999 I had the great privilege of being introduced to Norrie Woodhall by Olive Blackburn. Norrie, who was then 94 years young, was the last surviving member of the Hardy Players, the local amateur group who had formed in 1908 to perform Thomas Hardy's novels on stage locally and in London.

With our shared love of Dorset and Thomas Hardy, we soon became great friends, and when Olive and I asked her what she would like for her 100th birthday, without hesitation she said, "I would like the Hardy Players to be revived." This marvellous request took me on a wonderful journey resulting in 'A Life of Three Strands', a play I wrote about Hardy's life; and also adapting 'The Mayor of Casterbridge' and 'Tess of the Durbervilles', for stage.

In 2002 I wrote and published, 'The History and Mystery of Corfe Castle, which was illustrated by James Langan. This was followed by the publication of, 'The History and Mystery of Lulworth', The History and Mystery of Brownsea Island' and 'The Red Squirrels of Brownsea Island'.

I had long kept the stories of 'Old Dorset' in my head, and on and off had written them down, and many of the poems which stemmed from them have been published by the Dorset Year Book. Then in 2015, I finally brought all the tales together, including the true story of my father's WW11 adventure's in Russia, when he was on the first Arctic convoy with the RAF to leave Britain, and published 'Stronghold of Happiness, which is set mainly in Dorset during WW11, and is fiction based on fact. When I adapted it

for stage as a fundraiser, it was amazing to see the characters come to life.

Just recently a friend from the New Hardy Players, Liz Poulain, started up her own publishing company and was looking for children's stories. When I heard this I remembered a story which I set on the Dorset coast, and had written for my grandchildren. When I showed it to Liz, she said she liked it and would like to publish it later this year, which I felt very excited about.

So much has stemmed from that first publication in the Dorset Year Book, and like many other artists and writers I continue to be inspired by our wonderful county, with its breathtaking beauty and varied habitat and wildlife. And as I look back on fifty years of my work being included in the Dorset Year Book, I feel privileged to be a small part of this very special Dorset annual which has recorded the history, language, routines and richness of our county in a unique and accessible way. Long may it continue!

The 'Skimmington'

Jack Sweet

One of the forms of rough justice handed out in the past was called the Skimmington, Skimmington Riding, Riding the Stang, Rough Music, and many other variations of the same.

The Skimmington, and its many names and physical forms, was used to publicly embarrass, punish, or generally make foolish, individuals whose behaviour had caused some offence or upset, real or imaginary, to their local community or neighbours.

In 1834, the author of a History of Lyme Regis wrote that 'Skimmington Riding makes people laugh, but the parties for whom they "ride" never lose the ridicule and disgrace to which it attaches.'

On the north wall of the Great Hall of Montacute House there is an early seventeenth century plasterwork panel which depicts a hen-pecked husband having a quick drink of ale whilst he looks after the baby. On returning home, his wife is not amused and beats her husband, but this is witnessed by a neighbour who tells the village. The husband is then depicted riding the Skimmington on a pole and being paraded around the village to the jeers of his neighbours.

This rough justice, if justice is the appropriate word, took many forms, some harmless, others violent, and one which made the local news, was held at Whitchurch Canonicorum, in West Dorset, back on 5 November 1884. The Bridport News reported that at about 6 o'clock, the sound of tin trays and kettles being beaten heralded a strange procession in which three 'grotesquely attired figures", one male and two female, were escorted through the village. A Skimmington riding was in progress mocking the local individuals represented by the grotesques; one of the females had an extra long tongue tied back to the neck and holding some note paper in one hand and a pen in the other. After calling at several pubs, the procession, duly 'wetted', finished up in a field where a gallows had been erected and the three effigies were hung and burnt. The proceedings ended in a fight, with black eyes and bloodied noses, but the News wrote (with tongue in cheek), that the Riot Act was not read, the military were not called out, the crowd of some 200 dispersed and by midnight the village 'resumed its wanted quietude'. The reasons for the Skimmington were never revealed - at least not to the reporter of the Bridport News.

And now to Yetminster some eight years later.

James Wayman was an able seaman on board HMS Leander serving in the China Station, and his best pal was another able seaman, Henry Brookman. When Henry went down with a dangerous fever, James took great care of his shipmate, and was said to have 'nursed him like a mother'.

During his illness, Henry talked at length about his sister Florrie, who lived with her parents in Yetminster, and painted a vivid word picture of the delights of the village and the beautiful countryside.

As is often the case with lonely servicemen and in particular those overseas in distant stations, James wrote to Florrie and after a while expressed his love and eternal devotion in letters sealed in sweet-scented envelopes to his unseen sweetheart half a world away.

Finally James Wayman returned to England, and cemented his relationship with the pretty Florrie. A cottage was selected and taken on lease in Yetminster, presents and household articles were purchased by the sailor, and the wedding date fixed for Monday 22 August 1892.

The big day arrives; James waits in the Parish Church and looks forward to married bliss in Yetminster with the lady of his dreams. It is now, however, that things begin to go wrong, badly wrong. Florrie is late, in fact she does not arrive at all, there will be no wedding on 22 August or at any other time; James has been jilted at the altar. A distraught James Wayman goes looking for his intended and, incredible as it may seem, Florrie has not run away, but is found nearby in company with an able seaman from Evershot.

When a greatly saddened James returned to the 'matrimonial cottage', there was another shock awaiting him, the cottage had been broken into and the contents rifled through. The village policeman was called to investigate, but the villagers, putting two and two together, connected the rifling of the cottage to Florrie and her mother, and decided to take the law into their own hands. The Western Gazette later reported, that something approaching a riot occurred when the villagers 'paid them a visit in true Dorset style, accompanied with all the honours of a skimpily riding'.

On Thursday 8 September, an unnamed married woman and her unmarried daughter, were due to appear before a special session of the Sherborne Magistrates, jointly charged with wilful damage to a house at Yetminster by breaking the windows. At mid-day a crowd gathered outside the Sherborne police court to witness the arrival of the parties concerned only to be disappointed when it was announced that the matter had been settled out of court.

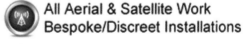

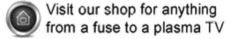
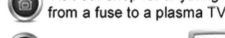

Worbarrow Bay

John Evelyn Swaine

On Bindon Hill, in my mind's eye,
I sat and mused twixt sea and sky,
watched the clouds like galleons sail,
heard the winds shrill lonely wail.

The rolling sea on eastward course,
assails with all its latent force
Mupe Rocks dragon's teeth,
in clouds of spray
on sunlit breezy summers day.

The waves are tamed at Arish Mell
to just a gentle swell,
but on the shingle neath Tynham Tout,
they break then turn about,
with grating roar
on the pebbled floor.

Climb up Gold Down
to Gad Cliffs scalloped edge,
but not too close
It's sheer to the ledge below,
then three hundred feet
via the tangled scree
to far below, and the surging sea.

To the east lies Tynham Cap
highest point on the district map,
down by the steep winding path
we wheel and lurch,
to the ghost village
and Tynham Church.

Tread the gravelled road to the beach
which turns and twists
so you'd never reach,
or so you'll think,
but soon on the brink
of the indigo sea we stand.

Watch out for oil
don't let it spoil,
but have no fear
the waters cool and deep and crystal clear.

Book Review - The Old Breweries of Weymouth

Reviewed by: Felicity Voisey

SUB TITLE: Devenish and Groves
AUTHOR: Terry Giles
PUBLISHER: Roving Press

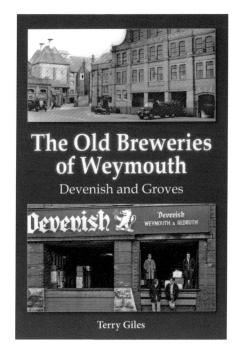

The story of the old breweries of Hope Square in Weymouth is told in this fascinating book. It is written in a lively and friendly style by an author who first took delight in the sights, sounds and smells of the breweries when visiting Weymouth on holiday as a child in the late 1940s. It tells the stories of the people, animals, buildings and area through the ages. The blacksmiths and the draymen, the maltsters and the coopers, the owners and the young lads, the women and the farriers are all featured. There are tales of the various family members and their sometimes odd behaviour. How the local church and even the future King were connected to the breweries. How important they were as employers, so much so that many workers from both sides of the harbour turned out for the funerals of senior family members.

Local history books are often seen as dry and dull but this one is lively and engaging and the writer's interest and passion for his subject is always evident. Personally I loved the pictures of the old beer mats and the story of the chalk circles. You will have to read it to find out what that was…

Price £9.99 Available in local outlets or from Roving Press Ltd, 4 Southover Cottages, Frampton, Dorchester, Dorset, DT2 9NQ

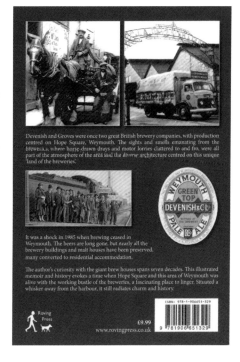

Tel: 01300 321531   E-mail: info@rovingpress.co.uk

Ghost Story

John Neimer

Julie and I enjoy motor cycling; we often load up the panniers of my big Honda Pan European and just head out to see where the road takes us. It's a great touring bike, comfortable, with plenty of torque just when you need it and it always feels light and controllable.

Which brings me to the story; we had decided to do a tour of the First World War battlefields, military history being another hobby of mine. We caught the ferry to Zeebrugge and headed for Ypres.

On our first evening we watched the very moving Last Post ceremony at the Menin gate leading to the battlefields. Then, after a good dinner with some excellent Belgian beer, we went back to the pension and studied our maps before turning in.

We wanted to see the great Lutyens memorial at Thiepval and some of the preserved trenches and battle areas and this we did. After a picnic lunch, feeling rather subdued by the vast scale of it all, we headed for some of the smaller cemeteries. One of the great things about a bike is the ability to explore very small lanes that many car drivers are reluctant to use.

It was up one of these, really a very muddy farm track we had taken in an attempt to follow a compass course across country that we stumbled upon a small British cemetery that wasn't marked on our map. There were about thirty graves, all with the War Grave Commission's dignified Portland stone headstones and all marked with the names of their occupants and some personal words given by their relatives. Most were from the same regiment, the Norfolks, with half a dozen Yorkshire men and one solitary New Zealander. The youngest was eighteen, the oldest twenty nine. We sat on the stone seat under the memorial, warmed by the sun, and felt the peace of the place as we sipped a cup of coffee from the thermos and speculated on the fates that brought a young man half a cross the world to lie amongst strangers in a foreign field.

Then Julie shivered and said, "You know, quite apart from these young men lying here there are countless others out there." She gestured at the surrounding fields scattered over the quiet down land. "The farmers here are always ploughing up old wartime scrap, shells, grenades, bullets and parts of skeletons. The whole land we can see must be packed with the remains of other young men who were never found." She is more sensitive to these things than I and has been known to sense strange events or echoes of them in old buildings. She shivered again and I put my arm around her. "Come on, let's get back to the ferry and find a cup of tea."

We climbed aboard the bike and put our helmets and gloves on and started up. As I did so Julie said, through the intercom, "I feel cold."

"OK, soon get you warm," I replied and let in the clutch. We bumped our way down the track and on to the main road back to Ypres and the ferry.

Julie complained several times on the way back to Zeebrugge of feeling cold but I was preoccupied with the bike, it seemed rather heavy and unresponsive, as if the back tyre was soggy. 'I'll take a look at it when we get aboard,' I thought.

But the tyre seemed perfectly OK when I looked at it, with no signs of deflating, but it was decidedly cold on the car deck and I didn't linger very long before joining Julie in the sunshine on the upper deck.

We live about a half hour's ride from Felixstowe so we were soon home beside the fire with a drink and something to nibble but it was a good hour before Julie had warmed up enough to cook us something and she was rather withdrawn through the meal.

"What's up?" I eventually asked. "I don't know," she replied. "I've just got this feeling of sadness and longing, just like I felt in the cemetery, the last one we went to."

I tried to comfort her and jolly her out of it and she was a bit better by the time we went to bed.

The next day she was still a bit depressed but I was preoccupied with getting my stuff ready for work so didn't take a lot of notice. It just so happened that, because the weather was still fine, I decided to take the bike to work. My office, where I work as an architect, is about twenty minutes ride across country and I can take the quiet lanes along the Suffolk/Norfolk border and across a disused WW2 airfield.

The bike still felt heavy and unresponsive and at one cross roads I nearly came off as it seemed to swerve across the road for no accountable reason, giving me quite a scare. I thought it was some fault with the forks or the brakes and so rode carefully to the office. Later, talking to Roger, my partner, I told him about the incident.

"Where did it happen?" He asked.
I got out the OS map. "Here, just near Crownland on the Walsham le Willows road."

"That's a funny old part of the world," he replied. "All sorts of odd things happen there, you know, they burnt a lot of witches there in the old days."

I laughed. "You're not suggesting that something haunts that cross roads are you?"

He looked at me seriously. "I don't know about that but that's the area where my old gran came from and she was a bit weird! Try going back that way this evening and see what happens."

"All right I will."

I approached the cross roads with some caution and so was not so frightened, or at least shocked, but still scared when the bike which, whilst still not feeling quite right, had behaved perfectly until then, once again swerved across the road only this time to the left rather than the right as happened in the morning.

I described the events of the day, and what Roger said, to Julie over our evening meal. She looked at me intensely. "I think we should take this seriously; why don't we take the day off tomorrow and follow it up?"

"What do you mean, 'follow it up'?"

"Well, ride to that cross roads and see where the bike takes us."

I snorted. "Probably take us into a ditch! But OK, I've nothing in particular planned for tomorrow. How about you?"

"As it happens my diary is light tomorrow. I'll get George to cover for me. Let's have a look at the map and see where that road goes."

So, after phoning George who owns the estate agency Julie works for and Roger who was very interested in our plans, we got out the large scale explorer map and some old aviation charts of mine, but, apart from locating a few abandoned World War two airfields, there was nothing of significance and the explorer maps had no clues for us.

The weather forecast for the next day was dry with a light northerly wind. We wore our lighter leathers and set out on our mystery tour.

We soon reached the cross roads and once again I felt the bike lurch to the right but this time I completed the turn and headed north. Julie, clasping me tightly around the waist, said, "I didn't like that, take it slowly."

I nodded my agreement and at a speed of about twenty mph cruised along the quiet lanes letting the bike dictate our route. I know this sounds pretty weird but it really seemed that at each crossroad and junction the bike would have a definite preference and I soon found by checking the GPS that we were heading in a general north easterly direction. We crossed the Diss and Thetford roads and the lanes were getting less and less frequented, with only the occasional farm or cottage.

Eventually we found ourselves in one of those East Anglian landscapes with a vast sky and almost no human habitation in sight. I stopped by an old stone bridge and we got off to have a sip of coffee and a sandwich. We leant on the bridge and stared down into the clear water. "Where are we?" Julie asked.

"Damned if I know," I replied. "I thought I had explored Norfolk quite well but this is right off my map quite apart from the weird experience of letting the bike show the way!"

"Look," she said pointing at a distant church tower looming over the hedgerows. "There's a village over there, let's see if the bike takes us there."

The road wound its way across the flat landscape, as ever in that part of the country. Because you can see your objective rarely means you can head directly towards it, but at least at each junction the bike seemed to want to head towards the church tower we could see over the intervening hedgerows and ditches and eventually we found ourselves in a quiet village street with the old church up a short lane past some thatched cottages.

I stopped by the lychgate and climbed off the bike. Looking around I could see poorly maintained cottages, three or four rather grander houses, one of which must have been the vicarage. As I opened the gate a breeze sprang up, quite suddenly, from the east and blew with increasing strength as we walked up the path to the church which was of flint and brick and quite low with a squat, strong looking tower. We wandered through into the church yard. "Look," said Julie, "there's some military graves over by the memorial."

As we approached the stern, grey stone memorial embossed with its powerful bronze sword-cum-cross-symbol of war and peace, the breeze grew even stronger, Julie grabbed my arm and pulled herself close. There were only a dozen graves, representing, I thought, probably a third of the young men of the village that went off so joyfully in those years before the world learnt the horrors of war on an industrial scale. All the graves were inscribed with the name, regiment and number of the occupants but one; Private Raymond George Everett had the added inscription, 'Having no known grave,' and named the battlefield where we had stood a few days before. The wind from the east had grown to gale strength but as we knelt to brush the grass away and read the inscription it died away and suddenly a joyful feeling swept over me of release and fulfilment.

"Did you feel that?" I asked and turned to look at Julie. Tears were streaming down her face. "Yes," she said, "he's come home; we brought him from France on the bike. He guided us here." She fell on her knees and prayed with her hands together and I followed, not knowing the words to say but thankful that, by trusting our instincts we had accomplished what that young man had longed for all those years in the heavy French clay.

The bike had lost its heavy, sluggish feel and accelerated joyfully, so it seemed to me, away down the road south.

Stalbridge to Siberia and Other Places

Hilary Townsend

My latest book was published using my own Silk Hay imprint in February this year and with it I finally managed to realise a longing – to recount and recall very many years of travels. As a child in Stalbridge I had always longed to travel but the war, petrol shortages and being, like everybody else then, very hard-up made this impossible.

STALBRIDGE TO SIBERIA
...and other places

A Dorset Woman's World Travels
- Volume 1 -

However, school at Gillingham encouraged me and the brilliant history master Mr. Wagner inspired me to go out and see for myself the places where famous figures in history came from. In 1948 I was able to join a school party to France and my passion for travel really took off. From that time the world was mine – open and exciting.
Friends in Europe asked me to stay with them. Later, friends at home were recruited as travelling companions and we realised that two young women travelling alone all over Europe was a bit unusual then.

Hilary Townsend

My world expanded to take in New Zealand and Brunei and the fulfilment of a lifelong dream to go right across Siberian on a train travelling from Moscow to Irkutsk, then on to Mongolia and China. It was the History Master who really inspired me to see for myself the mixture of races and the incredible landscape through which this railway line had finally been hacked.

In this book I have tried to recount the memories and the sheer joy my travels have brought me.

`Stalbridge to Siberia and Other Places` is available at
Silk Hay, High Street, Stalbridge, Dorset, DT10 2LH

It costs £7. 99 or with postage and packing £10.00.

A Tribute to the Dorset Regiment: 1914 - 1918

Devina Symes

When the call went out in 1914,
From all over Dorset our good men came
And volunteered for their King and country,
Landowners and labourers, all did the same.

Numbers of the Dorset Regiment swelled
And they were known as 'The Do'sets' locally,
Proudly they marched in their uniforms,
As the local bands played, rousingly!

Most farm workers could have stayed home,
Though some did join if the farmer agreed,
And many a labourer laid down his tools
To fight for his country in its hour of need.

How could they know of the 'hell hole'
That they would soon be living in?
That existed in France and Gallipoli,
Mespot, Egypt and Belguim.

Orders were given to 'go over the top'
Which was crazy and barbaric,
They lived in trenches with rats and lice
Many of them became very sick.
Such brave, courageous souls were they,
Determined to work through their pain,
Some came home very badly wounded
Then 'patched up' were sent back again.

4,500 of 'The Do'sets' were killed,
Leaving wives and mothers distraught; deprived,
After armistice, many injured couldn't get work
Some slept in ditches, where they died.

Many of the homeless became tramps,
And with tea-can in hand would ask a villager
For some hot water to make a 'brew'
As they walked from one workhouse to another.

Those who returned to work on the land
Never spoke of their horrendous ordeal
But at times were seen with a pocket knife
Quietly easing out the embedded shrapnel.

'Non dubious of the cause, non murmuring'
Words from Hardy's poem, 'Embarkation'
Are apt to those Dorset men in World War One,
Who fought for the freedom of our Nation.

And now as we mark this centenary
Many memories and thoughts will abide
As we gather on the 11th of November
To honour them all with love and pride.

To Commemorate the Ending of World War 1

Devina Symes

**(Dedicated to the 4,500 men of the Dorset Regiment
who fought and died for their King and Country in WW 1)**

Selflessly, with immense bravery
You fought for your country
and died.
Now we, in this centenary
Honour you all
With thankfulness and pride.

(Written on a poppy to be displayed at Flanders Field)

New Year's Eve 1866

(This piece is taken from my Victorian blog – Sue Hogben. The words used, though not nowadays politically correct, are ones that were used during the Victorian period. I did struggle to know whether to change them or to keep them, but decided in the end that to stay true to the Victorian values they should remain, after all, they had already been spoken and written so my avoiding them wouldn't make them or the subject disappear.)

New Year's Eve means many different things to different people. For some it's time to pull out all the stops and party long and hard. For others, it's a time for quiet reflection. A time to assess what has been and gone and that yet to come.

My main New Year's Eve tale isn't strictly, purely Weymouth and Portland, but no doubt many of its recipients were of a local nature. Folk who, through no fault of their own, had ended up somewhere they probably never thought they might. The headlines of the lengthy penned article

proclaim:-

'New Year's Eve at a Lunatic Asylum.'

It is 31st December of 1866, a reporter from the Sherborne Journal has been invited to attend the evening's festivities at the Dorset Lunatic Asylum. It is his report, but I have rewritten it in my own words, accompanied by quotes from the article. (This was the newly opened (1863) and much enlarged institute of what later became Herrison Hospital built upon Charlton Downs. A place where my own mother was taken in the 1950's when she suffered deep postnatal depression after my birth.)

It is 11 o'clock in the evening, the farewell night of the year 1866. I am sat in the great hall of the new Hospital, a place that is generally referred to as the County Lunatic Asylum. I have been invited here to partake in the evening's festivities along with the staff and inmates. As a reporter, I suspect there is a hidden agenda perhaps. These great monuments of incarceration

HERRISON. MAIN BUILDING.

have received nothing but bad press in the newspapers recently.

First to enter the hall are the men of the brass band who step up on the stage and take their places. Most are artists who give their time freely, but a couple of the band's members, so I'm told, are inmates of the asylum, one being an accomplished musician who plays the cornopean. Then from the side enters another musician, the leader of the band. He is physically carried in on another patient's back; because of paralysis of his feet he is unable to walk.

So his story goes. He was a sailor, who, whilst on board his ship in the West Indies, fell from the rigging and seriously injured his back. Arriving back in Weymouth some time later, he settled there, set up a school and "being a man of good abilities, did very well until he began to feel the effects of his accident, and it became necessary to send him where, kindly and humanely cared for, he might pass his days in peace." Not only did the poor fellow suffer from the unfortunate physical affliction caused by his accident but his mind has ultimately been affected also, "his chief delusion, I understood, was that he was chief heir to some immense estates; beyond that he was harmless."

Once he is sat comfortably at the front of the band the man is handed his violin. Hesitantly at first, he passes his bow across the strings a few times, eliciting discordant notes, but as he plays on so the sounds slowly begin to smooth out to more harmonious tones. Then the double doors to the room swing open and in file the male patients. "some staring vacantly upon the ground, others strutting in with all the swagger of 'my lord,' but all looking, clean, happy and contented." As they file past, a few turn their heads and nod at us, the guests seated at the front of the auditorium though one rather surly fellow "got behind his attendant's back, and did what is vulgarly known as taking a sight at me, all the time keeping his face as grave

as a parson's." I hasten to add, somewhat disconcerted, I do not acknowledge his sour greeting.

Now that the men are seated and settled quietly, it is the turn of the women to enter the hall. Like their fellow patients, as they pass by, their feminine faces reveal a variety of emotions and merely hint at their mental states. A couple of rather grand ladies make their particularly stately entrances, their full skirts sweeping the floor as they stroll imperiously across the hall to take their seats. One believed herself to be a grand Duchess so I'm told, the other no less a person than Her Majesty, the ex-Queen of Spain.

Seated in the front row with us is Dr Symes, the Superintendent in charge of the institute, and his family and friends. Of course, there are the hospital staff present, those men and women whose duty it is to care for their charges. Not "beetle browed men or women with iron wills and arms to match such as the sensation writers of late have rejoiced to put before their readers," these are "young men and women, neatly and modestly dressed, with good-tempered looking faces, laughing and joking with the rest."

During the evening's celebrations, I witness not the "slightest manifestation of violence" the patients behave impeccably, "indeed, the assembly would have set a good example to some where there is supposed to be more sense."

One or two of the more animated inmates catch my attention and I enquire as to their means of being admitted. Watching a man who dances in a very queer manner, "always on the hop," I ask why he had ended up in the asylum. His tale is a sad one.

Life for him, like many of us, had started out so good, so full of promise. He married a young, pretty lass and in their first few years they were happy. Then disaster struck the family, "the breath of the seducer coming over this like a cloud, a deserted home and the end-disgrace for the wife; for the husband a lunatic asylum." A valuable lesson to be learnt maybe, one never quite knows what life has in store for any of us really.

Another man, small in stature, catches my eye. He enters the room "with an appearance of being thoroughly pleased with himself." His thick head of hair is styled in the most elaborate of fashions, "it being parted in the middle, and evidently curled with great care." Upon his delicately featured face he wears his carefully manicured moustache with great aplomb.

This man of distinction, imaginary or not, passes through the hall, only stopping briefly while he nods to the chaplain. Upon that nod, "something was thrown across to him, which he eagerly caught at." Looking closer I can see the item being a pair of "white kid gloves," though they are far too large for his delicate hands and of a rather tatty state "ventilation was amply provided for by sundry slits and holes." This does not bother the man at all, in fact "they evidently gave the wearer the greatest satisfaction."

Once his hands are firmly ensconced within his gloves, he is convinced that he is complete in his full evening attire, then "he paraded up and down the room several times in great pomp." He passes me several times, and each time he stops before me, he elegantly stretches out one of his feet, keen to reveal his dancing pumps, which he admires himself so greatly, carefully turning his foot from one side to the other to enable a full view of their elegant styling.

Intrigued, I cross the room to talk to him. First, I take great pains to "compliment him on his general appearance." Something that obviously gives him great pleasure indeed as the widest of smiles stretches across his face. "Ah" he replies proudly, "we Blandford people can do it." With that social exchange having been successfully concluded in his eyes, off he lightly steps to impress some other person.

The music ceases, we are all requested to take our seats while members of the staff and some of the inmates give a musical recital. Having listened to a series of harmonious renditions from the singers and applauded their valiant efforts, the band strikes up once more.

I am now introduced to my new dance partner, a delightful young lady, "I believe she came from Cerne." As we waltz around the dance floor she proceeds to tell me that she is the "Duchess of Sherborne Castle"

and that she owns "various estates around the country." Pressing her gently, I remark that the "last time I was there a gentleman named Digby was in possession." That fazes her not the slightest, with the merest upward tilt of her chin, she simply decrees that the man is merely "an impostor."

During the evening's proceedings, this sweet lady takes to the stage and performs a couple of songs and "a sweeter voice I never heard." So pure and clear was its tone that "it sounded more like a silver bell than anything else I can compare it to." Her "highest notes were given with an ease and clearness that was astonishing."

That reporter from the Sherborne Journal wrote his sensitively drafted piece about the institution with a positive slant. The original was a lengthy article which appeared in its shortened version in numerous local and national papers.

A report created by "The Commissioners in Lunacy" from earlier that year reveals what exactly what and who this hospital served.

(Dorset County Chronicle 28 June 1866)

(I visibly cringe writing some of these words.)

"Three of the inmates suffered from religious monomania and one from over-study. But notwithstanding the large number of patients that have been admitted it appears that there are in this county no less than 12 lunatics, 156 idiots and 13 imbeciles..."

... "13 idiots and 9 lunatics in the Weymouth Union."

Out of the 397 patients at the start of that year, 41 belonged to the Weymouth Union. During 1866 the asylum employed 14 attendants, 10 nurses, 3 laundry maids and 3 kitchen maids. No one was on the wards to supervise patients overnight.

www.charltondownvillagehall.info/
about-us/our-history/

Drawn To Dorset

Claire Whiles

I'm a Dorset girl, born and bred, and although I have had the great pleasure of travelling widely, my home is whe re the heart is, that's for sure. I love to stroll in bluebell-laden woods and along wind-sculptured hawthorn and hazel hedgerows where nettle, dock, plantain, and cleavers grow on the rough paths, with pieces of flint catching my eye in the ground; ever on the lookout for an arrow head. These wonderful places looking every bit like a fairy grotto, the elementals surely inhabit this land of Dorset, watching and guarding it. "Tread carefully, hurt nothing, and make your peace with the world", they seem to say to me as I walk with my dog Olive, running wildly and madly, rolling excitedly on the wet grass, sniffing, and following trails of badgers and foxes.

Claire in tree

I know I am in very good company with all of you who are interested in history and the land.

Mankind has been 'Drawn to Dorset' since the beginning of time. The hunter gatherers, Vikings, Romans, Kings, Queens, artists and poets making history, and leaving their footprints and even their souls on this ancient land.

This history isn't always learned from books, it is felt, lived, becoming part of your life with a passionate need to know more.

I have had the great pleasure of meeting some amazing people who have researched particular periods in Dorset's rich past. They have been, dare I say it, as obsessed as I have to learn more about a time and a place; Mark Vine, author of the very powerful tale of Civil War in Weymouth, The Crabchurch Conspiracy, Josephine Sellers, author of Parallel Worlds whom I met many years ago recounting her fascinating experience of her past life here in Dorset, Rob Oliver who has dedicated so many years of his life to reuniting members and families of the WW2 Hyderabad Squadron based at Warmwell, Jonathon Harwood's research into the sacred geometry of Dorset Churches.

This inspired me to produce my book Drawn to Dorset, a collection

of real life stories spanning time, bringing the past to life through experience and discovery sparked by an unmistakable draw to this beautiful and extraordinary county of Dorset.

My own story began when I was just 14 sat in a French lesson whilst at Weymouth Grammar School in 1979.

Here is an extract from my own story in the book entitled "Escy".

"I hated school!

I wasn't academic, I was a dreamer, and a grammar school was not for people like me. I wanted to paint, write poetry, campaign for what was important, for animal rights, I wanted to be free on the land to be in nature!

Sat in a small, musty, smelly hut, bored, was somewhere I DID NOT WANT TO BE!

On this particular day, the poor teacher was attempting to elicit some French conversation from us 14 year olds, rather unsuccessfully.

Then, jerking me back from my daydream, I heard her utter the words Massif Central. I remember vividly shivering as if someone

Stag Tree

had walked over my grave and that, as they say, is where it all began!

I had no idea, back then, why those words evoked such a fascination for me and it wasn't until 20 years later I began to discover more about my journey through time…………..."

"Instinct took me down an old "cattle drove" path that ran adjacent to the private road to Ashley Chase Dairy. The track was lined with the most amazing contorted trees, and one in particular struck me, with its bent trunk, as looking like a magnificent stag.

Following downhill with a view to the left of Shipton Gorge and its hill fort behind, which, strangely, for no reason I knew of then, I have referred to as Healers Hill. I now know that I was taken on the death cart from Burton Bradstock to this incredible flat-topped hill that dominates the landscape in this area, as you can see it for miles. I had been so ill from my journey by boat from France that I received medicines made from local herbs, and healing from the local wise woman here on the healing hill.

Eventually, we came across a gate on our right, slightly hidden by brambles and very muddy, but it had a footpath sign pointing us into a wood. Immediately through the gate, an enormous ash tree greeted us – a real guardian tree it seemed and, on further inspection, I realised it was flanked by 2 more incredibly strong ash trees. Maiden, Mother, and Crone came to mind.

The wood was quite slippery underfoot initially, as it sloped down to a very windy stream, cutting its way through the soft ground, and I had to watch my step with the roots of trees prominent through the forest floor. Immediately, I felt you had entered another world, as it seemed so quiet and still. I didn't hear a bird or a tree rustling in the wind. The smell of damp leaves and water cleared our nostrils as we walked, not knowing if we were even in the right wood. Ivy twisted around some of the trees and

you could sense the ancient feel of the land on which we wandered. The remains of the bluebells and primroses gave clues to the beauty of this place in the spring, where a sea of yellow and violet would surely sweep you away in its glory.

As we continued enjoying the discovery of a 'new to us' path, Bruce running and sniffing with a very waggly excited tail, as dogs do when they encounter lots of new smells, I stopped dead in my tracks. I heard a voice say to me, as clear as day, as if you, the reader, were stood right behind me, talking to me – "You're nearly home!" I was startled and looked around to see if there was anyone but us in the near vicinity; I could see and hear no-one, and all was quiet as before. We carried on and, a few steps later, turned a bend on the corner of the path to see a magnificent stone arch staring right at us. This was the remains of St. Luke's Chapel in the woods.

Absorbing itself into the land, the ivy had taken hold of the stone, and the canopy of trees created a magical dappled light.

I suddenly felt very nervous and slightly shocked; the voice, this place, I was feeling uneasy! Strangely, I couldn't bring myself to walk through the arch, and I had to walk around it, which was rather odd!

I walked into what would have been the inside of the chapel, and a memory came flooding back. The image took me straight back to the past, around the year 1300, a tiny chapel with monks in pale robes going about their business in a gentle, soft way. To the left, a herb garden growing foods and medicines. I saw myself as I was then, and knew I had been brought to this place of safety. I recognised one of the monks as my friend in this lifetime, Duncan. This is where I now know I spent many years, safely, but in hiding after my escape from France with the document the priest had given me.

The chapel had been built by monks from Netley Abbey in Southampton. The monks were Cistercian, and the emphasis of Cistercian life was on manual labour and self-sufficiency. William of Litton had donated the land to the order in exchange for perpetual prayers to be said for him. The medieval villag of Sterte, or Sturthill, was very near to St. Luke's, so it is thought the monks served the village and worked on the farm.

CJ Bailey, in his book 'The Bride Valley', says, '...the Chapel of St. Luke was served by parsons from 1240 to 1545 when it became so impoverished that the living was left vacant. Whatever the reason, by approximately 1545, both Sterte and the Chapel were abandoned and St. Luke's descended into ruin'.

Inside the chapel lay the remains of a David and Olga Milne Watson. Sir David was a Scottish Industrialist and Managing Director of the Gas Light and Coke Company, and he and his wife, Lady Olga, owned the nearby Ashley Chase Estate. Falling in love with the ruined chapel, they commissioned the altar and cross that stands proudly at the other end of the chapel arch, and conserved what was left of the arch itself.

Previously, I had been researching Cistercians in Dorset for a few years for no apparent reason other than it felt right to do so. The Cistercian order of monks and nuns were reformed from the Benedictine Monks in France. Bernard of Clairvaux (1090-1153), a French Abbot, was the primary influence for this.

Dorset had Benedictine Abbeys such as Cerne Abbey, Abbotsbury Abbey, Cranborne Priory, and Sherborne, to name a few, but only a small cluster of Cistercian Abbeys. In 1149, William de Glastonia founded Little Bindon, near Bindon Hill on the coast near Lulworth Cove, as a daughter house to Forde Abbey, however, the terrain was too demanding and, in 1172, the monastery moved to a site near Wool, given by Roger de Newburgh and his wife Matilda, who was the granddaughter of the original founder.

How interesting that St. Luke's was Cistercian, and not linked with Forde, but Netley."

For many years my interest has been in Dorset's medieval past, poring over maps, visiting churches, walking ancient tracks, however in writing the book I've been led to research many other periods of time and what a Royal past we have here in Dorset.

"Dorset was the land of Saxon Kings. Ethelbald (meaning noble and bold) being King of Wessex from 858-860. He was the second of five sons born to Aethelwulf, and younger brother of Athelstan who died in 1851. His father had taken 13 year old Judith, daughter of the Carolingian King Charles the Bald, as his wife. After his father's death he created quite a medieval scandal when he subsequently married his step mother Judith".

"Bere Regis gets the Regis part of its name from Queen Elfrida, who was the mother of King Ethelred, but it was King John who held the manor here. It is recorded that he stayed in Bere Regis 16 times between 1204 and 1216, so he must have felt very at home there.

Bere Regis has a fascinating church, of which the earliest parts date before John's reign to 1050.

In the 15th century, the church acquired an amazing hammer beam roof, carved in oak as a gift from Cardinal Morton. There are incredible carvings in the church, all in beautiful colours and on the exterior, a very rare Sheela Na Gig carving."

Dorset abounds with wonderful artistic people and beautiful, enigmatic places. The book contains a multitude of information about some of these sites and the famous names that have visited or spent time here.

One such site is the iconic domed hill, topped with trees that can be seen from miles around the Bridport area; Colmers Hill.

This intriguing landmark situated near Symondsbury, taking its name from the "Colmer Tenemant", who were tenants in the 17th and 18th centuries. John Colmer was the Rector of Symondsbury from 1805-06.

The name Symondsbury derives from Old English, and means the hill or barrow belonging to a man named Sigemund. It was listed in the Doomsday book as Simondesberge.

The wonderful photographer Doug Chalk produces a calendar every year with stunning photos of the hill.

For me, I count my blessings every day that I was Drawn to Dorset and I trust you will find the real life stories in the book as fascinating as I have and enjoy accompanying the writers in their journeys of discovery.

Drawn to Dorset is a "not for profit" publication. All profits will be donated to Dorset Charities in the memory of Claire's parents; Henry and Norah Smith.

Claire loves to share her passion for Dorset and is available for talks. She can be contacted via email at drawntodorset@gmail.com or via her facebook page Drawn to Dorset.

'Drawn to Dorset' is available from Claire Whiles, local outlets and from Amazon and Waterstones.

ISBN 978-1-912400-11-9

Price: £11.99

Colmers Hill - *Photograph courtesy of Doug Chalk*
https://www.facebook.com/AperturePhotographics

Tribute to The Viscount Lord Trenchard

Air Chief Marshal Sir Patrick Hine, GCB, GBE

During a year that marks the RAF's centenary, it is most apt to pay tribute to Marshal of the Royal Air Force The Viscount Trenchard who was the RAF's first Chief of Air Staff and a direct descendant of a 16th Century High Sheriff of Dorset, Sir Thomas Trenchard of Wolfeton House, near Charminster. When Hugh Trenchard came to retire from the RAF in 1930, he was created Baron of Wolfeton and became the RAF's first peer.

Trenchard's early achievements, both academically and in his military service with the Royal Scots Fusiliers, were by any yardstick undistinguished, but he was an accomplished sportsman, and he showed courage and initiative during the Boer War during the course of which he sustained serious injury. By 1912, at the age of 39, it was clear that Trenchard's career in the Army had stalled, and one of his few close friends suggested that he learned to fly. While he showed no great aptitude as a pilot, Trenchard proved to be an able administrator and whilst on the staff of the Central Flying School at Upavon, he organised training syllabi which focused on preparing pilots well for future service with the Royal Flying Corps (RFC) and Royal Naval Air Service (RNAS).

With the outbreak of WW1 in 1914, Trenchard (now at last a Lieutenant Colonel) was given command of the First Wing of the RFC operating in France, the roles of his squadrons being to provide aerial reconnaissance for the artillery and rudimentary bombing support for land offensives. Trenchard's grasp for the strategic offensive potential of air power brought him to the attention of the Commander of the British Expeditionary Force, General (later Earl) Haig, and his star rose rapidly until by 1917 he had become Commander of the RFC and a major-general. In the summer of that year, London was attacked no less than 50 times by Gotha bombers and Zeppelins, causing considerable loss of life. In response to the attendant public outcry, the Government set up a commission to report on the organisation for air defence of the UK, which recommended the creation of an independent, third service for command and control of all the nation's air forces. Thus, the RFC and RNAS were combined and the Royal Air Force was born on 1 April 1918 with Trenchard appointed as the first Chief of the Air Staff (CAS). However, never easy in his personal relationships, Trenchard soon fell out with the new Secretary of State for Air, the press baron Lord Rothermere, and resigned his post of CAS. He was returned to France as the Commander of the Independent Air Force where he persuaded the French and by now American air elements to operate under his overall direction. Increasingly during the last few months of the war, the allied air forces were employed on strategic air operations interdicting the German Army's lines of supply and attacking industrial targets in the German homeland itself.

With the war over and Rothermere replaced by Winston Churchill as Secretary of State for Air, Trenchard was knighted, promoted to Air Marshal and on 31 March 1919 once again became Chief of the Air Staff, a position he was to hold for over 10 years. During that time, he had to ward off regular attempts by the other two Services, particularly the RN, to kill off the fledgling RAF which by now had been reduced to just over 30 squadrons, but successive government reviews always found in his favour. Trenchard strengthened his case by finding a new peacetime role for the RAF – air policing of the new mandates in the Middle East, notably Iraq, and of India's troublesome North-West frontier – which proved to be militarily effective and economically attractive to a cash-strapped British Government.

With typical foresight and zeal, Trenchard also set about laying some firm foundations for the RAF, initially with the creation of institutions such as the RAF Cadet College at Cranwell, the Apprentice Training School at Halton, and the RAF Staff College at Andover, and then later with the formation of Auxiliary Air Force squadrons and the establishment of the University Air Squadrons – the first 3 being at Oxford, Cambridge and London. He also ensured that money was made available to support our entries for the Schneider Trophy air races which Britain won 3 times with aircraft which were the catalyst for the designs of the Hurricane and Spitfire that helped save the nation in the Battle of Britain in 1940. It is not surprising, therefore, that Trenchard was dubbed 'the Father of the RAF' a description that he himself disliked but which de facto was accurate.

THIS WEATHERVANE COMMEMORATES THE ESTABLISHMENT OF A WORLD SPEED RECORD OF 406·92 M.P.H. ON THE 29TH SEPTEMBER 1931 BY
FLIGHT LIEUTENANT G.H.STAINFORTH A.F.C
AN OLD BOY OF WEYMOUTH COLLEGE AND A MEMBER OF THE SCHNEIDER TROPHY TEAM
THE AIRCRAFT OF WHICH THIS IS A REPLICA WAS THE PROTOTYPE OF THE BATTLE OF BRITAIN 'SPITFIRE'. ORIGINALLY ERECTED OVER THE COLLEGE IN JULY 1932 THE VANE WAS PRESENTED TO THE BOROUGH WHEN THE COLLEGE CLOSED IN 1940 AND WAS MOUNTED IN ITS PRESENT POSITION IN MAY 1952

Schneider Trophy weathervane & plaque in Greenhill Gardens, Weymouth

He became a man of great vision and was an unwavering believer in the offensive projection of air power; he set clear priorities and stuck to them; and he showed real tenacity, resolve and political nous in ensuring that the RAF survived its infancy. Trenchard's strong leadership of the RAF and major contribution to national security was further recognized in 1927 by his promotion to the highest rank (5-star) in the British armed forces – in his case Marshal of the Royal Air Force, an accolade so richly deserved.

It is worth adding that in 1931, Trenchard became Commissioner of the Metropolitan Police, a responsibility that he discharged with distinction. Amongst his many achievements was the establishment of the Hendon Police College, the creation of separate career paths for the lower and higher ranks akin to the military system of officer and non-commissioned career streams, the broadening of the Police recruitment base and the encouragement of graduates to join the police. During his last months as Commissioner, the Viscount Trenchard was made a Knight Grand Cross of the Royal Victorian Order. Thus, a start in life that offered little real promise became one of outstanding contribution to the nation he so patriotically served. But then, we should have expected nothing else from one whose ancestral roots lay in our beloved 'Dorset'!

The Trenchards and Wolfeton House

Peter Lush

Patronymica Britannica (1860) records that the name Trenchard is most probably derived from the O. Fr. trencher, to carve; and it may refer to the occupation of the original bearer, either as a carver of viands, or as owner of a trenchant blade in war. Ancestry tells us that 'Trenchard is an ancient Norman name that arrived in England after the Norman Conquest of 1066. It is the name for a soldier . . . . we found the name was originally derived from the Old French word trenchire, meaning a soldier, swordsman or man of war' and that 'the surname Trenchard was first found in Dorset where they were granted the lands of Hordhill in the Isle of Wight by Baldwin de Ripariis to Paganus Trenchard and his heirs about 1100 AD.'

The estate of Wolfeton was in the ownership of the Mohun family, a daughter of which, Christiana (born there about 1400), had married Henry Trenchard and they had a son called John who therefore inherited the estate. The Mohuns had come to England with the Conqueror and their family seat was Fleet House, now more familiar as Moonfleet Manor.

The foundations for Wolfeton House were laid around 1480 by John Trenchard and his son Thomas and it was originally conceived as a grand early Tudor mansion with Elizabethan additions. However, this was later demolished and the present building is the remaining south wing. Thomas, apart from his building of Wolfeton House also embellished the church of St Mary, Charminster, founded in the 12th century, by adding its imposing Perpendicular tower. His stylised monogram T can be seen in several places around the tower. In 1506, the house hosted Philip of Castile and his wife, Joanna, after they were shipwrecked off Melcombe Regis in a great storm.

The Trenchards lived in grand style at Wolfeton for 400 years and as was common practice in those days, intermarried with the other landed families of the county – the Strangways, the Sydenhams, the Ffooks, the Binghams and the Turbervilles – and so the branches of the family spread and nowhere in the line from John and Thomas have I found the strain that eventually begat Hugh Montague Trenchard.

The future Lord Trenchard had his roots in Somerset rather than Dorset having been born in Taunton on 3rd February 1873. His father was a former captain in the King's Own Yorkshire Light Infantry who was working as an articled clerk in a legal practice and his mother was the daughter of the Royal Navy captain John McDowall Skene. His grandfather was Henry Charles Trenchard (1812-1881) who had married Elizabeth Montague (1811-1840) whose maiden name would be given to their offspring and to their grandson. Although in the 1870s the Trenchards were living in an unremarkable fashion, their forebears had played notable roles in English history. Notable ancestors were Sir Thomas Trenchard, a High Sheriff of Dorset in the 16th century and Sir John Trenchard, the Secretary of State under William III.

In spite of his pedigree, Hugh did not enjoy the high life style of his ancestors and in 1889, when he was 16 years old, his father, who had become a solicitor, was declared bankrupt. After initially being removed from Hill Lands, a crammer in Wargrave, Berkshire, he was only able to return thanks to the charity of his relatives. He failed the Woolwich examinations twice and was then relegated to applying for the Militia which had lower entry standards, but even this proved difficult for him and he failed in 1891 and 1892. During this time, he underwent a period of training as a probationary subaltern with the Forfar and Kincardine Artillery. He finally achieved a bare pass in March 1893. At the age of 20, he was gazetted as a second-lieutenant in the Second Battalion of the Royal Scots Fusiliers and posted to India.

Wolfeton House also fell from its original grandeur. In an article for the Dorset Year Book of 1916-17, Sir Frederick Treves writes of a photograph of the house, 'Its fails to show the details of this ancient and stately mansion, which is claimed by many to be the best of its kind in Dorset. It affords no suggestion of the noble hall, of the grand staircase, of the elaborately carved walls, of the wonderful windows with their glories of stained glass. It shows, however, the view of the house that is most familiar to the people of Dorset – the view from what is always called the turnpike road.'

As with Hugh's branch of the family, and as recorded in The Dorset Magazine of April 2013, 'The Trenchards fell on hard times and so did the house, being let as a farmhouse in the late 18th century. By then it was owned by the Hennings, who had been both cousins and lawyers to the Trenchards. In the middle of the 19th century, they sold it on to yet more cousins, the Westons, who did have some money to spend. The Great Chamber was divided into five rooms and the windows bricked up. The Westons knocked down the ruinous parts of the house but conserved the rest, taking the stone from one end (the east) to rebuild at the other.'

The next owner was related to the Westons and a member of another of the great Dorset landed families, Albert Bankes, a younger son of the Bankes of Kingston Lacey and although he died in 1913 his widow, Florence lived on in the house until her own death in 1947. When Treves was writing in the Dorset Year Book, therefore, it was not many years since the interior had been restored to something resembling its original splendour. Wolfeton was now inherited by Priscilla Stucley, the granddaughter of the Bankes and unable to live there herself, gave it a new life by converting it to flats.

The house was now sold to a Mrs Thimbleby which brought the wheel nearly full circle for she was a distant connection of the Trenchards. The house is now open to the public on limited visiting hours.

As a then Major-General, Sir Hugh M. Trenchard, KCB, DSO, attended the Peace Dinner held by the Society of Dorset Men in the Connaught Rooms, London, at which he was one of the speakers. In 1923 he joined the Society as a Vice President, so we can legitimately look upon him as having been one of our own. Whether or not he ever visited Wolfeton is unknown, for the house had been sold by the Trenchards in the late 18th century although the two following owners were cousins. However, on being created a Baron on 27th January, 1930, he took the title of Baron Trenchard, of Wolfeton in the County of Dorset and retained that geographical connection when elevated to Viscount on 4th February, 1936.

Acknowledgments: - Sir John and the House of Trenchard (Dorset Ancestors), Dorset Year Book 1916-17 (Sir Frederick Treves), A Complete Jumble – Wolfeton (Dorset Life – The Dorset Magazine), John and Richard Travell

Uncle William's Temporary Lapse

David Downton

A granddaughter was leaving for Taiwan to teach English to Chinese children and I was hosting a farewell party for her family and friends. Despite many criticisms of young people today, it was a rewarding and joyful experience to engage in conversation with this group, who were far more articulate, at their age, than my generation and were well able to express their opinions on a variety of current topics.

The discussion turned to the subject of originality and spirit of adventure. Were these concepts 'alive and kicking' with the modern generation, who certainly had greater opportunities than we did, particularly for cheap travel abroad?

I suggested provocatively that despite many opportunities afforded, their generation thought the obvious thoughts and did the obvious things most of the time. A gap year for them was as predictable as my generation's gap of two years compulsory military service. Their peer group ruled the roost and to be different was a cardinal sin .They were a conforming generation, lacking originality and spontaneity, averse to risk taking so unlike past generations.

I was challenged on all fronts and asked to provide examples of the widespread risk taking behaviour of generations past, particularly in my own family.

I wanted to give them an example of extraordinary risk taking from people who would not normally behave in this manner, and I remembered my late wife's tale concerning her Uncle William who was a member of a Portland family going back several generations.

Her uncle had lived on Portland all his life, rarely leaving the island. He was a confirmed bachelor with conservative views and had worked as a quarryman from the age of fourteen until forced to retire with ill health, caused by back breaking work and dust inhalation, from mining the famous Portland Stone. He lodged with an elderly, devout, church going lady, who was so orthodox she forbade him to pick vegetables on a Sunday for lunch, had they been forgotten. William was a creature of habit and when he went out always carried three items; his cheque book, fountain pen and a pair of bicycle clips. Nobody knew why he carried the latter as he had never owned a bicycle.

Portland folk were traditional and didn't allow much thinking outside their comfort zone. It was not unknown for elderly Portlanders to ask their bank managers to visibly produce savings, to ensure their money was still in the bank and William was known to have taken advantage of this service.

In retirement William had more time on his hands, spent mostly attending his beautiful garden overlooking the sea near Portland Bill. He rarely had occasion to leave the island but one day decided to do something quite out of character and visit London for a short holiday. He was keen to see places of interest THAT he had only read about in newspapers. However, being a cautious and private man, William decided to keep his visit secret, in case relatives and friends became concerned for his well being in such a big city, and tried to dissuade him from taking such a trip. He thought it best to book the hotel with a travel agent away from Portland, where no one would know his business, so travelled by train to Bournemouth and did two things completely out of character. Firstly he chose to indulge himself by booking a room at the prestigious Dorchester Hotel, and secondly, which was even more bizarre, made the booking using a false name and address. He did not want to record his extravagance or his stay in London, worried that family and friends might think he had gone out of his mind.

On his return he could tell them as much as he wanted to, perhaps as little as "I've just been to Dorchester." William chose a name he knew didn't exist in Portland, and established a fictitious address in Poole, Dorset.

He told his landlady that he was going to stay with an old friend who had moved to the nearby village of Swyre. Hence William, under the name of Mr Jago Trenchard of 23 Steampacket Road, Poole, Dorset caught the early morning bus to Weymouth, then a train to Waterloo.

After a tiring journey and taxi ride from Waterloo station William, with some trepidation, entered the portals of the renowned Dorchester Hotel in Park Lane, Mayfair. He slid sheepishly past the liveried doormen and into the magnificent interior of one of the most luxurious hotels in the world. Looking at the ornate nineteen thirties furnishings and well dressed clientele, he realised immediately he had made a terrible mistake. Despite his foreboding, reception staff greeted him with great civility, but when signing in he almost   wrote William fortunately remembering, at the last moment, his alias, Jago Trenchard. A bellboy transported his suitcase to the room, which although the cheapest on offer had cost a small fortune. He was asked if he would prefer meals served in his room, which he accepted happily, realising how out of place he looked in this glamorous hotel.

William found an assortment of literature concerning famous attractions in and around London and cheered up somewhat planning the week's excursions. After a delicious breakfast he went into the city as quickly as possible to explore London's many attractions, visiting the Houses of Parliament, the Tower of London, Victoria and Albert Museum and was

delighted to see the changing of the guard at Buckingham Palace. Confidence soared when he booked a seat to see 'The Mouse Trap' in a West End theatre, something he had dreamed of but never thought he would achieve.

He crammed in as much as possible into his time in the City and towards the end of the week William even plucked up courage, after his evening meal, to visit one of the bars in the hotel for a quick drink.

Being used to his own company, he was not unduly concerned sitting alone with his drink, watching the world go by. But he was not alone long as a well dressed younger man asked if he could join him. William had no objection and was rather glad to have a little company for a short while. Initially the stranger made small talk, but soon turned to the subject of finance, pointing out that most clients of The Dorchester had a portfolio of investments ranging from shares to property. William, stated ,with some satisfaction, that he was himself both a property owner and had a portfolio of shipping shares that he had built up over a number of years.

He did, in fact, own two small cottages in Portland and had a quantity of shares in the successful Welsh shipping firm of Reardon and Smith.

The stranger introduced himself as Herbert Sykes, a partner in the solicitors Sykes and Emmanuel of Shoreditch. After buying William a drink he asked if he might be interested in making an investment in a block of flats soon to be built on a disused docklands in Millwall. London was expanding rapidly and accommodation would be much sought after, where demand would outstrip supply for some time to come. William was impressed with this offer and agreed to be taken to a meeting of potential investors next morning at 10 a.m. Mr Sykes said he would arrange for him to be picked up outside the hotel next day, which was William's last full day in the hotel as he was returning home on Sunday by train from Waterloo station.

He had a disturbed night's sleep, mulling over his decision to attend the meeting, as really he knew nothing about the fellow who had approached him in the bar. William did have substantial savings but was he not being reckless involving himself in a business venture so far from home.

However, curiosity won the day and he was picked up at the agreed time, taken by taxi to a rather seedy looking address in Soho, where he was greeted by the gentleman he had met the previous evening. He was shown into a small, dimly lit and sparsely furnished room, and not feeling happy with the situation, was about to leave when the door of the room was closed and locked.

Two other men in the room certainly did not look like professionals and the atmosphere was hostile.

"Good morning, Mr Trenchard," one of the men said, " we wish you to invest in a flat to be built in Millwall and you will now sign the paper with that intention, and pay the purchase price of the flat you are about to buy".

"How did you know my name?" asked William "I never gave it out last evening."

"We have a contact in the hotel, who regularly supplies us with potential clients to invest in our building schemes, we also know that you live in 23, Steampacket Rd at Poole in Dorset".

William was now becoming frightened, especially when a typed sheet of paper, indicating he had agreed to buy a flat on disused docklands in Millwall was thrust in front of him.

"I only expressed an interest" William pleaded, but the three men were menacing and he noticed one of them had a small stiletto knife in his right hand. "You will sign this agreement to purchase a flat and hand over the purchase price, or it will be the worse for you".

"Five   hundred   pounds!   "exclaimed William, looking at the so called contract". I don't have five hundred pounds with me,

and as it is now Saturday afternoon, the banks are closed so I can't withdraw any money. I only have twenty five pounds with me but I can give you a cheque for the rest as I have my cheque book with me".

His captors talked together, and reluctantly agreed to accept his cheque for the remaining amount. William, hoping his fountain pen was charged with ink, wrote a cheque for four hundred and seventy five pounds and signed it "Jago Trenchard". He was then blindfolded, bundled into a car and when it slowed down pushed out like a sack of potatoes. Having removed the blindfold and dusted himself down he saw Marble Arch nearby, so was soon able to find his way back to the hotel. How relieved he was to get back safe and sound, not even worrying about the looks he received at his dishevelled appearance. Fortunately William had kept enough money in his suitcase to pay for the extras incurred during his stay, or else would be forced to write a cheque in the name of Jago Trenchard, and commit a criminal offence .He did not wish to run into these men again, whom he now realised were crooks, so asked the hotel to call him a taxi for a very early departure to Waterloo station. He would lie low there until the train departed at nine o'clock.

William had a fretful night and had no appetite for breakfast. He made his way to reception to check out, hand in his key and pay what he owed for incidentals. But, as he was about to leave, two smart suited gentlemen approached and introduced themselves as the hotel manager and assistant manager. They asked if he had enjoyed his stay at the Dorchester and said they had a surprise for him. William really didn't want any more surprises and his taxi had arrived to transport him to the station The manager assured him that he need not worry about the taxi as the chauffer driven hotel car would be taking him to Waterloo station. "I am pleased to tell you that you are the millionth customer to stay in this hotel and the owners have decided to award you a cheque for £500 as well as a week in the hotel free of charge. "Consequently Mr Trenchard, please accept this cheque made out in your name and a voucher for a return visit to the Hilton". The colour drained from William's face as he accepted the cheque and thanked them for their generosity.

He could not leave quickly enough and after an anxious wait at Waterloo station had an uneventful journey back to Weymouth, sleeping most of the way.

Safe in his lodgings at Portland, William reflected on the consequences of his spontaneous behaviour and the thought of again meeting those London crooks tempered his enthusiasm for the urge to act impulsively ever again.

William framed the Dorchester Hotel cheque for five hundred pounds, and hung it over the mantelpiece in his living room. Underneath in italic script he had written "Unto thine own self be true".

After a few months passed, William, with new found confidence, felt able to share his story with friends and relatives, who gathered in the Red Lion public house for a memorable evening, which became part of Portland folklore.

My young guests had listened to the story intently and at its conclusion one of them plucked up courage to ask if the story was true or had it become embellished over the years.

I recalled the words of a great friend who was Editor of a Provincial newspaper and told them "One should never let the truth get in the way of a good story!"

Graham Wakely Elmes

Jenny Elmes

Graham Wakely Elmes, who joined the Society in June, 2007, was born, a war-time baby, in his grandmother's house in North Street, Wareham on 7th November 1943 (which Graham always says was the luckiest day of the year). His father, George, worked in Wareham Post Office, a protected profession, and his mother Kay had come to Wareham as a land girl from her home in Appledore, North Devon, housed in the next building to the Post Office where she could espy George at work through her bedroom window. They married and had Graham, followed by twin girls, Ruth & Mary 13 months later, and in time, a sister Sara was born.

Graham did not like school, preferring to be out on the heath catching snakes with his friend John Breeds (who was to become warden of Braunton Burrows Nature Reserve). When the opportunity came to leave Swanage Grammar School without completing his A Levels, Graham jumped at it, much to his parents' horror! He became an assistant at Furzebrook Research Station which involved digging holes on Hartland Moor and driving Landrovers.

After doing 'A' levels by correspondence course, Graham was awarded a bursary to study for a degree in Zoology at Queen Mary's College, London University. He spent much time there bell-ringing in the city churches and rowing on the Thames, captaining their eight. He returned to Furzebrook and continued helping Dr M.V. Brian, the station head, with his work on Myrmica ants. Later, Graham, in collaboration with his colleague and butterfly expert, Dr Jeremy Thomas, worked on the life cycle of The Large Blue

Butterfly which had become extinct in Britain due to changed farming methods and the absence of the correct ants. Thanks to their pioneering work, The Large Blue has been successfully reintroduced to sites in Devon and is now thriving. Graham eventually achieved a PhD and DSc from London University, and rose to the government position of Senior Principal Scientific Officer; in this Graham Elmes came closer than anyone to fulfilling the army saying that "there's a Field Marshall's baton in the knapsack of every Private".

In September 1975, a young teacher, Jenny Bell, arrived for her first teaching job at the new Wareham Middle School; she also happened to be a church bell ringer, and at that time, Graham was Tower Captain at Lady St Mary Church, Wareham, having helped mastermind a project to augment the then 8 bells to the present 10 bells. Soon they struck up a friendship and the rest is history; indeed they celebrated their 40th wedding anniversary on June 4th 2017!

Graham & Jenny were proud parents of two daughters, Elizabeth & Rosanna and delighted grandparents of four grandsons. Lizzy and her husband Chris, teach at Milton Abbey School. Rosie is a project manager at Thames Water in Reading, and her husband Will, is Director of Rowing for Reading University.

In Wareham, Graham had been a loyal member of the Ancient Court Leet, holding offices of Carniter, Ale taster and Juryman. He treasured his membership of The Society of Dorset Men and was very proud of being born, bred and spending his life in Dorset. However he also forged many working links internationally, and in his retirement wrote a 789 page book called 'Myrmica Ants of the Old World' with a Ukrainian ant expert Dr Alex Radchenko, as well as creating a unique collection of Myrmica specimens, which is now donated to the Hope Museum, Oxford.

Graham had three distinct threads to his life; he was a great family man, an accomplished campanologist (having rung a full peal of 5040 changes in every tower with ringable bells in Dorset), and a world-renowned myrmecologist (red-ant expert). He had suffered health problems for many years but these never stopped him living life to its full. There was a congregation of about 400 at his funeral/celebration of life in Lady St Mary Church on January 8th 2018, with bell-ringers coming from all over England to show their respects, entomologists, townsfolk and family members; it was a measure of the huge respect in which he was held. Professor Jeremy Thomas gave the tribute on Graham's entomological work, Tim Collins gave the church bell ringing tribute, and daughter Elizabeth Barnes gave the family tribute. A collection was taken to illuminate the glorious East Window of Lady St Mary Church, where Graham had been christened, confirmed, an altar boy and bellringer, and will serve as a memorial to the 74 years of his life, well-lived. He is missed by his family and all who knew him.

Origin of Pimps

Pimps date back to at least the 16th century. They were used long ago before the invention of central heating to light fires. In particular they were used for bakers' ovens as well as for homes.

It is an old-fashioned traditional craft brought about by coppicing. Silver birch is cut from heathland in the winter months to aid in heathland habitat maintenance. The birch is then stored under cover for a year to ensure that it is dry enough to work with. It is then cut by hand using a cleaver and chopping block, tied under pressure into individual bundles which are then tied with tarred string and then sisal to provide up to 25 fire lighters in one pimp bundle.

The word pimp is thought to have derived from the Welsh word for number 5. It is believed that the name was taken to describe these bundles because they were traditionally packed in 25s so 5x5 would be a pimps worth of wood. Both small individual bundles and collective bundles are called pimps.

As well as being really useful pimps look very pretty in a fire place or presented within a dried floral display.

For further details please contact 0773297048

Dorset Woodman's Smock

Alan Brown

Dorset Woodman's Smock by Alan Brown This smock is a traditional woodman's smock exactly the same as found in the Victoria and Albert Museum.

It was made for me by Rosalind Atkins of Winterborne Abbas. It is a beautiful piece of work, which incorporates the embroidered leaves which denotes the Woodman's work. There is also a great deal of

intricate smocking both on the front, back and on the sleeves and finished off with Dorset Buttons: an excellent example of Rosalind's outstanding ability: pure Dorset Craftsmanship.

I decided to have it made as my family have been making hurdles in the East Lulworth, Combe Keynes and Wool area since 1775 and who knows, maybe that smock in the Victoria and Albert could have been worn by one of them.

There are very few hurdle-makers left, my son is the eighth generation of our family to make hurdles but he had to give up when the market was swamped with cheap, mass produced factory imports from Eastern Europe. Within three months we lost output to seven companies that we were supplying.

The last order we had for sheep hurdles was 100 for the film 'Far from the Madding Crowd'.

John Blackmore, Musician

Marion Tait

John Blackmore's settings of William Barnes' poems originally formed a part of his undergraduate dissertation "West country Sound and Song". Inspired by Vaughan Williams' settings, John sought to return William Barnes' poems to popular consciousness through music, specifically for a twenty-first century audience.

While Vaughan Williams' piano and vocal arrangements have a distinct classical flavour, John uses guitar and voice to create a warm, folk-song feel, which certainly match Barnes' 'Hwomely Rhymes' In fact, made for each other.

During his performance, John drew attention to the musicality of Barnes verse and the beautiful but complex rhythms and structure that make Barnes work distinctly Dorsetian. Despite many of Barnes' poems sharing the five stanza structure, each of eight lines, John highlighted with sensitivity how the context and focus of Barnes' poems varied greatly, and demonstrated how he took this in to account with his settings.

John's song "Blackmwore Maidens" and "Blackmore by the Stour" sounded softened and gentle while "The Geate a-vallen to" setting was so meaningful, and sent emotional shivers down your spine. Both these poems were similar in style and structure and so very beautiful.

John also previewed a new Barnes setting: "The Stagecoach". He had visited his Irish roots to 'get a lilt' going. Here John recreated the driving rhythm of the wheels: went swiftly roun' rottle roun' trundle roun' truckle roun'. You could truly visualise the stagecoach on its journey through all seasons "while the whip did smack and the whip did crack on the ho'ses' back"

It certainly was a toe-tapping composition with feet tapping along to the beat.

The Stagecoach

Ah! When the old volk went abroad
They thought it vast enough
If four good horses beat the road
Avore the coach's rough
An' there they zot a-cwold or hot
An roll'd along the ground
While the whip did smack on the horse's back
An' the wheels went swiftly round. good so's.
The wheels went swiftly round.

No iron rails did streak the land
To keep the wheels in track.
The coachman turned his four-in-hand
Out right, or left, an' back
He'd stop avore a man's own door
To take him up or down
While the reigns fell slack on the horse's back
Til the wheels did rottle round again
Till the wheels did rottle round.

An' there when wintry wind did blow
Athirt the plain and hill
The sun were pale above the snow
An' ice did stop the mill
They laughed and joked with coat and cloak
So warmly roun' them bound
While the whip went crack on the horse's back
An' the wheels did trundle round, d'ye know,
The wheels did trundle round.

An' when the rumblen coach did pass
Where hufflen winds did roar
They'd stop to take a warming glass
By the sign above the door.
They'd laugh and joke and ask the folk
The miles they were from town
Till the whip did crack on the horse's back
An' the wheels did truckle round, good folk,
The wheels did truckle round.

An' gaily rode old age or youth
When Summer light did fall
On woods in leaf, or trees in blooth
Or girt folk's parkside wall.
They thought they past
The places vast
Along the dusty ground
When the whip did smack on the horse's back
An' the wheels spun swiftly round. Them days
The wheels spun swiftly round.

If you are interested in John's new CD
please contact Marion Tait, William Barnes Society.

Victorian Fayre

Marion Tait, Honorary *Secretary, William Barnes Society*

By popular demand the Victorian Fayre was back for a third year. This year Dippy the Diplodocus was on display in the Victorian Hall, Dorset County Museum, our usual venue. Consequently, the Fayre was held in the Corn Exchange, the very place where Barnes had given many of his public readings of his poems.

The event was hosted by the William Barnes Society and ably compared by Alastair Chisholm in his own unique style.

It featured the Dorset cultural heritage which would have been familiar to Barnes. There were many traditional crafts and skills, together with music, poetry and song all to celebrate William Barnes's birthday.

William Barnes was born at Bagber Common in the Blackmore Vale, Sturminster Newton, February 22nd 1801. He was the fifth of at least six children born to Grace and John Barnes. His father's livelihood was barely above subsistence level and they lived in a lowly thatched cottage.

Barnes was an extremely intelligent child and had a passion for books and learning. He loved the Vale and his retention of the sights and sounds of the working-class people in this area inspired his dialect poetry. He wrote nearly one thousand poems considered among the best in literature for their description of country life during the early part of the 19th century. Barnes was a prominent writer, philologist schoolmaster and subsequently a clergyman by profession.

The society hoped to raise awareness to a wider audience of the Dorset dialect poet as well as promote the traditional skills.

Through his poetry William Barnes left us an amazing legacy. We have a fascinating insight into a rural way of life of a bygone era that could have been so easily lost in time: preserving an endangered culture of Old Dorset. The poems portray the Blackmore Vale, its people, customs and culture and rural employment before mechanisation: traditional life slowly gave way to the modern age.

The Corn Exchange was transformed into a bygone era of a bustling Victorian fayre. The scene was set with stalls nestled cheek by jowl decorated with a symphony of colourful bunting and sellers dressed in traditional style garments: a feast for the eyes. There was a cacophony of sound from poets, musicians, sellers, demonstrators and shrieks of laughter from children having fun.

This was a family event with something for everyone to enjoy. Here were a wonderful array of traditional crafts and rural skills including Victorian style jewellery, Victorian style handmade wooden toys, corm dollies, Dorset buttons, and a fantastic display of Dorset Bonnets. Many visitors of all ages tried their hand at making corn dollies and buttons.

There were also rural craft demonstrations, including for the first time: hurdle-making, pimp-making and bobbin lace making, together with the popular net making, which visitors tried for themselves.

The children's corner was kept busy with activities to amuse all ages: wood cuts and printing, silhouette craft, drawing, dressing up in period costume that proved great fun, a name the bear competition, a pin the bustle on Queen Victoria invitation and much more.

The raffle and tombola stalls proved to be very popular, as usual. Local businesses had been very generous with donations and many were decorated in Victorian style packaging to complement the theme of the fayre.

There were refreshments savoury and sweet to suit all tastes: Freshly baked home-made scones with cream and jam, ploughman's lunch, an assortment of delicate sandwiches and a wide variety of tempting cakes and of course the priceless cups of tea and coffee.

The refreshment tables were adorned with vases of delightful freshly picked 'Tete-a-Tete' cyclamineus, delicate primroses and sprigs of green garden foliage, ensuring a comfortable seating area to relax, enjoy and watch the bustle of time.

A selection of Barnes's poems were read by Brian Caddy, Devina Symes, Dave Burbidge and David Guy. These included: Uncle An' Aunt, Zummer Evenen Dance, The Young Rhymer Snubbed, Lydlinch Bells, The Wold Waggon, Praise 0' Dorset and A Bit o' Sly Coorten.

My Orcha'd in Linden Lea

'Ithin the woodlands, flow'ry gleaded,
By the woak tree's mossy moot,
The sheenen grass-bleades, timber-sheaded,
Now do quiver under voot ;
An' birds do whissle over head,
An' water's bubblen in its bed,
An' there vor me the apple tree
Do lean down low in Linden Lea.

When leaves that leately wer a-springen
Now do feade 'ithin the copse,
An' painted birds do hush their zingen
Up upon the timber's tops;
An' brown-leav'd fruit's a-turnen red,
In cloudless zunsheen, over head,
Wi' fruit vor me, the apple tree
Do lean down low in Linden Lea.

Let other vo'k meake money vaster
In the air o' dark-room'd towns,
I don't dread a peevish measter;
Though noo man do heed my frowns,
I be free to goo abrode,
Or teake agean my hwomeward road
To where, vor me, the apple tree
Do lean down low in Linden Lea.

Linden Lea is still popular on the folk scene and has been recorded by many musicians including: The Yetties, Tim Laycock, John Blackmore and Aled Jones whose CD 'Duet' went to number one in the Classic list in 2016.

Devina Symes & Dave Burbidge sing Linden Lea
Society members Devina and Dave on accordion, also provided music and song
including: Rose in June, One Morning in May and Linden lea.

The Wold Waggon

The girt wold waggon uncle had,
When I wer up a hardish lad,
Did stand, a-screen'd vrom het an' wet,
In zummer at the barken geäte,
Below the elems' spreädèn boughs,
A-rubb'd by all the pigs an' cows.
An' I've a-clom his head an' zides,
A-riggèn up or jumpèn down
A-plaÿèn, or in happy rides
Along the leäne or drough the groun',
An' many souls be in their greäves,
That rod' together on his reäves;
An' he, an' all the hosses too,
'V a-ben a-done vor years agoo.

Upon his head an' taïl wer pinks,
A-païnted all in tangled links;
His two long zides wer blue — his bed
Bent slightly upward at the head;
His reäves rose upward in a bow
Above the slow hind-wheels below.
Vour hosses wer a-kept to pull
The girt wold waggon when 'twer vull;
The black meäre Smiler, strong enough
To pull a house down by herzuf,
So big, as took my widest strides
To straddle halfway down her zides;
An' champèn Vi'let, sprack an' light,
That foam'd an' pull'd wi' all her might:
An' Whitevoot, leäzy in the treäce,
Wi' cunnèn looks an' show-white feäce;
Bezides a baÿ woone, short-taïl Jack,
That wer a treäce-hoss or a hack.

How many lwoads o' vuzz, to scald
The milk, thik waggon have a-haul'd!
An' wood vrom copse, an' poles vor raïls.
An' bayèns wi' their bushy taïls;
An' loose-ear'd barley, hangèn down
Outzide the wheels a'móst to groun',
An' lwoads o' haÿ so sweet an' dry,
A-builded straïght, an' long, an' high;
An' haÿ-meäkers, a-zittèn roun'
The reäves, a-ridèn hwome vrom groun',
When Jim gi'ed Jenny's lips a-smack,
An' jealous Dicky whipp'd his back,
An' maïdens scream'd to veel the thumps
A-gi'ed by trenches an' by humps.
But he, an' all his hosses too,
'V a-ben a-done vor years agoo.

William Barnes poetry can be very musical and at times the words, rhythms and rhyme make you want to sing. Linden Lea A Dorset Song, words by W Barnes was set to music by Ralph Vaughan Williams.

A special feature this year was a performance by member and musician John Blackmore of songs he will include on his forthcoming album featuring his own musical settings of Barnes's poems. In addition, he performed his own compositions Great Western Railway, The Millers Daughter, Gone to London and Hardware Road.

The event to celebrate the life of William Barnes was a huge success with over 200 people visiting the fair and £800 taken. The doorman said that he had heard nothing but praise from people as they left the Corn Exchange.

Proceeds will go towards the publication of the WBS's new anthology of William Barnes poems edited by Alan Chedzoy, and also to St Peter's Church organ restoration fund.

Barnes was very much involved with St Peter's church, as for a time he was church warden and also one of three secretaries to the Fabric committee that undertook the major project to repair, modify and refurbish the building in 1856.

His beloved wife, Julia, is buried in the churchyard a few yards from Barnes's statue.

The Chairman, Brian Caddy, and committee members of the William Barnes Society wish to thank all local businesses, market traders and volunteers for their commitment and contributions to the event and all who made William Barnes's birthday extra special. It had been a truly remarkable day one which would be remembered for a long time to come.

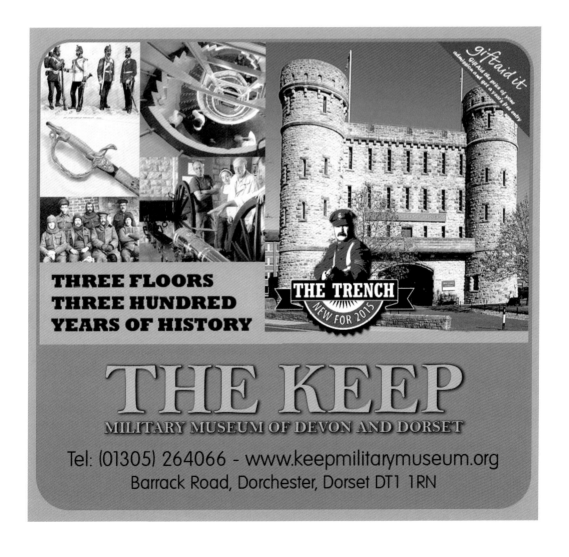

Toll Gate to Overcombe Corner

Today, the word Preston on a road sign along Preston Beach Road (the A353) clearly delineates the boundary line between itself and Weymouth. This road was once, around the 18th century, a turnpike road with a toll gate house near Lodmoor at which a toll or fee had to be paid by all who used it. A toll was a tax or duty paid by users of the road towards its maintenance, and constituted a major improvement in the condition of the country's roads since Roman times.

Long after the toll system was dispensed with, the toll house remained, the last occupants being the Shorey family who also ran a horse-drawn cab service. An old milestone along the way indicated the distance to Weymouth as 1 mile and to Wareham as 17 miles. In 1965 the café at Overcombe Corner, on the left-hand side of the road going towards Preston, was demolished and replaced with a block of flats that overlook the bay and Lodmoor. About the same time the petrol station opposite was replaced

A sea wall ran from the start of Preston Beach Road opposite Lodmoor to Overcombe Corner, combe being a short valley running up from the coast. This wall was built to separate the shingle beach from the road but was frequently breached in winter's strong and sometimes violent moods, especially at high tide. This caused intense problems including diversions via Littlemoor into Weymouth and vice versa, plus the cost of repairs and removal of debris and damaged vehicles.

Whereas some daring folk once walked dangerously along the narrow old sea wall, a wide and safe esplanade between the new wall and the sea now joins Weymouth promenade, the EC having contributed to the financial aspect of this substantial barrier.

The café at Overcombe Corner in 1929.

with a hexagonal toilet block, and the road divided, turning left for Chalbury Corner and right for Bowleaze Coveway which was once the old route to Osmington.

Eventually the old wall was replaced by the present sturdier one that slopes down to the road with a metal fence at its foot. Almost a mile long and reinforced with a steep bank of pebbles on the seaward side, this new stretch of road was given a 50 mph speed limit with one permitted crossing for pedestrians along the way. The esplanade is now a picturesque and interesting walk for old and young alike, especially parents with pushchairs and children on roller blades and scooters. It is not easy to differentiate between an esplanade and a promenade except that a promenade is defined as a paved, public walk usually beside the sea. The word is derived from the French *se promener* which translates as 'to walk' whereas an esplanade is a level piece of ground especially used by the public and is derived from the Latin *esplanare* meaning 'to make level'.

Originally, wooden seats were arranged along the esplanade with memorial plaques to lost loved-ones placed above. Due to wear and weathering, several of these much appreciated seats have been replaced with those of more durable limestone.

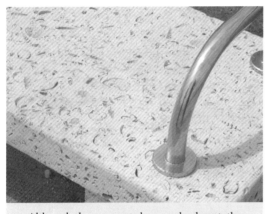

Although the new seats have no back rest, the slabs, which have been cut from Portland Roach limestone, provide seating that will stimulate interest in the wide variety of small fossils found along the Jurassic Coast, including one group of specimens known as Portland Screws.

Occasionally in late spring you may see a female duck and her ducklings scurrying anxiously towards Lodmoor either along the esplanade or at the seawater's edge. It is possible for them to reach the safety of the nature reserve via a small tidal inlet which links with the reserve, thus avoiding the busy A353.

Turning left soon after entering Preston Beach Road from Weymouth, a narrow road leads down to the Household Waste Recycling Centre or 'the Tip' as it is generally called. This 'tip' is a well-organised site which caters for the disposal of almost everything,

from old mattresses to garden waste; the latter mulched and made available later as compost. Apart from the good management of this site, one other factor is much appreciated – the help kindly given by the workmen and other 'tippers' who assist frail ladies and elderly gentlemen by dragging their garden refuse up the steep steps and into the container, and, surprising though it may seem, there are people who genuinely enjoy 'a trip' to this tip.

Very few waste disposal sites like this one can boast an attractive approach road along which something is in bloom or berry throughout the year. Each spring there is white May blossom on one side of the road and vivid yellow gorse opposite. Also in the spring, an unusual though not rare plant thrives along the wayside banks. This is dittander, a plant very similar to horseradish, found amongst long grasses near the coast especially in the south.

Preston, Bowleaze and Overcombe

"This is an extract from the book Preston, Bowleaze and Overcombe by D. Joan Jones, published by Roving Press. (www.rovingpress.co.uk, tel 01300 321531, on sale at £3.99)".

Lodmoor

From the Year Book: 100 Years Ago

John Travell

P3 Old Dorchester by Sir Frederick Treves

The Year Book for 1919-1920, the first full year of peace, begins once again with a poem by Thomas Hardy 'Autumn in the Park' and a long article by Sir Frederick Treves, on 'Old Dorchester' with no mention of the recent War, but describing the town as it was, from the time of James I at the beginning of the 17th century. Treves says, 'It was as square as a Roman tile...all the houses were shut in on every side by gates so thick they might have been the portals of a convent.' Because of the plague in London all travellers approaching the town from the London Road were stopped by two gate keepers, who were tradesmen of the town, carrying rosemary. A stranger could not enter the town without permission of the Governor. "The streets...were...precisely as they are today...the south part of the town was laid out in gardens and orchards from wall to wall.' The roads in Dorchester in 1610 were on a much lower level, and it was not until 1791 that the first paved footway appeared in East Street. St. Peter's Church was wholly surrounded and shut in by a jumble of old buildings. This was called 'The Bow.' The old Town Hall was in the Bow in front of which were the shambles, consisting of two rows of butchers' shops. The Bow was cleared away in 1790 to provide room for the new Town Hall. The Gaol was at the lower end of East Street near the 'White Hart.' The market was held in the centre of the town and sheep were penned in Pease Lane while the glovers' stalls were in the quiet South Street. At the bottom of Priory Lane, by the river, there was a mill '500

years old' where the Priory stood, which had been founded in the reign of Edward III. [The mill was still there in 1920]. The Priory had been built with stone from the Dorchester Castle which was where the prison was later built on the same site. The monks' chapel was pulled down in 1536, and in 1720 the Priory was being used as a Presbyterian Meeting House. Treves says that 'South Street was the most changed, with only two old buildings remaining; Nappers Mite, built by Sir Robert Napper in 1615, and the Free School (the Grammar School) built by Thomas Hardy of Melcombe Regis in 1567. [This was knocked down in the 1960s and replaced by the Hardy Arcade.] At the lower end of South Street was a garden to the 'Hospital' or 'Workhouse.' This was a hostel for fifty poor children who were taught a trade. The Dorchester Gallows stood on Gallows Hill, where the South and East Walks meet. Dorchester had a Governor until replaced by a Mayor in 1647. The town had sixty-eight trades recognised by the corporation; the chief industry was cloth, 'although a considerable business was done in malt and beer.' In 1620 there were 24 public houses in Dorchester, and the Corporation itself was engaged in brewing. Only the Freemen of Dorchester could trade in the town. The Town Beadle represented the dignity of the town, as well as its executive powers. He was the main law officer responsible for locking miscreants in the stocks and the pillory, and dragging 'scolds' down Glydepath Hill to be ducked in the Frome. Each night five watchmen and a bellman kept watch from twelve until six, according to the season. After the first coffee house was opened in London in 1652, the first license 'to sell coffee, chacolate [sic] sherbett and tea' in Dorchester was granted to Morris Gauntlet in 1679.

Dorchester was a strictly Puritan town and anti-papist. Treves says 'I doubt if Dorchester was a cheery place to live in. People were so particular and so intolerant of their neighbours' faults. Unkindly gossip, backbiting and tale-bearing made life bitter, and careless speech dangerous...The dress of the Puritan man was as severe...as the tailor could make it...Sunday was a day of crushing gloom...to fail to attend church was a crime.' In 1642 the Civil War broke out. 'A fort was built at the South gate, a gun platform at the West gate...there were thirty-seven barrels of gun powder in the Town Hall.' There were no soldiers in the town, so a militia of two companies was raised.

p18. THE VILLAGE INSTITUTE by the new President, the Earl of Shaftesbury

In an article on 'The Village Institute', the Society's new President, the Earl of Shaftesbury, said that 'The War has shown the need for a strong, progressive, virile and healthy agricultural industry, providing good employment, good wages and a prosperous outlook for the man whose work is on the land.' He went on to say that 'life is more than labour...reasonable recreation, of social intercourse, of mental development.. are as necessary to the rural worker as to the townsman...The village must be the unit of organisation and the Village Institute the centre of activity: the community spirit must be developed.'

p55. "THE GOOD OLD DAYS IN DORSET' Article by the late J. A. J. Housden

In another long article, J.A.J. Housden follows a journey through Dorset made by the antiquary, John Leland in 1533. He rode across the county describing the streams and rivers and places he visited, including Wimborne, Poole, Dorchester, Weymouth, Portland, Purbeck and Wareham. Dorset's first Lord Lieutenant, John Earl Russell, was appointed in 1549. Housden lists the names of the holders of the older office of Sheriff; these included John Turberville of Bere, John Sydenham and John Williams in the reign of Henry VII and John Trenchard, Giles Strangways, Thomas Trenchard and John Russell in the reign of Henry VIII. The duties of Sheriff included calling out armed men for the defence of the county. In 1577 the Justices of the Peace statistic listed 162 alehouses, 28 inns and 17 taverns in Dorset, plus '12 ale houses and 4 inns in the Town and County of Poole'. In Shaftesbury, 'beer was more readily procured than water.' The Domesday Book in 1086 listed 272 mills in the county, many of which were 'winter mills' which only operated in winter when the brooks and rivers were full. [At the time of the article in 1919 Housden says there were a hundred flour mills in Dorset.] Roads were better at the beginning of the 16th century than at the end – after the dissolution of the monasteries – because the monks had been road builders. Carriers were the main means of communication across the country. The post office first began to transmit ordinary letters (which were not relating to affairs of state) at the time of Elizabeth I. At the end of the 16th century the first post towns established in Dorset were Shaftesbury and Sherborne on the Plymouth Road. Referring to old Dorset families, Housden says that in the 1872 census, there were twenty Dorset estates of over 5,000 acres, and ten of these were over 10,000 acres. The ten were W.R.Bankes, Digby, Earl-Drax, I.B.Guest, Lord Ilchester., Lord Rivers, Lord Shaftesbury, R.B. Sheridan, H.G. Sturt and Weld. Ilchester and Shaftesbury were the only ones important in the county in 1501. In 1592 Parliament passed an Act for the "true" making of cables, hawsers and ropes 'and all other tackle' for ships in Bridport. The town had been making these for centuries but the Act said it was necessary because 'of late many evil-disposed persons...for their private lucre and advantage...made cables there, which cables be slightly and deceivably made.' Several Dorset men were involved in the Perkin Warbeck uprising which was defeated in Blackheath in 1497. Henry VII punished them by imposing fines on several Dorset towns, including Dorchester, Sherborne, Bridport, Beaminster and Bere Regis. The Franciscan Friary in Dorchester was dissolved in 1538. Between the Domesday Book census in 1086 and the dissolution in 1538, church estates had doubled and even trebled in size. Cerne had increased from 17 to 30, and Abbotsbury from 8 to 26. Among historically interesting Dorset people living in London in the 15th century Housden lists John Morton, Archbishop of Canterbury, who was born in Bere (or Milborne) about 1420. Educated at Cerne Monastery and Balliol, Oxford, he became a Privy Councillor and Chancellor of the Duchy of Cornwall and was also Rector of Bloxworth. Housden disputes Treves's story of the origin of the family and fortunes of the Dukes of Bedford in the Russells of Kingston Russell, and traces them instead from Henry Russell of Weymouth, who was a member of the House of Commons in about 1455, and married Elizabeth Herring of Chaldon Herring. Their descendants all married heiresses and it was their great grandson, John Russell, who became the first Duke of Bedford. His son, Frances, was Lord Lieutenant of Dorset and counsellor to Elizabeth I . There was also Lady Margaret Beaufort, who was born in 1441 and married Edward Tudor, the Earl of Richmond and half-brother of Henry VI. Her son became Henry VII after defeating Richard III at the battle of Bosworth in 1485. She held estates in Dorset and founded Wimborne School in 1496. She died in 1509 and is buried in the Henry VII Chapel in Westminster Abbey. The Year Book had not forgotten the War, and printed extracts from an article in the Daily News headed 'Dorset in War' which gave an account of the Dorset Regiment's service in France, Flanders, Gallipoli, Mesopotamia and Palestine. The peacetime Regiment of four battalions rose to seven during the war years. The Dorsets 'were the first English troops to be assailed by poison gas...at Hill 60 on May 1st 1915. A Dorset battalion was the first to set eyes upon Jerusalem when Allenby was chasing the Turk... "Primus in Indus" is their regimental motto...the 1-4th Dorsets were the first Territorials who landed in India in 1914...if it had not been for the valiant service of the 2nd Dorsets the British would have been driven out of Mesopotamia... The most spectacular thing of all was the whirlwind charge of the Dorset Yeomanry at Agagia.' When the yellow cloud of gas met them at Hill 60 on 1st May there were 337 casualties. Four days later the Dorsets lost 230 men when holding the trenches for sixteen hours until they were withdrawn with only 170 men left. At the siege of Kut in 1916, 370 officers and men of the 2nd Battalion were forced by sickness and famine to surrender to the Turks. 'Very few of the original survivors are alive today.' [1919] A new battalion was formed and moved to Palestine in 1918 and took part in the final battles in the Holy Land. The 5th Dorsets were among the first troops to land at Gallipoli in April 1915. Lt. Col. Bols who commanded the 1st Dorsets in the first months of the war became chief of staff to Allenby in Palestine.

The Year Book gives publicity to a just published book by Alfred Pope of Dorchester, 'A Wessex Family in the Great War' on the members of his family (more than any other family in Dorset) who served in the War. Thomas Hardy provided a foreword to the book.

p43. The Fighting Men of Dorset. No. 1. The 1st Battalion the Dorsetshire Regiment by Lt. Col. C.C. Hannay Commanding

During the War the Society was in constant touch with the Dorset units of the fighting service. The Committee felt that this should not lapse now the War was over. So this first article by the Commander gives a resume of the services of the 1st Battalion since it was re-formed in Dorchester in June, 1919. Hannay was sent to Londonderry to bring back the 3rd Battalion from Ireland. Eighty-six men also returned from service in Russia. The 2nd Battalion were sent to India in September, which left the 1st below full strength.

2nd. Batallion Dorset Regiment
Survivors of the Seige of Kut-el-Amara
Private J. Cole   Lance Corporal J. Wiliams
Brg. Q.M.S.F. Harvey   Reg. Sergeant-Major G. DeLara   C.O.M.S.R. Maidmont

that 'it was now the time for the counties and the county associations to do their duty in looking after the men who had been wounded and in finding employment… and seeing that the battalions of the county regiments were filled with willing soldiers so that if (God forbid) the occasion again arose and the country had to take up arms, the men of Dorset would rise once more.'

The Society of Dorset Men in London
Seventh Yearly Dinner Holborn Restaurant London May 9th 1911
The President Colonel J. Mount Batten C.B., in the Chair

P84. The Peace Dinner

The first Society Dinner, following the end of the War, was held as a 'Peace Dinner', on Dorset Day, 5th May 1919, at the Connaught Rooms in Kingsway. This was made the occasion for welcoming from the war the returned officers and men of the Dorset Battalions. The Year Book gives a detailed list of the chief guests and the members of the Regiment, from their commanding officers to the lower ranks, and especially the few survivors of the siege of Kut, who had recently returned from their internment as prisoners of war in Turkey. Among the main speakers was Major General Sir W.S. Delamain, who said

The next speaker was Major General Sir Hugh Trenchard (later to become a member of the Society) who had become famous as the founder of the Royal Air Force. He said 'it was a high honour to respond for the Air Force, who deserved honour from the whole nation. Never had any nation such pilots, observers, or men on the ground who kept the machines going, hour after hour, day after day...and pilots especially, who saw their fellows brought down in flames from 30,000 feet, and yet went on... and where ten machines went out and one came back, another squadron was up and out to the same place.' 'He wanted them to remember that the air service was a young force, with young officers and men...who had had no training for business, and he wanted employers...who could help...and if necessary, bear with them while they learnt their job...and could so obtain some recompense from the country for what they had done.'

THE EARL OF SHAFTESBURY.

Lord Shaftesbury, replying to the toast of 'Dorset our County,' referred to 'the great part the county has played in this war.' He said 'The farmers of Dorset have done their bit; the Red Cross have done their bit; the Dorset Guild of Workers have done their bit; and the men of Dorset have fought in every theatre of the war.' He went on to pay tribute to 'the great work that has been done by the Dorset Society in London' through the Comforts Fund, and the way the Society had endeavoured to keep in touch with those from the county serving abroad and keeping in touch with them when they had returned and been demobilised. He was sure that the Society would wish to take part with the county in preparing a great welcome to the regiments and units when they return home. Looking to the future, he said 'we must take our part with the rest of England in making the agricultural districts a better and a cheerier place for men and women to live in. We want to retain our population upon the land, and I for one hope some day to see a village green in every village in the county, and a village institute or village club.'

In response to the toast of 'the Dorsets,' several of the senior officers of the Regiment expressed their appreciation of the event. Colonel Radcliffe thanked the Society and all Dorset folk for their kindness and all they had done for the 2nd Battalion and the prisoners in Kut and Colonel Sir Randolf Baker spoke on behalf of the Dorset Yeomanry, which he had commanded for a year in the war and led in two charges.

A further toast was for 'the Dorset Men Athirt the Seas.' A number of men from Dorset who had emigrated to different parts of the world were present at the Dinner and spoke in reply. Captain Trowbridge from Shanghai said that he had lived in China for twenty years, and had only visited the Old Country twice in that time. Major A. Clark said he was a real Dorsetshire man, although he had spent the best part of his life in New Zealand. He had left New Zealand four years before at the outbreak of war 'to do what every decent NewZealander felt was his duty (for) the Mother Country.' In a closing speech, in reply to the toast of 'Our President', Mr Swinburne-Hanham said that owing to the extent of the war he had held the office of President for nearly four years. Thanking members for their support and generosity, he said 'The Dorset Society has been able to send out money and goods to the value of over £4,000 to his Majesty's forces fighting overseas.'

p91. The Annual Meeting

In November, the Society, described as 'undoubtedly one of the most cordial, as well as the largest, of the county fraternals in London,' held its Annual General Meeting at the Cripplegate Institute. The Earl of Shaftesbury was elected to be the seventh President of the Society. The year's report showed the membership of the Society to be larger than any time in its existence, a large addition having

been made since the armistice by serving men joining. The Committee had received a letter from the commanding officer of the 2nd Battalion, Lieutenant-Colonel F.W. Radcliffe, shortly before it left to India, in which he wrote 'most enthusiastically' 'about the liaison which exists between all ranks of the 2nd Dorsets and the Society' saying 'the more we see of each other the better for us all.'

Lord Shaftesbury had made an appeal to provide silver bugles and drums to go to the 1st and 2nd Battalions, and many members had already subscribed to this. The retiring President, Swinburne-Hanham, was re-elected as Chairman, and William Watkins was re-elected as Secretary. Thanking the Society for their support, Watkins said, 'They had been trying to enlarge the influence of the Society, and the Society

had become influential. One could not go to any part of the world now but one heard the word 'Dorset' and one heard the challenge "Who's a-fear'd?" He had heard it many times [having] just returned from Canada and the United States. During this visit he had come into contact with 'one of our Dorset land-owners...the Prince of Wales – and they had a most interesting talk about the county of Dorset and the Society of Dorset Men in London.' At the meeting Mr. Bellamy proposed that the Society 'confer an honour upon one of the lads of North Dorset – young Jack Counter, who had distinguished himself in the war and had had the V.C. conferred upon him by the King.' It was agreed 'with applause' that Jack Counter should be made an honorary member of the Society.

p93. Presentation to "Wold Charl."

In December, 'A large and representative gathering of the Committee' held a dinner to honour Mr. Charles Rogers. Sir Stephen Collins, who was in the Chair, said that 'Wold Charl had been a tower of strength to the Society ever since its inception, and was the right hand man of Mr. William Watkins. Next to Mr. Watkins he knew more about the inner workings of the Society than any other man...during the dark days of the Great War Mr. Rogers had unselfishly and willingly given his time and energy to visiting our sick and wounded soldiers...and carried words of cheer and sympathy to their relatives.' Wold Charl was presented with a hand case containing over one hundred pounds.

Mp97. To Darset Men Athirt th' Zeas. By Wold Charl

Wold Charl contributed his usual Dorset dialect article to 'Darset Men Athirt the Seas', telling them 'the good work that has been done was made possible by our

Society sent a report of its seventh annual general meeting held in Sydney in August 1919. The President, A. J. Hare, expressed their appreciation of the London Year Book, though in a letter to the Secretary, Captain Caines, Mr. A.J. Hunt of Bondi wondered why 'there were no pictures of the fine avenues of trees entering the town of Dorchester...the only town in England where you cannot enter or leave without passing through an avenue of trees.' An 'old Blandfordian' had contributed a nostalgic

Photo by C. R. Stride

Wold Charl tellèn Gaffer Clarke teäles o' the long ago.

Society having at its head brains that give willing workers a job to do, knowing full well that it would be faithfully done...The more members we have in the County the larger will be our power of doing good in London, and I do hope you will bear in mind that the Society is not for men in London alone, but for every self-respecting Dorset County Patriot wheresoever he may be.'

p103. Seventh Annual Report of the New South Wales Branch.

The New South Wales Branch of the

article on 'Old Days in Dorset', and Captain Caines had written a letter about the Spanish flu epidemic, which had meant many meetings could not be held. Several members had died from the epidemic, which was now on the wane. The death of the Vice- President, Thomas Warren, was recorded. He had been 'one of the pioneers of the Society in New South Wales, having been in the colony for over half a century. He had been a member of the Bridport Volunteers when they paraded at Queen Victoria's Review in Hyde Park. As they marched past, a news boy had shouted 'Here comes Dorset butter!'

The Beam

The William Barnes Society

Photographs by Mark North / William Barnes Society © 2018

Williams Barnes' poem 'The Beam in Grenley Church' was inspired by the folk story of the Miraculous Beam in Christchurch Priory.

When Ranulf Flambard decided to build a Norman Church here to replace the Saxon building, he is thought to have decided to erect it on top of St. Catherine's Hill, two miles away to the north of the town; an ideal position for it to be seen and to give it prestige similar to that enjoyed by the new cathedral just started at Durham high above the River Wear.

The townspeople, however, wished the church to remain in the town itself where they had always worshipped. They also knew that the hill, being gravel, had no water supply for the community of priests who would live there.

However Flambard insisted, and the stone was taken by cart up St. Catherine's Hill, but when the workmen appeared the next morning they found the site empty and the stones returned to the site of the Saxon church. After this had happened several times, Flambard concluded that this was divine intervention and gave way to the demands of the people.

When building began on the present site, it was noticed that

a mysterious carpenter worked on the construction but was present neither at mealtimes, nor when wages were paid.

One day, a large beam cut for the roof was found to be too short and had to be lowered back to the ground. As evening was coming on, the embarrassed and worried workmen went home. Such huge timbers, cut from trees in the New Forest, were costly and scarce.

On their return next morning they were made speechless on finding that the beam had been placed in the right position and with length to spare.

The mysterious carpenter was never seen again and it was assumed that he was Jesus the Carpenter who had come to help them in their work.

Until then the Church had been known as the Church of the Holy Trinity, to which the

parish altar is still dedicated. After the events described above it came to be known locally as Christ's Church of the burgh of Twynham, with the monastic High Altar being dedicated to Christ the Saviour. As the town grew it adopted the name of Christchurch Twynham, eventually to become Christchurch.

Grateful thanks to the William Barnes Society and to Mark North for the photographs.

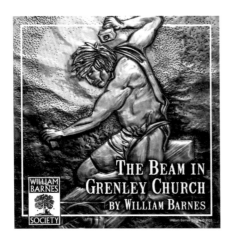

THE BEAM IN GRENLEY CHURCH
BY WILLIAM BARNES

In church at Grenley woone mid zee
A beam vrom wall to wall; a tree
That's longer than the church is wide,
An' zoo woone end
o'n's drough outside,--
Not cut off short, but bound all round
Wi' lead, to keep en seäfe an' sound.

Back when the builders vu'st begun
The church,--as still the teäle do run,--
A man work'd wi' em; no man knew
Who 'twer, nor whither he did goo.
He wer as harmless as a chile,
An' work'd 'ithout a frown or smile,
Till any woaths or strife did rise
To overcast his sparklèn eyes:

An' then he'd call their minds vrom strife,
To think upon another life.
He wer so strong, that all alwone
He lifted beams an' blocks o' stwone,
That others, with the girtest païns,
Could hardly wag wi' bars an' chaïns;
An' yet he never used to staÿ
O' Zaturdays, to teäke his paÿ.

Woone day the men wer out o' heart,
To have a beam a-cut too short;
An' in the evenèn, when they shut
Off work, they left en where 'twer put;
An' while dumb night went softly by
Towárds the vi'ry western sky,
A-lullèn birds, an' shuttèn up
The deäisy an' the butter cup,
They went to lay their heavy heads
An' weary bwones upon their beds.

An' when the dewy mornèn broke,
An' show'd the worold, fresh awoke,
Their godly work ageän, they vound
The beam they left upon the ground
A-put in pleäce, where still do bide,
An' long enough to reach outzide.
But he unknown to tother men
Wer never there at work ageän:
Zoo whether he mid be a man
Or angel, wi' a helpèn han',
Or whether all o't wer a dream,
They didden deäre to cut the beam.

The Great German Offensive 1918

Greg Schofield

Part 1:

Early 1918 was a window of opportunity for the Germans. In January a peace treaty was signed with the new Communist Government of Russia, which ended the war on the Eastern Front. For the first time, the Germans were able to concentrate their army on the Western Front. However, the window was narrow; the USA had entered the war in April 1918 but had not yet arrived in any numbers, however, that would not now be long delayed and an offensive against the allies had to take place before they could be reinforced.

The German General Ludendorff planned to attack the lines where the French and British lines met and cooperation and communication was at its least effective. New tactics were to be used which had been successful against the Italians in 1917; instead of a prolonged bombardment, General 'Breakthrough' Bruchmuller organised a short concentrated barrage, after which 'Stormtroopers' armed with flamethrowers and machine pistols burst through the gaps created, ignored strongpoints and kept moving forward, forcing the allies to fall back in confusion.

The blow fell on 21st March on a stretch of the line held by General Gough's 5th Army, which had just taken over some French trenches and had no defence in depth. The onslaught of 47 German divisions on 28 British and French divisions was immediately successful, the 5th Army disintegrated and the allies fell back in confusion, with a huge gap threatening to open up. All allied forces were put under the command of Marshal Foche and a defensive line hardened as the Germans ran out of steam. They had advanced 37 miles in two weeks, but outrun their artillery and supplies, become exhausted through poor diet caused by the British blockade, and disillusioned by the evidence of the allies' plentiful supplies which they stopped to loot.

During the retreat, the following Weymouth men were killed:-

GEFFAL George	2nd Lieutenant, 2nd/ 4th Ox and Bucks Light Infantry. Killed 23rd March, 1918
HANSFORD P. E. C.	Company Sergeant Major, Royal Engineers. Formerly volunteer artillery. Killed 9th April, 1918, aged 31. Awarded DCM for conspicuous gallantry 24th August, 1916. Son of Charles (One of the Weymouth Town Sargeants) and Sara Hansford. Husband of Mary. Lived 106, Northwood Road, Thornton Heath, Surrey
HOOPER Thomas George	Gunner, Royal Garrison Artillery. Killed 21st March, 1918.

HUNTER Nigel Duncan Ratcliffe	Captain, Royal Engineers. Awarded M.C. and Bar. Killed in action 26th March, 1918, aged 23. Son of Mr and Mrs Duncan Hunter. Lived 'Chesildene', Rodwell, Weymouth.
JARVIS Arthur Charles	Private, Royal Army Medical Corps. Killed in action 25th March, 1918, aged 27. Son of Thomas and Emily Jarvis. Brother a prisoner of war. Lived 61, Franklin Rd., Weymouth
LANGFORD William George	Private, 6th Dorsetshire Regt. Killed 24th March, 1918.
PITMAN Harry E.	Rifleman, 1st/ 17th London Rifles. Killed 21st March, 1918, aged 33. Only son of Mrs Pitman. Lived12, Spring Gardens,
SARGENT Frederick Charles	Private, 7th King's Shropshire Light Infantry. Killed 28th March, 1918, aged 27. Son of Mrs S. T. Sargent. Lived 1, Terrace St., Weymouth.
SCRIVEN Francis Henry	Private, 1st Wiltshire Regt. Killed 24th March, 1918, aged 19. Lived 22, Ilchester Rd., Weymouth. In 1917 his mother had appealed for exemption from conscription for Francis, her youngest son and only support at home. One son had already been killed and three more were serving in France. At home she had only a daughter and two sons under 15. The appeal was refused.
SMALE Stanley A.	Private, Royal Engineers. Killed 21st March, 1918, aged 21. Initially reported missing, confirmed dead in 1919. Enlisted August 1914; left for France 1915. Son of William and Phoebe Smale, 13, Kempstone Rd., Weymouth.
SQUIBB William Clive	Private, 2nd/ 4th Royal Berks Regt. Killed 21st March, 1918., aged 29. Husband of Katherins Elizabeth Squibb. Lived 10, Terrace St., Commercial Rd., Weymouth.
STEWARD Edward	Private, 8th The Queen's (Royal West Surreys). Killed 21st March, 1918
WALBRIN James H.	Private, 6th Dorsetshire Regt. Killed 1st April, 1918, aged 28. Son of M. A. Walbrin, Glyde Path, Dorchester. Husband of Amelia G. Walbrin.
WENLOCK William	Private, 7th Duke of Cornwall's Light Infantry. Reported missing 22nd March, 1918; confirmed dead 2nd April, 1918. Aged 19. Youngest son of Theophilus and Lucy Wenlock, 18 King's St., Weymouth.

We insure it.
You enjoy it.

BESPOKE
THE NFU MUTUAL
INSURANCE COLLECTION

It's no surprise that over 95% of our NFU Mutual Bespoke Home Insurance customers choose to stay with us.

NFU Mutual Bespoke Home Insurance is specially designed to cover larger properties and more complex insurance needs with contents valued from £100,000.

For more details, speak to Matthew on 01258 473299
email sturminsternewton@nfumutual.co.uk or visit us at
The Creamery, Station Road, Sturminster Newton,
Dorset, DT10 1BD

🐦 @nfum_Stur

NFU Mutual
INSURANCE | PENSIONS | INVESTMENTS

Counterattack

Greg Schofield

After the great German offensives of 1918 ran out of steam, the allies on the Western Front had an opportunity to catch their breath and reorganise and prepare for their own counter-offensive.

The initial attacks were made by the Americans and French in July in the South of the Front, while the British launched a number of diversionary attacks, but the main British blow fell on 8th August at Amiens with 15 Divisions, 430 tanks and 1700 aircraft. The Germans were shattered and in what became known as the 'Black Day of the German Army', whole Divisions abandoned their trenches and surrendered or retreated under the onslaught. By the end of the first day, the British had advanced 8 miles!

The following Weymouth men died:-

• William CLARKE — Sergeant, Royal Garrison Artillery. Died of gas poisoning 04/07/1918, aged 36. Lived 58, Emmadale Road, Weymouth.

• Walter James CROAD — Lance Bombardier, Royal Garrison Artillery. Died 19/07/1918, aged 23. Son of James & Mary Croad. Lived 111, Chickerell Road, Weymouth

• Gerald Arthur HAWKES — 2nd Lieutenant, Royal Garrison Artillery. Died 03/07/1918 of severe gas poisoning, aged 25. Educated at Hardye's School, Dorchester, matriculated at 16. A notable athlete, he won the Dux Ludorum at London University. Served in H.M. Office of Works at Westminster, at first refused permission to join up, so served in the AA Corps of the RNVR on searchlights.

June 1915 enlisted in 'Queen's Westminster Rifles' and arrived in France in November. Wounded in the Somme battles of 1916, then commissioned in the RGA. Returned to the front in 1917, then gassed at Armentierres in July. Selected for Household Seige Battery. Returned to France April 1918. Gassed 24th June, died 3rd July.

Youngest son of Mr & Mrs T. Barling Hawks, his father a magistrate. Married Frances Bessie Hawkes 21st November, 1917. Lived 'Savernake', Rodwell, Weymouth.

- William John MARTYN   Private, Royal Army Medical Corps.
Killed in action 30/07/1918, aged 27.
Son of Inspector Eustace & Mrs Lillian Martyn.
Lived 98, Dorchester Road, Weymouth.

- E. S. SIMMONDS   Corporal, 9th Royal Fusiliers. Died 10/08/1918, aged 23.
Son of Ellan and the late Edward Simmonds.
Lived 6, Little George Street, Weymouth.

On the 11th August the 1st Dorsetshire Battalion wasinvolved in particularly heavy fighting in the Artois region, during which the following Weymouth men died:-

- Arthur Buckenham FISH   Private, 1st Dorsetshire Regt. Died 11/08/1918, aged 20.
Son of Rev. John W. Fish.

- Frederick Charles LEWIS   Sergeant, 1st Dorsetshire Regt. Died 11/08/1918.
Reported wounded and missing 11/08/1918, confirmed dead June 1919.

- William RIGGS   Private, 1st Dorsetshire Regt. Killed in action 11/08/1918, aged 26. Son of Thomas & Emily Riggs. Lived 6, Avenue Road, Weymouth.

- W. SIDDONS   Private, 1st Dorsetshire Regt. Died 11/08/1918.
- Frank WEBBER   Private, 1st Dorsetshire Regt. Died 11/08/1918

Whilst it is true that the Germans were starved of raw materials and food by 1918, and were particularly affected by the Spanish Influenza, their morale had been particularly shaken by the failure of their own offensives earlier in the year and the evidence of the allies' plentiful supplies. But more significant were the new British tactics; all the lessons of the previous four years had been learnt. Improved field communications, better cooperation between the different arms of the forces, and rapid deployment to change the point of attack when impetus ran out all led to success.

In 1917, the Germans had retreated to specially built and fortified defences known as the Hindenburg Line, which they thought were impenetrable. From 21st August in 1918, the British, using their new tactics, broke through three powerful positions in the line, and the Germans, despite holding American and French attacks elsewhere were forced to undertake a fighting retreat. For the German

AUSTRALIAN WAR MEMORIAL   ART03021

High Command, their priority was to extricate their armies from France; the allied priority was to maintain the pressure and establish a new fortified line. Losses were high on both sides until the Armistice finally came on 11th November, 1918.

During those campaigns, the following Weymouth men died:-

- Frank BOLT — Sergeant, 5th Dorsetshire Regt. Died 01/10/1918, aged ?????? Lived 1, Garibaldi Row, Weymouth.

- Alfred George BOWN — Private, 8th Somerset Light Infantry. Died 24/08/1918.

- William George BRINKLEY — Private, Lord Strathcona's Horse (Canadian) Killed in action 09/10/1918, aged 26. Only son ofGeorge and Mary Brinkley. Lived 43, Brownlow Street, Weymouth.

- James CORBIN — Private, 16th Devonshire Regt, Died 02/09/1918, aged 18. Son of John and Thomas Corbin. Lived 77, Dorchester Road, Weymouth.

- Samuel CURLING — Private, 5th Connaught Rangers. Killed in action 09/10/1918, aged 26. Married to Ada Curling. Lived 9, Albert Terrace, Portland.

- Lionel William Pellew EAST — Brigadier General, Royal Regiment of Artillery. Died 06/09/1918, aged 52. Severely wounded 1891, on NE frontier, Assam. When war broke out Garrison Commander, Cardiff. Transferred to France; Mentioned in Dispatches June 1916 and January 1917. December 1917 raised to Brevet Colonel and awarded C.M.G. and D.S.O. Son of Admiral J. W. East and Ruth Cunningham. Husband of Margaret Reith Stephen East.

- George R EMINSON — 2nd Lieutenant, 21st London Regiment, (1st Surrey Rifles). Killed in action 01/09/1918, aged 21. Lived Bond Street, Weymouth.

- Herbert Henry FENNEMORE — Private, 1st Hampshire Regiment. Killed in action 31/08/1918, aged 41.

- Ernest William FLEMING — 2nd Lieutenant, 13th King's Royal Rifle Corps. Killed by machine gun fire 04/11/1918, aged 22. Scholar of St John's School; clever painter in oils and water. Apprenticed at the 'Beehive', St Edmund's Street, Weymouth; then worked for Dunford in Dorchester. Volunteered 23/10/1915, whilst training for a government position. Promoted to Corporal in the RAMC, and then commissioned. Two other brothers joined the RAMC at the same time; Louis, in a Liverpool hospital with a head wound; Freddie, in hospital in Egypt with malaria. Eldest son of Frederick and Eleanor Fleming. Husband of Kathleen Ellen Fleming. Lived 34, Walpole Street, Weymouth.

- Edward E. FOX — Private, Queen's Own (Royal West Kent). Killed in action 25/10/1918, aged 34. Husband of Fanny Fox. Lived 11, Abbotsbury Road, Weymouth.

- W. GLOVER — Private, Army Service Corps. Died 31/10/1918

- J. Leonard Wilfred GREENMAN — Private, 8th Somerset Light Infantry. Died of wounds at a casualty clearing station 23/08/1918, aged 18. Lived 4, Argyle Road, Weymouth.

- Ernest HANSFORD — Private, 8th Somerset Light Infantry. Killed in action 10/10/1918, aged 21. Lived 18, Walpole Street, Weymouth.

- E. L. HARDY — Lieutenant, Royal Engineers. Died of wounds 07/10/1918, aged 28. Lived 59, St Thomas Street, Weymouth.

- Joe HIGGINS — Squadron Sergeant Major, 6th Dragoon Guards (Carabiniers). Killed in action 26/08/1918, aged 32. Landed in France 06/08/1914. Mentioned in Dispatches; awarded Medal Militaire (France). Brother Bert was a prisoner; brother Rowland convalescing after wounds. Left a baby son called Joe who served in his father's regiment in World War Two. In May 2006 he visited his father's grave and left the message: '… I know you so well, I think about you every day…'. Lived 6, Wesley Street, Weymouth.

- Edward Victor IREMONGER — Private, 9th Royal Fusiliers. Died 14/09/1918, aged 31. Son of Edward and Fanny Iremonger.

- George William KNIGHT — Lance Corporal, 1st The Queen's (Royal West Surrey) Killed in action 21/09/1918, aged 30. Awarded Military Medal. Lived 5, Charles Street, Weymouth.

- Reginald George LOWE — Private, 1st Somerset Light Infantry. Killed in action 02/11/1918, aged 19. Lived 7, Newstead Road, Weymouth.

- Herbert W. LUCAS — Private, 5th Dorsetshire Regiment. Died 01/10/1918.

- James Thomas MARSHALL — Private, 1st Somerset Light Infantry. Killed in action 02/11/1918, aged 37. Bootmaker and repairer at 6, Victoria Arcade. Married to Edith Eliza Marshall. Lived 27, Abbotsbury Road, Weymouth.

- Albert Charles MORRIS — Sergeant, Royal Field Artillery. Died of wounds 16/08/1918, aged 27 Awarded the Military Medal. Lived 6, New Street, Weymouth.

- Charles James NEW — Corporal, Queen's Own (Royal West Kent). Died 08/10/1918, of wounds received the day before. Lived 1, Newberry Gardens, Weymouth.

- William Ernest NORTHOVER — Private, Royal Army Medical Corps. Died 17/10/1918, aged 21. Lived 'Railway Arch Hotel' Chickerell Rd, Weymouth.

- Ernest Edward OZZARD — Private, 5th Dorsetshire Regiment. Died of wounds 28/09/1918, aged 32. Son of Daniel and Emily Ozzard of Weymouth; husband of Jane. Lived Stoke Abbot, Beaminster, Dorset.

- George W. PITMAN — Sergeant, 2nd/6th Durham Light Infantry. Killed in action 05/11/1918, aged 33. Husband of Alice Mary Thomas (Formerly Pitman). Lived 80, St Leonard's Road, Weymouth.

- Joseph Ernest PRINCE — Lance Sergeant, 1st Dorsetshire Regiment. Reported missing 30/09/1918, confirmed dead September 1919, aged 43. Brothers killed, Bertie Leopold and Reginald Luke. Employed at the 'Victoria Hotel', Weymouth. Son of Mary Prince, husband of Eleanor Millie Prince. Lived 2, Upper St Alban's, Street, Weymouth.

- Edward J. F. SARTIN — Private, 1st/1st Oxford and Bucks Light Infantry. Killed in action in a night attack 26/08/1918, aged 25. Joined up in 1916. Wounded and gassed June 1918; killed immediately on his return to action. Had four brothers also serving a 5th brother a policeman. Worked for Mr Prideaux (Dental Surgeon) for 12 years. Lived 4, Harman Terrace, Westham, Weymouth.

- Bertram David SWAN — Quartermaster Sergeant, Royal Field Artillery. Killed in action 05/09/1918, aged 29. Sailed to France 1914 and fought at Mons. Due for home leave on the day he was killed. Lived 4, Mitchell Street, Weymouth.

- George William TISDALE — Private, Army Service Corps. Killed 08/10/1918 whilst on ambulance duty.

- Sydney Victor WOODCOCK — Private/Signaller, 1st Wiltshire Regiment. Died 17/09/1918 of wounds received the day before, aged 19. Enlisted 02/03/1917 in North Somerset Yeomanry (Cyclists). Sent to Ireland January 1918; April 1918 transferred to Wiltshire Regt. and transferred to France. Worked as a member of Milledge's clerical staff. Son of Mr Reginald and Mrs Woodcock. Lived 10, Crescent Street, Weymouth.

Narrow Lanes

Fran Gardner

Narrow lanes

with

high hedges

ancient holloways

rooted

in the land

and

in history

linking

one community

with another

and us

with the past

Near Beaminster.

Pevsner and Silk Hay, Stalbridge

Hilary Townsend

In 1972 my mother died and I inherited her house, Silk Hay, in Stalbridge High Street. The house looked old and had been listed cursorily in the 1960's but nobody seemed to know anything about it. In 1975 the roof of

huge hand cut forest marble tiles threatened to fall off the roof and into the High Street, killing people I had grown up with.

I went to County Hall for advice where the Planning officer then was Miss Pamela Cunnington, an expert in vernacular architecture. She identified the house at once as one end of a medieval merchant's house with a Tudor extension, recommended a firm of builder's experts in medieval restoration and secured invaluable grants for the work.

In 1987, when I was finally able to live there, a highway drain was discovered to have been leaking into the foundations of Silk Hay for about thirty years. The hollow floors throughout the ground floor and all the plaster on walls and ceilings had to be

replaced, and the highway drain renewed. This work revealed the original Tudor fireplace and curing cupboard and a crude sketch of a Crusader knight on a reused stone, probably from the Commanderie of the Knights Templar at Templecombe, where the Templar buildings had been pulled down in 1549, shortly before the Tudor extension was added to Silk Hay.

In the 1930's a German-born architect named Nikolaus Pevsner (1902 - 1983) came to the UK and between 1951 and 1974 created The Buildings of England series of county volumes, but when he published the Dorset volume in this series nothing could be included about Silk Hay because nothing whatever was known about it. However, when Michael Hill an architectural historian and expert in Dorset buildings undertook the revision of Pevsner's book for Yale Press, he came to examine the house. In the revision published in May 2018 it now merits an entry under Stalbridge.

In 2012 an Angel Award from English Heritage was presented for the restoration of Silk Hay and also in 2012 my book was published about the thirty year long struggle to do the work. Entitled `Silk Hay – One Woman's Fight for Architectural Heritage` it is available from Hilary Townsend, Silk Hay, High Street, Stalbridge, DT10 2LH and costs £9.99 or £12 with postage and packing.

Our Ancient Land Scape

Fran Gardner

There's something

about trees !

Their tall

dark strength.

Their cool

green shade.

Their strong

permanence in

Our ancient

Land scape.

Near Throop.

The Home Guard Lydlinch Platoon

As recorded by Home Guard member Frank Palmer

Philip Knott

Following the fall of Dunkirk, and with the imminent threat of invasion, the Secretary of State for War, Sir Anthony Eden, announced in a wireless broadcast on the 14th of May 1940, the proposed formation of a Citizens Army, to be known as the Local Defence Volunteers. He asked for men between the ages of seventeen and sixty-five, who were willing to join, to report to their local police station. Men of all ages and backgrounds, who were not eligible for call up volunteered. During the next few weeks officers were appointed, and local platoons were formed. At the start volunteers were asked to provide whatever weapons they had of their own. An assortment of old rifles, farmer's shotguns, antiquated swords and knives were used, and as a last resort pick axes and pitchforks. Lee Enfield rifles and Lewis Guns later replaced these weapons. The volunteers from Stourton Caundle formed part of the Lydlinch Platoon. We were all issued with an armband, to show that we had enrolled as members of the Local Defence Volunteers. We did little at first, apart from attending lectures in the village hall and taking an occasional turn at keeping a lookout for German parachutists during the hours of darkness We used to patrol the high ground at Holt Lane on a rota basis, two of us from 10 pm till 2am and another pair would arrive to take over until 6 o'clock in the morning.

During the autumn of 1939 army manoeuvres took place at Lydlinch Common, air raid shelters were also constructed in the gardens of local houses and cottages. These were often little more than a hole in the ground, covered by sheets of corrugated iron. These were desperate times and we were often told that we should arm ourselves by making our own weapons. For example, it was once suggested that a sharp knife on the end of a pole would come in handy as a make do pike. Some were able to arm themselves with their own shotguns. Then came a day when we were given the order to report for a fitting of our army uniforms in the village hall. I remember it mostly for my having arrived rather late and that there was little left from which I could pick. My denim trousers were far too big but I was told that I would have to manage with these until we were next in line for an issue of army battledress. I even had to pack my boots with cardboard. The only items that seemed to be fit for purpose were my leather spats and forage cap.

Army manoeuvres were now taking place on a large scale, and with an ever-increasing frequency, over much of the countryside and locally on Lydlinch Common. The army vehicles used to leave the road covered in mud and it was my job to clean up the mess at every given opportunity. I was engaged on this task when a spotter plane hit the top of a tree, crashed to the ground and burst into flames at the roadside on Lydlinch Common. It was a horrific moment and something I have never forgotten.

On May 16th, 1940 an evening football match was arranged between Stourton Caundle and a team of Scottish soldiers, on a hastily marked out pitch in Messlem Field. The soldiers came by lorry to the Trooper Inn, changed into their blue and white kit and then marched with military precision to the field. I enjoyed every minute of my being a stopgap goalkeeper for our side. Highland dancing took place outside the Trooper Inn after the match and I doubt if the locals had ever seen anything like it before. These soldiers were wearing full Scottish dress and they danced to the accompaniment of drums and bagpipes. The soldiers were stationed at Crendle Court, near Milborne Port. The return fixture was cancelled at short notice as they were due for embarkation to France, where sadly, a number of them were to perish before, and during, the retreat to the beaches at Dunkirk.

In June 1940 all of the road direction signs were removed and buried deep beneath the ground at various locations throughout the district. Four sets of "tank traps" were installed on the approach roads into Sturminster Newton. This task was given the utmost priority over any another job of work. Barriers could be slotted into position at short notice and were large enough of an obstacle to stop a military tank. An underground shelter had been constructed into the sloping land at the front of the Roads and Bridges depot, located opposite the Bull Inn and it was here that the council's employees took a turn on night duty. Road stone was held in reserve at various sites and was used after a bomb had blasted a hole in a narrow lane at Crate Hill, Fifehead Neville. Much more stone was needed after an exploding landmine had left a huge crater in the road at Holebrook Lane, Lydlinch.

Invasion Scare

I was awakened by a loud knocking on the door of our home Hays Cottage during the night of September 7th 1940. A youth called out to say that we were all being put on an emergency stand-by until daylight, then he was gone without saying another word. I hurriedly dressed, went outside and then ran down the road to join those who had already gathered near the Trooper Inn. We were not told anything but had guessed that it might have had something to do with an anticipated invasion. The night was spent either telling

of each other's stories or just milling around in circles to keep warm. Rumours were rife after this invasion scare and I remember hearing that our forces had sprayed oil on the sea and then created a wall of fire by setting it alight. We were also to hear reports of burned German bodies being washed up along the south coast. The following is an explanation of what actually happened. On the night of September 7th the code word "Cromwell", meaning "Invasion imminent", was issued, putting both the army's Eastern and Southern Commands on Number One Alert. There was never any invasion attempt by the Germans. The bodies washed up on our shores were those of Germans bombed by the RAF in French ports and swept across the English Channel by the tide.

Formation of the Home Guard

In the July of 1940 Winston Churchill announced a change of name, to the more professional sounding Home Guard. Later that year denim battle dress was provided, and was worn over everyday clothing. Eventually proper army battle dress was provided, with black boots, leather gaiters, belt greatcoats, haversacks, gas masks and helmets.   Many changes were made following the invasion scare. We were also issued with three rifles and a few rounds of ammunition to share between us while on guard duty. The decision was taken to use our cricket pavilion as a guardroom and to relocate it from the cricket field, at the rear of Veale's Cottage, to a site in a corner of the field at the junction of Cat Lane, at Brussels Knapp. A dugout was excavated in the grass verge at the same time. A derelict thatched cottage at Goldsneys was requisitioned for use as our headquarters. We were issued with a .22 rifle and would occasionally go to the rifle range located in an orchard at the rear of Barrow Hill Farm for target practice. A small Nissan hut was constructed at the bottom end of the orchard for an ammunition store. There was a gradual tightening up of military discipline in the Home Guard and service became compulsory.

Back row left to right- Charlie Dennett, Dick Winter, Frank Hollex, Dennis Jeans, Eddy Bond, Frank Palmer, Sonny Bealing and George Lane.
Middle row- Albert Bealing, Roy Brown, George Brown, Leslie Woods, Joe Walden, Len Lake, Jack Watson and Alex Smith
Front row- Billy Bugg, Charlie Lake, Cecil Orchard, The Sergant, George Furnell, Bob Green, Jack Pye and Jim Gray.

Basic Military Training

We were taken by lorry one Sunday to Bovington Camp and shown a collection of German and Italian tanks in the museum, presumably a crash course on identification. We were taught a variety of ways in which a military tank could be knocked out, one of which was to go running up alongside an enemy tank and then to smack a "sticky-bomb" into position near its metal tracks. We tossed hand grenades over the top, from within the quarry at Garvey. One failed to explode and had to be blown up with a small amount of plastic explosive material. A member of our squad was scared stiff and had dropped a grenade in his fright. We were more than a little fortunate in that he had not pulled out the safety pin. We did a route march in full kit on a hot summer's day resulting in many grumbles of discontent, much sweating by all and some with blisters on their feet. We fired our .505 rifles for the first time on a recently constructed range

at Okeford Hill. I was chosen to be one of four who did the marking down of scores in the butts for much of the morning. Some could not shoot for toffees and we would hear their bullets either thudding into a mound of earth or go whining past overhead. Several had failed to register a hit and so an old soldier in our party had helped them out by poking a few holes through a target with his pencil. He knew all the tricks and was as artful as a monkey.

There was a Rifle Meeting on the range at Oborne. Many hundreds of men were there from the 4th Battalion on a long tiring Sunday. I was the only member of the Lydlinch Platoon to win a prize and it had given me a feeling of great satisfaction. I attended a follow up event at the same venue arranged to select those who would be going to a tournament somewhere in Sussex. I lost out by one point and was bitterly disappointed.

A night training exercise was arranged to take place in Stock Gaylard Park, a battle-craft test between our platoon and a rather secret unit of the Home Guard. We had been ordered to try and stop them from getting through our defensive positions around both the large garden and several outbuildings at Stock House. Many of them were to fail and give themselves up before the night was out, probably to get under cover after hours of teeming rain.

The next exercise for Lydlinch Platoon of the Home Guard took place on Lydlinch Common against a Commando unit. We went there early in the evening and prepared their arrival at around midnight. I had been quick to realize what might happen and had used many leafy branches in an effort to camouflage my chosen position for the heavy machine gun. The officer in charge had then told us all to take things easy until hearing a loud blast on his whistle. We did not have to wait long before getting the signal that a lorry was travelling at high speed in our direction. The vehicle was then brought to a juddering halt, after a member of our group threw a thunder-flash under it. He was hidden from view near the roadside. Commando after Commando could be seen jumping over the tailboard, all emitting a blood-curdling cry when setting forth to flush us out. Our place of concealment had remained undiscovered through the evening and my colleague and I were both trying to stop ourselves from laughing aloud while watching the action as it unfolding before our eyes.

Night Patrols

The Stourton Caundle Section of the Lydlinch Platoon was summoned to undertake night duty at Sturminster Newton. We were taken by lorry to an old house in Bath Road, and then given our orders for the night by the Officer in command of the 5th Platoon. We were told to stay fully clothed and to get some rest. There was much rowdy behaviour, by a few of the younger members, and sleep had been nigh impossible for most of us in the room. Some of these youths were wrestling on the floor with live grenades in their shoulder pouches. We were not in any danger however, as I had taken the precautionary measure of bending the safety pins, whilst engaged on the task of priming the grenades with fuses on the previous night. The phone rang at about two o'clock in the morning. Our Lieutenant received a message giving him a reference number

on the map. The location as soon identified as Honeymead Lane. He then gave orders to get there as quickly as possible by lorry. It was decided that we should split up into two groups on our arrival. One to walk the hedgerows and the other stay on guard at the entrance to the lane. Everything went according to plan, until the silence came to an abrupt end with loud laughter, after one our younger members broke wind. Two high-ranking officers of the Home Guard had observed our every move, although we were not aware of it at the time. But they sure did tear us off a strip afterwards, especially about the laughing and also for the noisy way in which we had clambered down from out of the lorry. There were many soldiers stationed in the area and it soon became the norm for the Home Guard to take over at night, if these regular troops had moved out, or were going on military manoeuvres.

HOME GUARD SPECIAL UNIT
Charlie Lake, George Harris, Frank Hollex, George Furnell, Bob Ashford and Vernon Caines

Advanced Training

In the October of 1943 I attended a training course held at the Barracks of the Dorsetshire Regiment at Dorchester from Friday night until the Sunday evening. We were a class of twelve, all of whom had volunteered in the hope of passing a test on our knowledge and skills at map reading and weaponry. I arrived by Jeep and was told to report to a Sergeant Shackle. I slept well on a top bunk in the barrack-room and on the Saturday morning had a breakfast of fried eggs and bacon. Sergeant Shackle lined us up for inspection and then marched us off to the lecture-room. He was astute with his questioning when enquiring as to our interests outside of work and gave us each an appropriate nickname before the morning was out. I was rather flattered to be called "the Musician". In the afternoon we were given a short break and watched from a window as a squad of soldiers were being put through their paces on the square below. There was an officer on parade and we were somewhat confused as to why he waved his hand at us on a number of occasions. He then headed in our direction with a very purposeful stride. We did not know what why but made ourselves scarce in an area at the rear of the building. The Sergeant told us later that we could have been disciplined, as it was a breach of military regulations to stare from out of the windows, when drill was taking place on the square.

On Sunday we spent much of our time stripping down, and putting back together, all of the moving parts on several types of automatic weapons. We were expected to have satisfactory answers to many a searching question. I did quite well on the range, with .22 rifle during the afternoon. We were to leave for home soon afterwards, probably wondering if we had done well enough to gain for ourselves a good report. I passed in the following subjects: General Knowledge, Rifle, 56 M Grenade, Sten Carbine, Browning Automatic, Battle Craft and Map Reading. I was rewarded with a second stripe and promoted to the rank of Corporal.

Air Raids

Village men of all age groups had volunteered to learn the correct way to deal with incendiary devices, dropped from enemy aircraft. They were known as 'Fire-watchers'.

Mr Harry Holdway, who lived at Barrow Hill Farm, had been appointed Air Warden. At the height of the German bombing campaign, in 1940 and 1941, a unit consisting of three men would be on duty throughout the night. When a red alert was received, by telephone from military command, the wardens would sound the alert by blowing short blasts on their whistles, as they toured the village to warn the sleeping residents. After the all clear had been given, the exercise would be repeated, but this time giving long blasts on the whistles. During this period wave after wave of German bombers could be heard passing overhead, on their way to the industrial cities and ports, in the Midlands and north of the country. Wave after wave of German bombers flew overhead and on such nights we would be on the go all night. Only but once did I actually hear a bomb come hurtling down from an enemy plane. I admit to having been very, very frightened at the time. After the explosion we had gone in search of the crater but could find nothing out of the ordinary in the nearby fields and lanes. We heard at daybreak that it had fallen in a field at Rowden Mill. A stick of about five bombs fell in a field at Brunsells Knapp. I came home from work the following evening and walked around the area with several other young men. We clambered over mounds of earth and down into craters at the spot where the bombs had fallen, penetrating deep into the ground. An officer from the Bomb Disposal Unit had duly arrived to carry out tests. I seem to recall that no trace was found of any unexploded bombs. A search light battery operated by a small unit of regular soldiers was located at Rowden Mill Lane, in Brookhill field. When it was in operation, fingers of light could be seen criss-crossing the night skies above the village. In addition to the 'fire-watchers' there was also an Auxiliary Fire Crew. The Fire Engine was located in a garage at Drove Road, opposite the Old Vicarage. Members of the Fire Crew included Sam Harris and Jack Osmond.

A line of bombs were dropped across a field at Brick Hill with the last one dropping down a disused well quite near to the pair of cottagers at Brick Hill. There was some structural damage but no casualties. Searchlights were dotted across the countryside the nearest being located at Rowden Mill Lane operated by a small detachment of regular soldiers. The beam from the searchlight lit up night skies above the village. Bullets were fired down a beam of light by the crew of a German bomber and on another occasion the crew were fired at by a 'sneak' German raider as it swept low over the field at the break of dawn.

Daytime Air Raid at Sherborne

On September 30th 1940 I was trimming a hedge on the Kingstag side of Berry Lane at about four o'clock in the afternoon. A woman came from out of her house to ask if I had heard the sound of a loud explosion in the direction of Sherborne. I heard the roar of many aeroplane engines and had looked upwards into the sky to watch a formation of nine planes between a break in the clouds. I was told later that fifty Luftwaffe planes had dropped more than three hundred bombs over a wide area of Sherborne.

The following morning I travelled to Sherborne by lorry with a gang of my workmates from Division 5. We were told on our arrival that our first job of work would be to make good the damage caused by bombs to both the road and drains at Horsecastles. A huge crater had to be filled in and compacted by hand. Three of us were then given orders to join up with a gang of men from another district at Lenthay. The devastation appalled me, as the result of a direct hit on the cemetery, and was too horrified to give it anything more than a cursory glance. During our first week the town siren was heard and the man in charge had ordered us to take shelter in a nearby ditch, as a dogfight was taking place high up in the sky. I remained standing but did not feel quite so brave when some small objects began to whistle through the air thudding to the ground nearby. These were later identified as being spent cartridges from the machine guns of a Spitfire. I assisted with the removal of some kerb stones from out of the back bedroom of a house, most of which were undamaged, after having been hurled through the roof by the force of a massive explosion in the roadway outside. A work mate had tried to wash his hands clean afterwards, only to discover that he had dipped them into a sink where a baby's dirty napkins had been left to soak overnight, as the water supply was still cut off.

Demobilization

Following the D-Day invasion the Home Guard was no longer required.

Demobilization took place on the 31st of December 1944. The final act was to parade to St Peters Church to take part in a service of thanksgiving. There was a small amount of cash in a Benevolent Fund. The money came from the organizing of a few whist drives and dances, raised to give a little financial assistance to anyone in our unit suffering an injury whilst on Home Guard duty. It was never required for this purpose and was used to provide the local children with a tea party in the village hall. Our very last time together was a day out in Southampton with grandstand seats at the Dell to watch Southampton play Tottenham Hotspur.

Flanders Poppies

Brian C. Moore

Britain's teenage soldiers
Rose before the dawn
And died before the sunset
In the war to End all wars.

Teenage blood filled trenches
From Ypres to the Somme
While seeds from Flanders poppies
Crossed the sea to home.

And seeds from Flanders poppies
Fell in Britain's fields
Giving birth to Flanders poppies
On downland, hill and weald.

And every Flanders flower
Is a British mother's son
Come home again to live again
In the scarlet fields of home.

2,000 Miles of Dorset Coast

Steve Belasco

It's more than seven years since I started photographing the waters of the Dorset coast with any sense of purpose. I'd sailed these waters for many years before but relatively recently decided that I could establish an online library of images captured from offshore.

It struck me that only a limited number of people have the opportunity to view the Jurassic Coast's splendour from the sea (its best viewpoint) and I wanted to share my pride in my home county by utilising two of my passions, boating and photography. Plus, it gave me an excuse to get out on the water when I could, (alongside a full-time job and a growing family) and I soon became a proud Ambassador for the Jurassic Coast Trust.

There are now more than 5,000 downloadable images on my website, jurassicphotographic. com, many of them unique and nearly all captured from offshore. They record not just the incredible geology and geography of our World Heritage Site, but the humans and animals that come to enjoy it and the people and creatures that depend on it, whether for commerce or survival. It's probably the only library of its kind on the internet.

The geology and history of our ancient coast is well served by people far more clever than I, so my mission has been to creatively record our 21st-century custodianship to share with as many people as possible and to provide a visual record for future generations. We're all part of evolution and I believe that long into the future, human interaction with the coast, whether that be pleasure, exploration, industry – yes and thoughtlessness – will be just as relevant as that of the dinosaurs.

I've pottered around 2,500 nautical miles back and forth along the 100-odd miles of coast between Poole and Exmouth - more than 2,000 of them in Dorset - with a few forays into darkest Devon. My average speed has been around five knots (six mph), meaning 500 hours at the helm, and many more stopped to actually take photos.

In a small boat the longer excursions like Lyme Regis or Studland are not really practical in one day and have to be planned (weather being the major factor) so I've spent many nights in the small but cosy cabin aboard my boat Strange Weather.

But the waters nearer to my home port of Portland still see me nipping out for a couple of hours here or a morning there. There's always something to photograph, boats of every description, coasteerers plunging into the water, wildlife in its element plus amazing cloud formations, sunrises, and sunsets and all with the glorious backdrop of our coastline.

Perhaps serendipitously, I find myself working now as a berthing master at Portland Marina, which means messing about with boats most of the day, right at the centre of the Jurassic Coast.

Allow me the indulgence of sharing a few of my favourite Dorset spots to visit on my boat. It seems strange that, although I'm very interested in how humans interact with and enjoy the 21st-century Jurassic Coast, this selection of my 'ace places' is often totally bereft of them!

Gad Cliff and Brandy Bay

Gad Cliff towers over Brandy Bay

The shallow Brandy Bay to the west of Kimmeridge Bay is hard-bottomed and shallow, and going close inshore requires cautious navigation. In many ways austere, with low shale cliffs to the east and large, fallen rocks to the north, the bay can be wonderfully peaceful and quiet on a sunny morning with just the echoing call of raptors on the hunt high above. Brandy Bay is prosaically-named after the nefarious smuggling activity that was based here in the past…

The mighty Gad Cliff towers above reminding me, from some angles, of the presidents of Mount Rushmore in South Dakota.

If you're lucky, and very observant, you might just catch sight of the feral goats that have lived here for centuries. Apparently, there are also a great number of adders here, so watch out…

Gad Cliff, a little like Mount Rushmore?

Portland Bill from the south

Portland Bill

I reckon the Bill area to extend a kilometre or so up either side of the island from the actual point. When close offshore at the point the rocks, lighthouse and Trinity House obelisk dominate. Move out a little and the view broadens abruptly, from Pulpit Rock on the west side to Gode Nore in the east. It all encompasses a fascinating collection of rock ledges, deep caves, quarries and even a couple of tiny 'islands'!

Bottlenose dolphins with colourful beach huts behind

Though a little sinister on a dark day, and strictly out of bounds when it's blowing, there's a surprising amount of colour here when the sun shines, from the reds of the lighthouse itself and a couple of ancient cranes, to the warm yellows created by the raised beach along here, not to mention the colourful beach huts.

The Undercliff 'The Lost World'

Although much of the Undercliff is in, ahem, the next county, the first section is in West Dorset and has been much written about as a unique wilderness of dense undergrowth with its own micro-climate. I love the 'primordial' look of the place. Dark green foliage dominates, vaguely reminiscent of the mangrove, with patches of white and red cliff shining out, and the plateau of Goat Island, the Jurassic Coast's

The Undercliff has a primordial feel to it

answer to the classic movie, The Lost World.

When I gaze at the interesting but narrow strip of foreshore here, I half expect a tribe of loincloth-clad savages to come rushing out of the greenery hurling spears at me, like an Indiana Jones movie!

Tough work to transit on foot, it's not surprising that from seaward it's rare to see any signs of humanity except for the ubiquitous fishermen's floats.

A colony of guillemots under St Aldhelm's Head

A Coastful of Quarries

The stretch of rugged, and sometimes inhospitable, coast between Anvil Point and St Aldhelm's Head in Purbeck has been much-hewn by man. There is fairly deep water close in and all along these five miles or so are cubes and perpendiculars, straight lines and box-like shapes caused by the major quarrying that peaked here in the 18th and 19th centuries. (The Romans started it much earlier). Brooding rectangular caves, or galleries, peer out to sea like giant eyes.

The last coastal quarry to close here is Winspit, which shows an interesting mix of ancient and relatively modern techniques and is a popular visit on foot. It was Winspit that the BBC chose to represent the Daleks' home plant Skaro in the Doctor Who TV series and several episodes were filmed here.

(This is wonderfully appropriate in the sense that the foreword for my next book, 'The Jurassic Coast From The Sea' has been written by the creator of TV's Broadchurch, Chris Chibnall. Chris has written several episodes of, and is indeed the new head writer and leading executive producer of Doctor Who!)

Winspit Quarry with Worth Matravers beyond

I've only highlighted a handful of Dorset diamonds here, but I equally love to visit The Chesil, Worbarrow, Man O' War Cove, Lyme, Old Harry… actually, all of it!

Red Arrows above Golden Cap

FACT BOX

Steve's images are available as canvases of all sizes and as framed, fine art prints.

The popular photobook Dorset From The Sea, ISBN 978-1-845847-62-3 is available direct from him at £9.99, plus £2 p+p, for the 'coffee table' edition.

Contact:
stevebelasco16@gmail.com
or
01305 871904
or view the website:
www.stevebelasco.net

Nuremberg's Voice of Doom

The Autobiography of the Chief Interpreter at History's Greatest Trials

Author: Wolfe Frank Edited By: Paul J Hooley

Highlights:

· With the British War Crimes Executive, Frank was engaged in collecting material for the prosecution of many of the major Nazi war criminals.

· Frank gained the nickname 'Voice of Doom' for his role in translating and announcing the final sentences to the war criminals and 400 million radio listeners.

· This is a remarkable insight into the Nuremberg trials, including conversations struck up with all the war criminals on trial, particularly Hermann Goering.

· He held the first Chief of the Gestapo in his home, where he produced a list of names and events that proved vital to the prosecution at the Nuremberg Trials.

· He coaxed full confessions, later used as evidence, out of: the man responsible for the manufacture of Zyklon B; and the SS General who designed the mobile gas chamber.

Description

The memoirs of Wolfe Frank, which lay hidden in an attic for twenty five years, are a unique and highly moving behind-the-scenes account of what happened at Nuremberg – 'the greatest trial in history' – seen through the eyes of a witness to the entire proceedings. They include important historical information never previously revealed. In an extraordinarily explicit life story, Frank includes his personal encounters with the war criminals, inside and outside the courtroom, and describes some of the official and unofficial meetings and exchanges he had with Goering, Ribbentrop, Keitel, Ley, Speer, Hess and others. This book therefore is a unique record that adds substantially to what is already publicly known about the trials and the defendants.

A unique character of extreme contrasts Frank was a sybarite, a womaniser, a risk taker and an opportunist. He was also a highly intelligent man of immense courage, charm, good manners, integrity and ability.

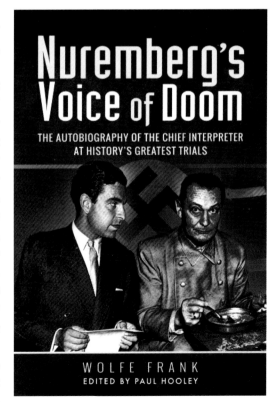

He undertook the toughest assignment imaginable at Nuremberg and he played a major role in 'materially shortening the enormously difficult procedures by an estimated three years'.

Nuremberg's Voice of Doom is a story of two interwoven themes: one of love, adventure and excitement; the other of a former German citizen's ght for the right to become a British officer and his extraordinary commitment to service, duty and justice – that was seen to be scrupulously fair to, and by, the Tribunal, the prosecutors, the defence lawyers and the war criminals alike – throughout what was described as being 'the greatest and most important trial the world has ever seen'.

Whilst this book is therefore an important military record that will appeal to those interested in the history of World War II and the rise and fall of the Nazi Party, as well as being a definitive account of all that happened at Nuremberg, it is also an enthralling human-interest story that will intrigue and fascinate a much wider audience.

Author Details

Born on St Valentine's Day 1913, WOLFE FRANK was a strikingly handsome man and one of the twentieth century's most charismatic figures. He was married five times – to a German Baroness, an American actress, a suspected Russian spy, an Italian hostess and an Austrian interpreter – and he had countless affairs. In a packed lifetime he was, at various times, a linguist, financial advisor, racing driver, theatre impresario, broadcaster, journalist, salesman, businessman, restaurateur, skier, and property developer. In 1949 he risked his life again by going undercover, on forged papers, to write an acclaimed series of articles (exposing the subterfuge and uncovering evil in post-war Germany) for the New York Herald Tribune, during which time he single-handedly tracked down, apprehended and took the confession of one of the 'most wanted' missing Nazi war criminals.

PAUL HOOLEY was born and educated in Surrey. He founded a design and printing company that grew to be ranked amongst the industry's top 1%. He has also been a director of a building society, a private hospital and companies involved in advertising, entertainment, publishing, finance, building, transport, property and engineering. He retired from business in 1990 since when he has devoted much of his time to studying, writing and lecturing on a wide range of historical and military subjects. A former town and district councillor, he was Mayor of Bedford in 1978. Amongst other involvements he has been a magistrate, a tax commissioner and a prison visitor. He has been married to Helen for over fifty years, has three children and now lives in Dorset. He was appointed a MBE in 2003.

How Paul Hooley uncovered the story.

About two years ago a friend of mine, Mike Dilliway (who also lives in Gillingham) was about to move house. Knowing I was a writer and a historian, Mike asked me if I would look at several boxes of papers that had been stored in his loft for over 25 years – to see if there was anything there that might be of historical importance.

After an initial period of trepidation as I sorted through several thousand sheets of paper, my heart soared when I realised that I had stumbled across a treasure trove of documents consisting of the memoirs, family records and other material concerning the life and times of Wolfe Frank who was Chief Interpreter at the Nuremberg Trials, and who was one of those involved in the pioneering days of simultaneous interpretation.

Wolfe, who retired to Mere and became something of a recluse, spent his final years in the village completing his memoirs. He left his archive to Mike in his will. Mike not realising what he had placed them in his loft where they remained undisturbed for a quarter of a century.

By the time I had concluded my investigations I knew it was my duty to ensure that Frank's involvements at, and remembrances of, the Nuremberg Trials, as well as his participation in the setting up of the world's first simultaneous interpretation system, were more properly documented. It was also very clear to me that he hoped his insights of these events, as part of his life's story, would be published posthumously. This led to me compiling, editing and expanding Wolfe's story which is to be published under the title 'Nuremberg's Voice of Doom' in the UK and USA in October.

To give you a little more information at this stage – the book consists of a posthumous autobiography of the first half of Wolfe Frank's astonishing life – that stands up to the closest scrutiny – plus a potted biography of his later days (based on his memoirs) and further added information that chronicles the life, times and involvements of one of the 20th centuries most charismatic figures and a brave, dedicated and gifted man whose exploits and achievements should not be allowed to fade into obscurity.

Frank's participation throughout the trials at Nuremberg places him in the quite unique position of having been totally immersed in the proceedings from the very first day of the war crimes investigations – he was asked to translate the then only known piece of evidence. He then became one of the most active players in the forensic and interrogations processes and the setting up and pioneering of the world's first ever system of simultaneous interpretation (a triumph in itself). Once the International Military Tribunal (IMT) started, Frank became a central figure in all stages of the trials. He interpreted the Tribunal's opening remarks, was used more than any other interpreter during the ten month duration of the IMT, and then finally brought proceedings to a close by informing the defendants of their fate – a duty, simultaneously listened to by an estimated radio audience of four hundred million – which is why the world's media dubbed him the Voice of Doom.

It is true to say therefore that the first and last words the defendants heard in their own language at Nuremberg were uttered by Wolfe Frank, a man they – like the Tribunal, the prosecutors and their own counsels – trusted implicitly and for whom they had the highest possible regard and respect.

These memoirs add substantially to what is already known about the trials and add further important insights about what went on behind the scenes. They include details of Frank's personal encounters with defendants Goering, Ribbentrop, Keital, Kaltenbrunner, Speer, et al. as seen through the eyes of one (perhaps the only one) who was involved at every stage of what has been described as having been 'the greatest trial in history.'

'Nuremberg's Voice of Doom' is a record of two interwoven themes, one of love, adventure and excitement (he was married five times – to a German Baroness; an American actress; a suspected Russian spy; an Italian hostess; and an Austrian interpreter and he had countless affairs), the other of a former German citizen's fight for the right to become a British soldier and his extraordinary commitment to service, duty and justice that saw him rise to become a Captain in the Army and, it was said, 'the finest interpreter in the world'.

I cannot stress enough that whilst this is an important military record that will appeal to those interested in the history of World War II, the rise and fall of the Nazi Party and the inside story of all that happened at Nuremberg, including the introduction of simultaneous interpretation, it is also very much a human interest story that will appeal to the wider public.

Email: enquiries@pen-and-sword.co.uk
Website: http://www.pen-and-sword.co.uk

The Great Globe at Swanage:Who put it there?

Kay Ennals MBE

The Isle of Purbeck in the south-east of Dorset extends from the limestone cliffs of the english channel across the heaths to Poole Harbour. In this delightful setting is the town of Swanage. The town is a very popular resort and residential area. (Swanage Bay is sheltered from the prevailing winds with beautiful sands, safe bathing and boating).

Many new and older buildings in Swanange are constructed from the locally quarried limestone. Purbeck stone has been widely used for building. As it became known it was requested for building in many large towns and even abroad. Workings in the quarries date back to as early as 1650. Transport was a problem and men handled huge blocks of stone, initially using horses, and having to heave the stone on boats, but when the railways came the problem of transport was eased.

John Mowlem (1788- 1868) was a stonemason and the founder of a quarrying construction company. He was born in Swanage, the son of a quarryman. He was one of a poor family of six children. He worked with his three brothers at tilly whim stone quarry, but the quarry closed down in 1812. John looked for other work, and was determined to improve himself. He applied for jobs outside Swanage.

His first opportunity came at Norris Castle Quarry on the Isle of Wight. His work was recognised by an architect, James Wyatt, who persuaded him to go to work at the masonry of all government departments in London. There he worked on contracts at Greeenwich, Kensington Palace, the Royal Mews, and Somerset House as foreman.

John then set up his own company ordering the stone he needed from Swanage to pave London Bridge and re-pave Blackfriars Bridge, and the Strand. A shortfall in supply led him to purchase a quarry in Guernsey where he oversaw the shipping from the Channel Islands of granite setts.

When his fortune was made he returned to Swanage for his retirement. His nephew, George Mowlem-Burt- (1845 - 1918) who also worked for him was made a partner. A relative of George's wife whose name was Joseph Freeman, became a partner, too. The firm was renamed: Mowlem Burt and Freeman'.

George Mowlem-Burt took over the entire company from his uncle and brought many new ideas and effects to Swanage from London. One of the effects was a clock tower commemorating the Duke of Wellington which once stood at the Southwark end of London Bridge but was set up as a feature of Swanage sea-front.

George also undertook a huge landscaping project in Swanage, which is today Durlston Park. On this estate is the Great Globe. George felt he would like to give something back to Swﾠ ge for his love of the town and appreciation of his joy in living there.

The Great Globe was, and is, a massive 40 ton stone ball made at Mowlands Works in the stone yard. It was shipped in 15 segments to Swanage and was set up on a platform just below the castle. It is amazing how it rests on its lip and seems as if it would be easy to push it over.

Reading, or trying to read, the detail of the map inscribed on the globe is quite captivating. Around the globe area are a set of stone plaques carved with quotations.

This huge ball of stone cannot be missed. It stands within Durlston Country Park and Nature Reserve which stretches along the south coast of Swanage. It is one of the curiosities on the Isle of Purbeck. It is also a reminder of those who worked in the quarries over the years. Stone masons and builders who created so much from the natural resort of Purbeck stone.

George Mowlem Burt was knighted in 1902. He represented Swanage on the Dorset County Council for a number of years. He died at Carthion (his home), in Durlston Park, aged 73 years.

DORSET WRECKS sea shanty group, based in Weymouth, are available for weddings, birthdays, Trafalgar night & corporate events. Among recent gigs are Folk Festivals at Wimborne, Bridport, & Weymouth; Shanty Festivals at Coastliners in Poole, & Teignmouth. Singing on Tall Ships: - [?] Marite, Nao Victoria, & Pelican. Sea Food Festivals at Lymington & Weymouth, and Camp Bestival. Contact 07805 884786 for enquiries. www.facebook.com/DorsetWrecksSeaShanties/

Village Trades and Tradesmen in the 1920s

Philip Knott

Shop and Post Office

In the 1920s the main village shop and post office at Stourton Caundle was located at the top of Golden Hill. The shop premises were divided into two compartments, with the grocery business located in a room to

the right of the entrance doorway. There were some tinned foods and jars on the shelves, but most of the provisions were delivered to the shop in bulk and weighed up to the customer's requirements. Foodstuffs, such as sugar, rice, lentils, and dried fruit were delivered in Hessian sacks and other products including margarine, lard and dried fruit were delivered in wooden boxes of varying sizes; tea came in three-ply chests.

A small room to the rear of the grocery section served as a store for such items as a barrel of malt vinegar and seven-pound tins of corned beef, which was sliced with a sharp carving knife to the customer's requirements. Cheese was cut by means of a wire, with wooden handles attached to each end. Metal scoops were used to weigh up other items such as rice, which were then placed in a brown paper bag. Sometimes dried fish could be purchased. The fish arrived at the shop in a wooden barrel and had the appearance of a

piece of leather. However after an overnight soaking in a bowl of water, it provided a nutritious meal when cooked.

The small centre room, just inside the entrance door, served as the post office, boots clothes and stationery were also stored here. Jars of sweets were displayed on a shelf in the window, in a prominent position so as to attract the attention of the children. The normal price of toffees and boiled sweets was a penny an ounce, and better quality sweets were six pennies per quarter. As far as the small children were concerned the best buy of all came when the jar was almost empty. A child could expect a large bag of misshapen sweets for only a penny. Empty orange boxes were in demand for use as nesting boxes in hen houses, while tea chests were suitable for winter storage of potatoes.

In 1926 a public telephone was installed in the room to the right hand side of the entrance door, with no privacy for the person making the call. Two wires, supported by a line of poles connected the post office with a manual switchboard in Stalbridge Post Office.

Postman Alec Roberts delivered the post to the village from Stalbridge Post Office, riding a pedal cycle. The delivery round started at Stalbridge Weston, from there he pushed his cycle along the footpath to Haddon Lodge, where he stopped for a coffee break. After delivering to Woodrow, he then rode down Sherborne Way to commence delivery through the village High Street, collecting the outward going mail from the

Post Office on the return journey to Stalbridge. Rural Postmen worked long hours in the 1920s, delivering the mail twice a day and also on Sunday mornings. The postmen sorted the letters in a room at the rear Stalbridge post office before setting out on their rounds. Outgoing mail was taken in mailbags to Stalbridge Station for transportation to the the main sorting office at Blandford.

The proprietors of an adjoining shop at Golden Hill were Mr and Mrs Chaldicott. Groceries were delivered to remote dwellings and outlying farms by pony and trap, with the pony kept in a stable at the rear of the premises. The property fell into disrepair and was demolished in the late 1930s.

Chaldicotts Shop at Golden Hill c1930

🌾 The Bakery

Mr Walter Hays was the proprietor of the bakery which was located in a building on the opposite side of the road from the post office. Mrs Hays made large cakes including seed, dough, fruit, and lardy, which were sold at a price of nine pence each. When a dozen buns

Baker Hays on his delivery round

were purchased thirteen buns were handed over, this was known as the Baker's Dozen. The baking oven was fuelled by either coal or coke making it difficult to maintain an even temperature in the oven.

At the weekends local residents could take their joints of meat to the bake house to roast for a cost of one penny and kneaded dough could be purchased for pastry making. The local baker Mr Hays delivered his bread and cakes cart by horse and cart. The cart was fitted with a fixed semi-cylindrical canvas tilt, on the sides of which were displayed in bold lettering his name and trade.

Other Tradesmen

Mr James (Jimmy) Walden was a carpenter, wheelwright, undertaker and made wooden hay rakes. For many years he did a good trade by taking a cart laden with rakes to the local markets held in May and June. Mr George Smith was a carrier and also slaughtered cottagers' fattened pigs. Fred Ford another carrier also delivered coal collected from Stalbridge station. Mr Louis Jeans was a thatcher and also had a reputation for being able to charm warts. The Parsons family were tailors and Jimmy Lambert' repaired boots, shoes and leather leggings. On the Thursday afternoon of each week he would set out in his pony and trap to deliver the local weekly newspaper the Western Gazette. Mrs Jeans was frequently being called upon to perform the duties of midwifery and the after-care of mother and baby. Mr Jeans worked for Sturminster Newton Rural District Council as a 'Stone Cracker', repairing the unsurfaced roads, using stone hauled by horse and cart from Garvey quarry. Joe Walden, who had lost an eye in the First World War, worked as full-time photographer, taking photographs at private sittings, local events, going around the schools and by paying regular visits to the Blandford Army Camp. His transport was a belt driven motorcycle, with his equipment carried in the side-car.

Mr Ambrose Stainer, was one of several men in the village, including my own grandfather, who cut men's and boys' hair on a Sunday morning to earn a little

The Smithy at Bishops Caundle

The Blacksmith's shop at the Pound (far left) closed in the first decade of the 20th Century. The building at the front was the cattle pound used for holding stray cattle, which were released to the owner on the payment of a fine to the village Waywarden.

tobacco money. During the winter men were regularly engaged in the task of sawing logs to keep the home fire burning, providing work for Mr Stainer and my grandfather, who were proficient in the skill of sharpening hand saws. A charge of 6d was made for each saw sharpened.

A building, on the right hand side of the entrance to Church Farm, was a blacksmith's shop. The premises were rented by a Mr Ayres who was the village blacksmith at Bishops Caundle.

Village Inns

The Trooper Inn was owned by Wykes Brewery of Gillingham. The landlord was a

The Trooper Inn in the early 1920s

Mr Walter Green, who also owned a pony and trap, and provided a local taxi service. He was also the local coal merchant, the coal being collected by horse and cart from Stalbridge station and stored in the yard at the rear of the Trooper.

During threshing time the threshers would call at lunchtime, with their bread and cheese wrapped in a handkerchief.

Gypsy families were also regular visitors to the pub when encamped at Holt lane. The Hughes and the Penfolds were well known gypsy families and everyone was careful not to upset them. Sometimes they would sing and dance all night long and there was often fighting. General Elections were also very exiting times, with lots of discussion and arguments and customers were often bribed with free drinks, to vote for one party or the other. The games played in the pub at this time were 'shove-

hapenny' table skittles, darts and dominoes. Miss Guest's hunt met outside every season, and drinks were served to the riders. After the death of Mr Walter Green in 1928, his wife Charlotte took over the tenancy. In the wintertime it was not unusual to see her sitting in front of the open fire in the public bar plucking chicken. Her son Robert owned several horse and putts, which were used for road building contracts for the District Council. He was also an expert at catching rabbits, either by ferreting or the use of wire snares. Rabbits were also hunted at night with the aid of a portable light, powered by a car battery and using specially trained dogs, known as lurchers, to catch them. Rabbits could be purchased at the back door of the Trooper for a tanner a piece.

In the 1920s Cider making in the stables at the rear of the Trooper Inn was one of the highlights of the year in the village social calendar. Hurricane lamps were suspended from the rafters and the stronger boys were given the task of turning the handle of the apple crusher. The only incentive for doing this was to be allowed to drink the apple juice

Gwyers Alehouse in the 1920s

in the tub under the press. If a boy was foolish enough to drink too much juice, then he was soon in for a surprise, as the outcome was likely to be a sudden opening of the bowels, a lot worse than a periodical dose of laxative. A single or double handled cider cup was used for drinking cider in the home, but the men preferred to use a short length of cow horn when working in the fields, because it was easier to carry and was unbreakable. A young lad was expected to carry the jar of cider out into the fields to serve a cup, or horn full, of cider to each workman, using the same drinking vessel. This task was referred to as doing the honours. Many farmers made cider on their farms, for the provision of free cider to the workmen was an added incentive to get the work done.

George and Mary Stokes purchased the small holding at Gwyers fom the Stourhead estate in the 1850s. As well as being a farmer George was an entepeneur and he obtained a licence to sell beer brewed on the premises. He is also listed in census returns as a plumber and glazier.

Visiting Tradesmen

Many different tradesmen people delivered in Stourton Caundle on a regular basis. Two Stalbridge bakers, Dikes and Bryants, provided stiff completion for Baker Hayes. In addition to the bakery Dikes had a grocery shop and supplied pork from either their own pigs or from pigs reared on local farms. Stalbridge butchers, Fred Bugg and Sydney Eavis, delivered meat to the village by horse cart. Both had their own slaughterhouses and retail premises in Stalbridge. Sydney Parsons at Stalbridge Weston was mainly a rabbit and egg dealer but also retailed meat.

The ringing of a loud bell, would herald the arrival of a travelling bazaar from Wimborne Minster. The motor van was large and the carrying capacity increased by fitting an external wooden framework to both sides of the vehicle, in which was carried racks of crockery packed in straw. Saucers, plates, dishes, pots, pans, buckets, brushes, soap and a hundred other items were carried inside the van. Earthen ware pots were hung by the handle from hooks along the rows of shelves. A glass case had been built in behind the driver's seat to house the more special items that a customer might ask for. The salesman would use a 'u' shaped attachment on the end of a pole, for lifting down such items as buckets and large jugs. The proprietor made use of the roof space by erecting a guardrail around the perimeter, providing a suitable location for the storage of a small stock of his larger wares. Access to the roof area was by means of a vertically fixed ladder on the side of the vehicle.

A chimney sweep visited farms, outlying hamlets and villages in the Sturminster Newton area, with a small donkey cart. He trudged from job to job, transporting the tools of his trade on the cart. He always acquired plenty of trade on his regular visits to Stourton Caundle. A donkey and cart was sometimes parked outside the Trooper Inn at lunchtime. The owner made his living from offering bloaters in exchange for rags and bones and the skins of moles and rabbits. Old Jack was a well-known character selling reels of cotton thread, skeins of wool and sewing needles from a tray suspended from around his neck by a leather strap.

A copy of the "Old Moore's Almanac" could be purchased from a man who would visit Stourton Caundle every autumn throughout the 1920s. He would go from door to door, departing at the end of the day in time to catch the last train from Stalbridge station. Gypsy families were regular visitors to Holt Lane parking their caravans on the wide grass verge. The men were mainly horse dealers and made wooden clothes pegs and artificial flowers for their womenfolk to sell on the doorstep. These women were never at a loss for words when it came to a tale of woe, especially if they were trying to persuade someone to either buy their wares, or begging for some cast-off clothing.

On many a summer's Sunday afternoon a group of noisy men could be heard shouting out: "Fresh Weymouth Mackerel". They must have done good business, judging by the large number of people who went to the back of their lorry, with a china plate in one hand and a small amount of money in the other, checking first that the quality of the fish had not deteriorated during transit.

A man from Shaftesbury used to visit Stourton Caundle twice a year on his specially adapted bicycle, to use as a mobile workbench, for the sharpening of knives, scissors and shears. He would operate this contraption by setting the cycle firmly onto its stand and then using the pedals to drive the belts and pulleys to turn the grindstone. Three men would arrive in a lorry

and then go from door to door trying to sell floor mats of all sizes, rolls of linoleum and coconut matting. Every week a horse and dray from the Wyke Brewery in Gillingham made a delivery to the Trooper Inn.

One particular horse-drawn cart had the unmistakable smell of death about it. It was known as the 'Knackers cart'. This purpose built cart was used for the transportation of dead cattle and horses to the kennels at Inwood House, at Henstridge, for feeding to the fox hounds belonging to the Merthyr Guest Hunt. Herby Parsons, a fishmonger from Stalbridge, came once a week, his means of transport was a pony and cart.

Three coal merchants delivered to Stourton Caundle. One had a lorry while the other two still relied on a horse and wagon. During the winter months one coal man would seldom return home without a cartload of hazel sticks bought from a local farmer. These sticks were eventually sold forty to the bundle for use as runner bean sticks and for supporting peas. Two men delivered cleaning materials for use in the home and also paraffin for heating, cooking and lighting. These men were known to us as being "the Oil Men".

F.C. Cox and Son had three retail premises, including a drapers shop in Manchester House. On the opposite side of the High Street were soft furnishings and linoleum, boots and shoes, and gents tailoring and outfitting

F Cox and Sons retail premises on both sides of Stalbridge High Street

Other Goods and Services

To obtain goods, other than those available in the two village shops or delivered house to house, a journey to Stalbridge was required, either on foot, or by bicycle, or pony and trap. All basic goods and services were readily available in Stalbridge.

Charles Bollen was the proprietor of a tailor and outfitting business. Suits, made to measure, were supplied by Henry and Leslie Hobbs. The Cobbler, Herbert Taylor, was the main boot and shoe repairer, with his premises the corner shop at the top end of Station Road, opposite the Post Office. Arthur Day repaired working mens boots with thick leather soles and hobnails in his workshop at Gold Steeet. The adjoining house is still called the Cobblers. Charles Meader, a jewellers and ironmonger's shop, also sold a variety of other items, including glass, and china, ironmongery, furniture, toys and stationery, from his premises at the junction of Station Road with the High Street. Graces draper's shop, with separate ladies and gentlemen outfitting departments, was located on the right hand side of the junction at the bottom of Barrow Hill. On the other

side of the High Street was Herby Parsons fishmonger's. Herby, who was a real character, set up the business on his return from the First World War; he also had a mobile fish round, delivering weekly to outlying villages including Stourton Caundle. Mr Vincent had a saddlers shop in the High Street selling and repairing horse harness. Messrs Jeanes were blacksmiths making and repairing impliments for the local farmers and shoeing horses. Walter Lovelace established a garage for repairing and hiring cars, employing several mechanics and drivers for the car hire business.

Supplies for the local shops, coal and corn merchants, flour for the bakery and daily newspapers all arrived by train at Stalbridge Station, along withn the incoming mail. Messrs Moggs, a local haulier, delivered goods arriving at the station to the shops. Two coal merchants had depots in the station yard delivering coal by horse and waggon. Stalbridge tradesmen of the 1920s could not have imagined that some fifty years later the railway line, so vital for the transportation of goods to supply their businesses, would no longer be in operation.

Graces Draper's Shop is the white buiding on the right

The Powys Society

Hon. Secretary Chris Thomas

John Cowper Powys was a writer with an extraordinary ability to convey to his readers, in passages of luminous prose, not only the great beauty of landscapes under certain conditions of weather and light, but also the minute details of the natural world as well as the unique and special quality of the spirit and atmosphere of certain places. In his novel *A Glastonbury Romance* (1932) he refers to *"...the immemorial Mystery of Glastonbury"* and says *"Everyone who came to this spot seemed to draw something from it, attracted by a magnetism too powerful for anyone to resist..."* In *Obstinate Cymric* (1947) he described his identification with the mountains and rivers of Wales. But of all the places he wrote about it was Dorset, associated so closely with his intense recollections of childhood, which continued to inspire his imagination and provided him with evocative locations and settings for his major novels and a background for his many characters.

The work of Thomas Hardy was an acknowledged early influence on his writing. He dedicated his first novel, *Wood and Stone* (1915), to Hardy: *"with devoted admiration to the greatest poet and novelist of our age"*. In the Preface to *Wood and Stone,* JCP refers to Hardy as the *"monarch of that particular country"* meaning, of course, Wessex, and says that he embodies the *"atmosphere of the large mellow leisurely humanists of the past"*. This is a style that JCP, early in his writing career, seemed keen to emulate. In a letter to his old friend Louis Wilkinson JCP said that *"from T. Hardy I learnt long, long, ago to see all human feeling, gestures and actions & everything else against the Inanimate Background of Nature..."*

Places in Dorset are powerfully evoked in JCP's novels in, for instance, *Wood and Stone,*

with scenes set in Weymouth; *Ducdame* (1925) with scenes set in Charminster; *Wolf Solent* (1929), with scenes set in Sherborne, the Trent Lanes, Honeycomb Woods, the Vale of Blackmore and Weymouth; *Maiden Castle* (1937), with scenes set in Dorchester and its environs and of course *Weymouth Sands* (1934), where the town of Weymouth is itself a character. For anyone coming to John Cowper Powys for the first time these are some of the books that are eminently worth reading before you tackle his later historical romances such as

Owen Glendower (1941) and *Porius* (1951) because they will give you a real taste of JCP's prodigious descriptive powers and an insight into his Wordsworthian, sensualist, philosophy of life.

There is no doubt that Weymouth was, for JCP, a very special place which he returned to in his mind many times in his old age. *"That's where my real life began"* says Wolf Solent to himself, *"that's the place I love"*. JCP confided his devotion to Weymouth in his diary describing what he called his *"vivid memory conjurations and evocations"*, declaring that *"Weymouth is my home and ever will be..."* He referred to the *"rapturous epoch"* of his youth spent in Weymouth during summer holidays. He even confesses, in 1940, to having devised a personal *"Weymouth Te Deum"* which he repeats to himself, whilst shaving, every morning, whilst he meditates on memories of *"the shells and sea anemones and sea weed and pebbles of Weymouth, Portland and Chesil beach places where I am more at home than anywhere else in the world. I have ever 'gone to Weymouth'. Thus I daily go back to the edge of the sea..."* In his *Autobiography* (1934) he refers to Weymouth as *"the centre of the circumference of my mortal life"*. Weymouth always seemed to be associated by him with an ideal place and especially with sunshine and brilliant light, the *"dazzle of sun on water"* and *"warm diffused sunlight"*. He knew very well all the main places in Weymouth which he reconstructed faithfully in *Weymouth Sands*: the Jubilee Clock, the statue of George III, Sandsfoot Castle, Greenhill Gardens, the Nothe Fort, Chesil beach, Lodmoor, the harbour bridge and Portland as well the views across the wide sweep of Weymouth Bay to the White Nose, Redcliffe Bay and St Albans Head. He called these places *"sacred hieroglyphs"* and "landmarks of the inanimate". He says that they sunk into his mind with *"transubstantiating magic"*.

Some of the most powerful passages in JCP's *Autobiography* deal with JCP's childhood memory of summer holidays in Weymouth spent with his paternal grandmother, Amelia, at Penn House in Brunswick Terrace at the eastern end of the Esplanade. JCP described his grandmother as a *"beautiful, refined old egoist"*. Llewelyn Powys remembered *"a little old lady, exquisite, dainty, with cheeks flushed like the petals of dog roses."* Amelia died at the age of 87 in 1890. At Weymouth JCP remembered *"the glitter of the sun-path on the sea"* glimpsed from the front room of Penn House overlooking a shelving bank of pebbles which became the source of JCP's later philosophy of mystical sensuality. He vividly recalled the smell of dried seaweed, sand, fish scales, and the sun blistered, fragrant carved wooden entrance door of Penn House. As he wrote many years later, in the preface to a new edition of *Wolf Solent* (1961), Penn House was *"the gate to the waves and tides and pebbles and sands of the salt sea."*

Penn House is now a guest house run by David and Maureen Bennett who know all about the connections of their residence with John Cowper Powys. Inside some of the original decorative features have been preserved perhaps just as JCP knew

them in the 1870s and 1880s. The world of Victorian interiors is well described by JCP in *Weymouth Sands* no doubt drawing on his memories of the interior of Penn House. Certainly it's still possible to see the same view JCP describes, in *Autobiography*, from an upstairs room, of the spire of

St. John's church and it is still possible to gaze at the same vision of the sun-path on the sea viewed from what used to be Amelia's drawing room and which is now the dining room of the guest house.

David and Maureen witnessed the terrible storms of 2014 which lashed the Esplanade. But of course this was not the only storm to have hit the Weymouth coast so dramatically for in November 1824 the town suffered the effects of a terrible "Great Gale" which destroyed much of the old and new development and was reported at length in *The Gentleman's Magazine* and

Penn House Hotel

the *Bath Chronicle*. This storm arrived only just after the construction of Brunswick Terrace had been completed (although Penn House was probably built some years afterwards). The name of Brunswick Terrace was also a late invention for according to the London *Morning Post* (20th August 1824) and the Salisbury Journal (23rd August 1824), it was the Duke of Gloucester, on a visit to Weymouth, who named the terrace Brunswick Row (it was later renamed Brunswick Buildings before becoming Brunswick Terrace).

The harmonious Georgian architecture of Brunswick Terrace and Penn House with their distinctive bow windows made a deep impression on JCP. Brunswick Terrace and Penn House are accurately represented in both *Wood and Stone* and *Wolf Solent*. In *Wood and Stone* JCP says *"The houses they now approached were entitled Brunswick Terrace and they entirely fulfilled their title by suggesting in the pleasant liberality of their bay windows and the mellow dignity of their well proportioned fronts the sort of solid comfort which the syllables Brunswick seem naturally to convey."*

The most moving account of JCP's relationship with Dorset can be found in the diary of his niece Mary Casey (the daughter of his youngest sister Lucy). Mary Casey describes how JCP's ashes were scattered on Chesil beach on 26th June 1963: *"...we hired a taxi to carry us to that beach beyond Abbotsbury...the high waves came crashing over on to the shingle, spread in immaculate foam and withdrew sucking back the noisy pebbles. Where the stones were already wet and dark Gerard [Mary's husband] spread the ash, then we stood still and silent looking upon the sea until one of the arching waves was shed over them and sank back carrying with it the last earthly remains of John Cowper Powys."* JCP had already identified the special qualities of Chesil beach which he described in *Weymouth Sands*: *"What a place this*

Chesil was. The great embankment stretched away westward heavy with moanings and sobbing and inarticulate storm wails."

Meetings of the Powys society held in 2018 provided plenty of opportunity for discussion of the writings of the Powyses. In April, at Ely, we looked, in depth, at a single chapter of *A Glastonbury Romance*, called *Mark's Court*, and scrutinised the character of Cordelia as she appears throughout the novel.

At Dorchester, in June, we held a meeting in the marvellous library of the Dorset Natural History and Archaeological Society, at the Dorset County Museum, where we discussed short stories by T.F. Powys *(Nor Iron Bars)* and William Somerset Maugham *(A Friend in Need)*. We concluded that T.F. Powys's story was much more sophisticated and held our attention much longer. Like a parable it seemed to point to something fundamental in the human condition.

Our annual conference took place in Street, near Glastonbury, in August. The talks ranged from a study of appearance and reality in *Wolf Solent*, an analysis of 'close reading' of some selected passages from the works of JCP, Llewelyn and T.F. Powys, to a study of 'pan-psychism' in *Wolf Solent* and *A Glastonbury Romance* and an examination of reader responses to the style of JCP's writing. Our speakers included Nicholas Birns, Associate Professor at the Centre for Applied Liberal Arts, New York University, Charles Lock, Professor of English Literature at the University of Copenhagen, and Taliesin Gore, graduate student at the University of Exeter. Unfortunately, our guest speaker, Professor Anthony O'Hear, Professor of Philosophy at the University of Buckingham, was unable to attend the conference due to a family bereavement but his talk was read by our Chairman, Timothy Hyman. Walks were organised visiting places in the town of Glastonbury associated with *A Glastonbury Romance* and further away, following a route across meadows, field paths and green lanes, surrounded by high hedges, to Splotts Moor, and Harty Moor, to Whitelake river, where we enjoyed views of the Tor and listened to readings from *A Glastonbury Romance*.

dedicated to Llewelyn Powys, and organiser of the event has provided this description of the walk: "The breeze from the south-west had swept away the ominous looking dark rain clouds by the time the majority set off

The Sailor's Return, East Chaldon

Immediately after the conference, on Monday 13 August, some of our members joined other colleagues at the Red Lion in the village of Winfrith and then travelled the short distance to the Sailor's Return in East Chaldon to raise a toast to the memory of Llewelyn Powys. From here members commenced the 23rd annual Llewelyn Birthday Walk to Chydyok farmhouse. This was where Llewelyn lived with his wife, Alyse Gregory and his sisters, Philippa and Gertrude, in the 1930s. The group then progressed to Llewelyn's memorial stone located on the Downs of High Chaldon. Neil Lee, founder of the Dandelion Club,

on the Birthday Walk…[we] followed… the long and occasionally wildly undulating flint track which leads ever upward from the village… I noted one or two changes along the way; there were new signs erected near the gate at the end of the short Chydyok Road, (which leads from the village green up to the afore-mentioned track): "Private Road": "Pedestrians only"; and "no vehicular access without permission". The track itself had deteriorated, the ruts widened and deepened, especially on the steep extremes of Chalky Knapp…vehicular access was certainly not advisable! There were changes at Chydyok too, most notably in the part of the garden where Llewelyn had constructed his 'Terrace Walk' in 1933. The wire mesh boundary fence which divided it from the track appeared to have been crushed and mangled, and the 'Terrace Walk' beyond had been torn up and was no more than a turmoil of broken ground and dead or dying shrubbery... The walk along the footpath up and over Tumbledown was as exhausting and as exhilarating as ever, and the panoramic view eastward from the field gate above Bat's Head as equally breath-taking and spectacular. A large herd of young bullocks grazed the cliff top downs as we walked westward along the old 'Gypsy Track' towards the Obelisk Field, causing some consternation and concern as they obstinately refused to move as we approached...

We gathered at the stone beneath darkly glowering but swiftly flying clouds which stretched from the northern horizon as far as Portland in the south, beyond which an azure sky back-lit the island which appeared to float in perfect silhouette on a silver sea... The breeze off the sea strengthened and gradually blew away the clouds as we walked back along the old Gypsy Track chatting about all things Powys, whilst drinking in the atmosphere...The Sun finally escaped and bathed the afternoon landscape in golden light as the familiar tall chimneys of Chydyok came into view across Tumbledown, and we made our way back down the long, steep and winding flint strewn track to the village."

Towards the end of 2017 The Powys Society launched a new Facebook page which in 2018 attracted a large number of visitors. This is now the place to go if you wish to exchange views about books by the Powyses with other enthusiasts, join the on-line Powys Reading Group, keep up to date with latest news and Society events or just learn more about the Powyses. The Facebook page helps to supplement our website which includes more details about our publications, associated web-based links and information about how to join the Society. For more information please visit www.powys-society.org , e-mail Hon Secretary at chris.d.thomas@hotmail.co.uk or write to Hon Secretary, Chris Thomas, at 87 Ledbury Road, London W11 2AG.

Llewelyn Powys Memorial Stone on Chaldon Down

Our publications programme continues with the production of Newsletters and a scholarly journal each year packed with informative details and analysis of the life and works of the Powyses. Our March 2018 issue of the Newsletter included the first translation in English of Max Brod's review of the original German edition of *Wolf Solent* in 1930. The Newsletter and Journal are sent free to all members of the Society. The Journal can already be accessed on-line, in a subscription library, through digital platforms such as ProQuest and JSTOR. In 2018 we published a new collection of letters from JCP to the novelist, short story writer and playwright, James Hanley (1897-1985), called *Powys and Lord Jim*. This important collection, the testimony of a significant close personal friendship, provides useful information about the two writer's literary development, and their interests in philosophy and current affairs, over a period of 30 years, beginning in 1929 until shortly before the death of JCP.

We are now planning events in 2019 when we will celebrate the 50th anniversary of the Society. We plan to visit Ely, Exeter University, Llangollen (the venue of our annual conference) and London. Everyone is welcome to attend and participate in these events. Details of our meetings and activities will be posted in due course on the Society's website and Facebook page.

The Powys Society is a recognised charity (801332). The Society was founded in the late 1960s with the aim of promoting public education and recognition of the writings, thought and contribution to the arts of the Powys family, particularly of John Cowper Powys,

T.F. Powys and Llewelyn Powys. The Powys Society publishes three Newsletters and a scholarly journal each year. The Society produces other books by and about the Powyses, under the imprint The Powys Press, and organises discussion meetings and an annual conference. The Powys Society is international, attracts scholars from around the world, and welcomes anyone interested in learning more about this very talented and unusual family.

The historic Old Town Hall in Weymouth is a Grade 2 listed building, originally being three Tudor cottages. It has been restored and retains its unique atmosphere. It is available for hire for a variety of events, wedding receptions, art or history displays, music nights, band practice, pilates, meetings and many other uses. To hire ring 07805 884786 or email selles.macuquina@btinternet.com.
To check facilities visit http://weymoutholdtownhall.co.uk/

Review of Philip Browne's book
The Unfortunate Captain Peirce

Judi Moore

Philip Browne won Dorchester Literary Festival's inaugural Local Writing Prize in July 2018 for this book, so it seemed appropriate to offer the review I wrote of it in February (before it was famous …) to 'The Dorset Year Book' so that others may become aware just how interesting and well-written the book is; a worthy winner that beat off 57 other entries (including one from me). The author is a lecturer from Dorchester; the unfortunate Captain met his end under the cliffs at Seacombe on the Isle of Purbeck.

I have been in thrall to this book since the beginning of 2018, having found it in Weymouth library.

The Dorset coast is spattered with wrecks, so one comes across books about them quite often. The title of this one immediately piques interest. Why should Captain Peirce be more unfortunate than any other captain who has experienced shipwreck? The cover gives a clue.

It is a reproduction of one of several paintings about the disaster which appeared soon after the event. The young

Prize-giving ceremony for the inaugural Hall & Woodhouse DLF Local Writing Prize.
From left: Chip Tolson, Philip Browne, Kate Adie (who presented the Prize)
Christopher Little and Cathie Hartigan. Photograph © Janet Gleeson for DLF.

ladies in various states of distress in the painting are mainly daughters and nieces of Captain Peirce. They are the reason the shipwreck became a cause célèbre for several years after it happened. Everyone in the painting died.

However, this is much more than a book about a disaster. Philip Browne has been forensic in mining contemporary records for information about the life of Captain Peirce, his connections, the East India Company and the faraway places it sent its ships to. When Browne says 'it is likely that ...' one feels confident that he is right. This is a man steeped in the time and places of his book, who probably knows Captain Peirce, and his wife, better than their own family did.

The book begins with Captain Peirce's first command of a ship. It follows him around the globe, eastwards, then westwards, on each voyage, showing his growing skill as a sailor and navigator, the profits he made, his rise in the world, and not forgetting the baby he gave his wife each time he returned home!

But the disaster looms. As with the movie 'Titanic', one knows the ending from the outset. But when it comes one immediately understands why Captain Peirce was designated 'the Unfortunate' from the day the Halsewell struck.

I went to hear Philip Browne talk about his research for the book, at Weymouth library in February, 2018. Actually, the talk wasn't about that. Instead he spoke, with great enthusiasm, about how the ship got into difficulties in the English Channel, which compounded until ... It is a shipwreck almost in slow motion, as the Halsewell set sail on New Year's Day 1986, ran into vile weather, experienced more bad luck than one ship should ever be confronted with, and finally struck on the 6th of January.

At the talk I discovered that his research took Browne five years, into the bowels of the British Library and other archives (including those of the East India Company), to the Netherlands, and all the way to India. The wreck is his passion.

Browne wears his learning lightly and has written a pacy saga, almost as if it were a novel of the eighteenth century on the high seas and in fashionable society. It is a rare achievement and I commend him highly for it. He has a real talent for turning research into a proper, rollicking, story. Enjoy.

That Very Lucky Girl

Graham Richard Allard

Looking at this year's Newsletter I noticed the photograph of some members of the Society attending the Blessing ceremony of our founders tomb in Dorchester. For some reason this enticed me into looking at the life of our first Society President, Sir Fredrick Treves. I thought that I knew quite a lot about him already and some of his achievements in life, but I was totally intrigued when I came across the story of the little girl who fell down the tallest cliff face at Lulworth Cove on the 7th September 1892 and was treated at the scene by Sir Fredrick.

The young girl was Edith Hope Lecky aged eleven and she fell down the cliff face dropping some 380 feet to the beach below. Staying at his Lulworth cottage at the time Sir Fredrick was called and was very quickly on the scene administering aid to Edith and her most horrific wounds. Sir Fredrick is reported as saying at the time something in the vein of "As the girl had her back to the cliff side whilst falling her clothing was ripped to shreds and therefore a combination of these shreds of clothing continually catching the rough surface of the cliff along with her hitting the several protruding ledges of rock, probably slowed her decent slightly resulting in her thankfully surviving the fall".

She was indeed so very lucky that day, her fall being broken by her shredded clothing and also being tended to by one of the leading surgeons in the country at the time at the very scene of the accident. Coincidently at the time of the accident Sir Fredrick was actually reading a book written by the little girl's father. So who was this little girl's father and what became of the little girl later in her life?

The eleven year old girl, as previously mentioned, was Edith Hope Lecky and at the time of the accident was living at 1 Morningside Road, Bootle, Lancashire. She was baptised on the 3 April 1881 at St Mary's Church, Walton on the Hill, Lancashire. Her father was a Master Mariner and went by the name of Squire Thornton Stratford Lecky, her mother was Elizabeth Susan nee Henderson who was an Australian. Elizabeth was Squire TS Lecky's second wife.

His first wife whom he married on the 26 February 1863 as a bachelor was Mary Lloyd, a widow, whose father was a brewer by the name of Roger Dutton. This first wife Mary gave Squire TS Lecky two sons, Charles Beresford Lecky born on the 6 December 1863 and Arthur Goulstone Lecky born on 28 July 1865, sadly Arthur died when he was only five years old. So what became of Mary nee Lloyd, Squire T. S. Lecky's first wife? Well worthy of note and some interest perhaps is the fact that Mary Lloyd nee Dutton had married Robert Lloyd who was also a Master Mariner on the 24th September 1856 and their witnesses at that wedding are recorded as Squire Thornton Stratford Lecky and the groom's sister Anne Lloyd. We know that Squire T. S. Lecky then married her in 1863 when she was a widow, however on December 14th 1875 with a decree nisi Squire Thornton Stratford Lecky divorced his wife Mary for adultery in that between 1872 - 1873 and 1873 - 1874 whilst he was away at sea she had been having an affair with a married dock engineer secretary by the name of Thomas Armstrong Drought Slack.

He married his second wife and Edith's mother, Elizabeth Susan Henderson at St Mary's Church, Liverpool in 1878. Squire Thornton Stratford Lecky was born in Downpatrick, County Down, Ireland. In 1852 he went to sea and carried out many sea surveys that involved him with their nautical charting. He was also commodore captain of the American Line and Marine Superintendent of the Great Western Railway. Much of his published works dealt with navigation. He was elected to the Royal Astronomical Society in March 1881 where he is listed as Squire Thornton Stratford Lecky, Esq, 1 Morningside Road, Bootle, Liverpool. Squire T. S. Lecky, Edith's father, died on the 23 November 1902 in Las Palmas.

Edith Hope Lecky, our lucky girl, grew up and had a happy childhood despite her accident, then at the age of 29 married Joseph Brooke Harte who was 37 and a Clerk in Holy Orders at All Saints Church, Clapton Park, London on the 15th July 1910. They were to have three children Mary K Brooke-Harte born in September 1911, Clement F. J. Brooke-Harte in June 1914 and Charles A. B. Brooke-Harte in December 1923. The Reverend, Joseph Brooke-Harte, or as he was known Reverend Joseph of Ashreigney Rectory died at the age of 66 in the Royal Devon & Exeter Hospital.

Edith Hope died in September 1942. She left a will 'Edith Hope Brooke-Harte of the White Horse Hotel, Exford, Somersetshire, widow, died 16 September 1942. Administration Llandudno 21 December to Mary Kathleen Brooke-Harte spinster and Clement Francis Joseph Brooke-Harte Captain H.M Army. Effects £1921 16s 2d. So it seems that our 'Lucky Girl' had another good fifty years of life with a husband and a family after that most horrific day in September 1892. Well done Sir Fredrick!

I am not sure if it still exists, as it may well have rotted away, there again it may have been replaced, but on the beach at the foot of the highest cliff in Lulworth Cove there used to be a wooden board with the following inscription on it which was commissioned by Squire Thornton Stratford Lecky (S.T.S.L):

This marks the spot whereon E.H.L aged 11 years fell from the summit of the cliff, a descent of 380 feet, September 7th, 1892. She miraculously escaped without sustaining lifelong injury. S.T.S.L

Quarter Days - *Hayne Russell*

The expression "Come next Quarter Day, we mid be out o' house an hwome" was very significant to the tenants in a Dorset village whether they be a cottager or a farmer. The Lord of the Manor usually owned everything as far as the eye could see and rents were due on Quarter Days. These were Lady Day - 25th March, Midsummer Day - 24th June, Michaelmas Day - 29th September and Christmas Day.

So if payment could not be made promptly on these days and unless you had a sympathetic landlord you could find yourself homeless.

Mumming in Dorset

Chris Preece

"We put up no holly or mistletoe, and the mummers had no heart in them".

This quote, from January 1796, comes from the diary of a young woman living on Portland, describing the mood of the people during a winter of severe storms when several ships were wrecked on the "dreadful rocks" around the island.

Over a thousand sailors died that winter and as well as describing their awful cries and the helplessness of the brave fishermen of Portland who could do nothing to save them, she also makes a passing reference to mummers and their muted Christmas celebrations of that year, which suggests that mummers' plays were not an uncommon sight on Portland over 200 years ago.

This is not unusual. Research has shown that towns and villages all over the country had mummers at this time, some walking over thirty miles in a day to perform their plays in as many places as possible. In the years between the two World Wars though this Christmas tradition died out apart from a dozen or so. Many were revived during the 1960's and 70's often due to the enthusiasm of Morris sides.

Research into early performances of mummers plays shows that acting ability was a minimal requirement; plays were performed with little characterization. The players would stand in a semicircle around the action, stepping forward to declaim their parts in a rhythmic and stylized manner, returning to the line once their part was over. Audience participation was not encouraged. The words of the script are important and were kept to by the players,

Frome Valley Mummers

although the words were handed down over generations by word of mouth. The event was considered more important than the way it was performed.

All this sounds a bit mysterious, indeed some of those involved with mummers today say that these plays should be performed not as entertainment, but as a ritual intended to keep life in balance and the seasons turning as they always have, in much the same way as our ancestors would light bonfires in midwinter to remind the sun to return in the spring. It is often assumed that these plays are relics from our pre-Christian past, with links to the old gods and beliefs, however researchers believe this is romantic nonsense, based on the rumour that these plays are very very old when in fact there is no real evidence that they existed prior to three or four hundred years ago. This may be the case nevertheless as the rumours of ancient origins are very persistent.

Hardy Players

It is not my intention to describe these plays, their history or purpose, except in a perfunctory way. Experts and enthusiasts have done this very ably already. I will point to a number of Mummers plays that can be seen in Dorset today. A good place to start is a play performed regularly on Portland and in the surrounding area by Frome Valley Mummers.

The script of this play was deposited in Dorset County Museum in 1962. Later research indicates that it was probably performed in Broadway before the 1st World War. Although it is speculation that the performance of this play ceased because performers did not return from the fields of France but it is feasible that this was the case. Whatever the truth, a relative of one of the soldiers/mummers deposited the words of the play in the County Museum for safekeeping. The script was 'found' by a member of the Frome Valley Morris side in 1978 and the play has been performed by them every Christmas since.

It is not beyond imagination, given the distances travelled by mummers in order to perform their play, that this was the play seen on Portland in 1796, the mummers having braved the ferry crossing of the Fleet on a winter's day.

Although it is the intention of Frome Valley Mummers to keep to the traditional interpretation of mummers plays as described above, ad-libs and departures from the script occur in almost every performance. Presentation has varied too over the years, ranging from deadpan to wholly comic and including explosions and fireworks. The play is always evolving.

Wessex Mummers

The costumes worn by the Frome Valley Mummers have also changed over the years, mostly at the whim of the person playing the part. Recently there has been an attempt to co-ordinate costumes to include, what have become known as, Dorset shaped hats and ribbons. Similar to those made famous by the old Hardy Players in the photograph of them posing at Thomas Hardy's home Max Gate in 1921. Original research has indicated that costumes were aimed at disguise of the performer, not to emphasize the character being played.

Thomas Hardy famously included a mummers play in his novel 'Return of the Native'. In addition to his many talents Hardy was a folklorist and would have seen and known about mummers. Although the play appears in a work of fiction, his description of the play and how it was prepared for and performed would have been based on his observations. The play of his novel, including the mummers play (a play within a play), was performed by the Hardy Players in 1921 in the Dorchester Corn Exchange.

Stourvale Mummers

Frome Valley Mummers are not the only mummers in Dorset and the presentation of mummers plays varies a good deal. Towards the North of Dorset, Wessex Morris also regularly perform a mummers play. Based in Cerne Abbas they looked for the 'local' play but unfortunately none could be found, so they "imported" a play from Quidhampton, near Salisbury; and after thirty years the play has become traditional to Cerne. It is a lively play with ad-libs and audience participation encouraged.

Staying in the north, at Corscombe Babylon Morris include a play in their Christmas and New Year tours. To the north east of the county Stourvale Mummers perform a play from Sixpenny Handley, "a survival of the old pagan notions of sympathetic magic" they say. That "rumour" again. The play is described in the Dorset Year Book of 1955/56 so I don't need to repeat it here.

Purbeck Mummers

In the south based in Poole, Anonymous Morris and nearby Purbeck Mummers, a colourful group, describe their play as broadly comic.

Finally in the west of the county, near Bridport, are the Symondsbury Mummers. Their play is considered to be the fullest surviving version of a mummers play. It was performed regularly up to the 1st World War, resumed briefly between the wars and then revived in 1953. The play holds lots of records, probably the earliest 'revival' and, timed at forty minutes, the longest play. It also features Tommy the Pony, a hobby horse claimed to be the oldest in the country when I saw him once in the museum at Dorchester.

This has been a brief and personal look at mummers plays in Dorset, I hope it has provoked some interest. Most of the groups mentioned have websites that will tell you where and when the plays can be seen over the Christmas period, many include a script and other information. Most of the plays can be seen on Youtube. Seeing them on Youtube though is

Tommy the Pony of Symondsbury

no substitute to seeing them performed in a local pub, hall or in a street, so this Christmas search one out and be a part of an old Christmas tradition.

The quote at the beginning of this article came from 'Old Portland', a book edited by Jean M Edwards. Other books used to inform this article were 'The English Year' by Steve Roud, 'A Wessex Nativity' compiled by John Chandler, 'Return of the Native' by Thomas Hardy and many others. A leaflet that accompanies the Frome Valley Mummers, produced by Dave Milner, was also used. The Master Mummers website, www.mastermummers.org is a mine of information.

The Broadwey mummers play ends with a song, very similar to a Celtic blessing, a fitting way, I think, to round off this article:

> A loaf in your locker and a sheep in your fold
>
> A fire in the hearth to keep out the cold
>
> A pocket full of money and a cellar full of beer
>
> And a fat pig in the sty to last you all the year
>
> Merry Christmas and a bright New Year

In Comes I - Mummers in Bath

Chris Preece

In comes I.
Words spoken by mummers, intrude over the
bustling background buzz of the square. The city square,
grand buildings on all sides, none the less belonged to the Abbey.
The Abbey dominates all, the west wall, stone upon stone, soars.
Carved stone angels climb to heaven and return over the centuries
bearing God's word. It is as if it always was.
The Abbey is the reason for the square,
the reason for the city, it speaks of perpetuity, of power, of sacred duty.
Ignored, this day, by weekend shoppers, wrapped
against the cold in scarves and hats, absorbed in finding the right
Christmas gift.
They scurry through the square or sit around the edge, outside cafes,
drinking their hot chocolate or steaming mulled wine with festive stollen.

Here comes I.
Words from the mummers,
words not as old, words not as powerful as the silence of the abbey stones,
but, maybe, pointing to an older religion, a time before the abbey was.
vulnerable, transient words.
Words not written into the pages of history with sword and fire by Abbot and nobleman,
words passed from mouth to mouth, from generation to generation by artisan and mason.

The mummers continue with their play, their ritual. The words process,
Spoken by a collection of unconnected characters, Father Christmas, St George, Beelzebub.
The Turkish Knight is dead and brought back to life.
Uncomprehending shoppers, pause as they pass by
in a spate of consumerist frenzy. Curious tourists, their itinerary
of culture and religion interrupted, take photographs.
Buskers watch with irritation, waiting for the interruption to be over and attention to
return to them. Instrument cases in front of them open like hungry oysters.

Here comes I
Words that died on the lips of men of Dorset. Men whose mouths now full of mud
lie forever in the corner of a foreign field. Words remembered and treasured by mothers,
sisters and sweethearts.
Discovered words that echo, this day, around the square, and re-echo with the
crimson poppies and stark white crosses planted before the Abbey.
Poppies, keeping the memory of these men, now dead, alive. A forlorn gesture towards
us learning from the past.
Words, bringing life to their customs and traditions, pointing, for those who will hear,
to who we are and to where we come from.
The play reaches its climax. St George speaks to the resurrected Turkish Knight, "let's
shake hands and fight no more."
The mummers leave their stage. The men lie in their graves. A moment has passed.
The world goes on.

John Castleman Swinburne-Hanham J.P.
President of the Society of Dorset Men 1915-1919
Fifty years a Dorset Magistrate

Laurence Clark

John Castleman Swinburne-Hanham was a founder member of the Society of Dorset Men in London as it was initially called and was elected chairman at the first meeting in 1904. He continued in this office, including the years when he was president, until his death in 1935.

Photo by]   [*Messrs. Elliott & Fry.*

Mr. J. C. SWINBURNE-HANHAM, J.P.
(Chairman of Committee).

The Society's sixth president was the eldest son of Major John Swinburne and Edith Mary, daughter of Edward Castleman of Chettle near Blandford Forum. He was educated at Rugby school, then studied law and was later called to the Bar. In 1889 he married Elizabeth Marion, daughter of Sir Thomas Spencer-Wells. They had two daughters.

In 1884 he qualified as a Justice of the Peace for Dorset and served on the Sturminster Newton bench. In 1909 he became deputy chairman and in 1923 chairman. He was also chairman of Dorset Quarter sessions, resigning these positions in 1933 due to increasing deafness. Swinburne-Hanham was also Recorder for Faversham from 1903–1934 and at one time he was a member of the Dorset County Council. For some years he was chairman of the Licensing Committee for Dorset and the Assessment Appeals Tribunal. Apart from the legal positions he held Swinburne-Hanham was Hon. Treasurer of the Anti Vaccination Society of England and a vice president of the Cremation Society of England. A staunch Liberal he unsuccessfully contested for that party the parliamentary seats of Hampstead in 1892 and East Somerset in 1895. Swinburne-Hanham was also a Freemason and a member of the London Dorset Lodge where he held various offices. During his time as a magistrate he was described as the personification of shrewd judgement, patience and consideration. He had the right temperamental equipment as a chairman and his outstanding traits were his kindly human understanding and never failing geniality. These qualities were displayed during his long chairmanship of the Society of Dorset Men and his re-election year after year was a tribute of esteem from all the members.

It has already been stated that Swinburne-Hanham was vice-president of the Cremation Society of England; this was probably due to the influence of his step-father, who was a known advocate of cremation. He was seven when his father died and in the following year his mother married Captain Thomas Hanham R.N. of Manston House, near Sturminster Newton, who had built a mausoleum and crematorium in the grounds of his house. When his wife died in 1876 and his mother in 1877 their bodies were placed in the mausoleum. Captain Hanham died in 1883. All three were then cremated. This was said to be the first cremation in this county.

After the death of his step-father John Castleman Swinburne added Hanham to his surname and so became John Castleman Swinburne-Hanham. He inherited most of Thomas Hanham's estate, including the house and grounds where he lived for a time. The society's longstanding chairman and former president died at his London home on 15th January 1935 aged seventy-four and was cremated at Golders Green crematorium. There were no flowers by request. Instead donations were to be sent to the Dorset County hospital.

Sources
Dorset County Chronicle and Somersetshire Gazette
Dorset Year Books
Kellys Directory of Dorset
The Greenwood Tree Magazine of the Somerset and Dorset Journal of the Family History Society

Two Linked Book Reviews

Philip A. Hunt

Wyn George: Traveller & Artist
(Wimborne Minster, Dorset: The Dovecote Press Ltd, 2013) 160 illustrations (including 104 colour plates) plus 67 photographs and plans; 245 pp, paperback, £20, ISBN: 978-0-9573119-7-8 (If out of stock at publisher, still available from author: Jessica.christian@btinternet.com)

and by the same author:

Dorset Brothers at War: Three Blandford Yeomen 1914-18
(Stroud, Gloucestershire: Amberley Publishing, 2017) 144 black and white photographs, 6 map pages, coloured photograph cover; 223 pp, paperback, £16.99, ISBN: 978-1-4456-6684-6; e-book £16.99, ISBN: 978-1-4456-6685-3

It is appropriate to review these two recent books together in this centenary year of the 1918 Armistice in the Great War, since that ordeal is central to both.

Jessica Christian, an art historian and now a superb biographer – even impressive military historian – has written these two studies of her Dorset relatives. The first describes her great-aunt, Winifred Ruby (Wyn) George (1880-1951).

Wyn George, eldest daughter of a Blandford Congregationalist family with a thriving grocery business, was a talented artist. She attended London's Slade School of Fine Art in the second half of the 1890s, a friend and contemporary of many now well-known artists, including Gwen and Augustus John. In 1896 she kept a diary, the only known student-days journal of that distinguished school's heyday.

Anemones, 1900 (oil on wood)

During the Great War, Wyn served as a driver based in Étaples, close to the Western Front (where in happier days she had worked as an artist). Her duties were to look after visiting relatives of seriously wounded and dying servicemen, collecting them on arrival, transporting them to the military/field hospitals and often to funerals, and taking care of them until their departure. After the Armistice she remained in France to help in the Devastated Areas.

After the war, Wyn circumnavigated the globe, sending home to Dorset a series of diary-letters. Her remarkable experiences, love of regional costume, and exploitation of her talent as a child portraitist, enabled her career to prosper. She concentrated on

'The Old Elm (Blandford)', 1933 (watercolour)

producing a series of rapid pastel studies of – mostly – women and children in the numerous countries she visited, paying her way by taking regular portrait commissions in pastel, and selling loose, and impressionistic landscape watercolours. Wyn George was a successful professional female artist; an achievement in her time – and not least of all because she was disabled. Her biographer has used Wyn's diaries, other family documents, and first-hand recollections, to present a vivid picture of an intrepid Dorset woman. This biography, beautifully written, with superb colour reproductions of Wyn's works, inspires interest in the George family and Dorset in the period.

Thomas George, early 1930s (charcoal, chalks and pastel on toned paper). A prominent Blandford business man, leading member of the Congregational (now United Reformed) church, and father of eight including Wyn, Bertram, Stanley and Roy

Principal temple dancer, Angkor, 1925 (charcoal and pastel on toned paper)

The 1918-2018 centenary makes it apt that Jessica Christian's second family account describes the Great War experiences of Wyn George's brothers, Bertram, Stanley, and Roy George, based upon their (again) hitherto unpublished accounts. This second book narrates the brothers' experiences as volunteer soldiers in the Queen's Own Dorset Yeomanry, training in Norfolk, and then posted to Egypt and on to Gallipoli. Stanley later served with the Imperial Camel Corps in the

A group of Queen's Own Dorset Yeomanry volunteers, Norfolk, late 1914, all identified by Stanley

Nile Valley, the Western Desert, and in Palestine. Bertram, eldest and sole survivor of the soldier brothers, was subsequently commissioned in the Royal Garrison Artillery and served at Passchendaele.

Stanley's 1915 diary and the brothers'

Back to camp after a patrol in the desert with the Imperial Camel Corps, autumn 1916

Left to right: Roy, Stanley and Bertram George of Blandford Forum, Queen's Own Dorset Yeomanry, Autumn 1914

letters home contrast descriptions of the different campaigns and theatres of war. These invaluable contemporary Dorset soldiers' narratives are illustrated with their own photographs. The fascinating accounts of daily cavalry life and duties, and the depictions of service abroad and in action, are remarkable in their detail and in their evocation of experiences far outside those of almost all readers today (just as Wyn's travels reveal a world we have lost, where so many places under British influence had a relative stability and safety lacking today, and a Dorset female could travel, and work creatively, long before the late 20th century phenomena of mass tourism and more general female emancipation).

Each book is written engagingly, and illustrated beautifully. Each contains a superb scholarly apparatus. These set Wyn's artistic travels and her brothers' campaign experiences in context for the generation of modern readers unfamiliar with the geography and history of the world these Dorset folk encountered. The military book includes excellent, helpful maps. Its biographical index of service personnel will interest greatly anyone, including those currently seeking information on ancestors in the Queen's Own Dorset Yeomanry.

Jessica Christian has composed two fascinating accounts of her remarkable Dorset relatives. They deserve reading. The stories they present of Dorset family life, and experiences abroad in peace and in war, of these four siblings are a fitting tribute in the centenary of the Armistice. They commemorate the resolute sense of duty, the endurance, the love of equines, and the encounters with places far from home, that Dorset men and women showed and experienced in that titanic ordeal. Stanley and Roy did not return to their beloved Dorset. Roy fell at Gallipoli in 1915; Stanley was killed in Palestine in 1918, rescuing wounded comrades whom as a stretcher bearer he refused to abandon, despite impossible odds.

'Who's a-feard?' indeed: these two books are a fitting tribute to Jessica Christian's Dorset family.

2 August 2018.

The Weather Forecasting Stone - *Hayne Russell*

Forecast	Condition
Stone is wet	Raining
Stone is dry	Not raining
Shadow on ground	Sunny
White on top	Snowing
Can't see stone	Foggy
Swinging stone	Windy
Stone gone	Typhoon

(The stone should of course be hung from a suitable tree)

A witch down your chimney! - *Hayne Russell*

"If thee want t' kip a witch be a comin' down yer chimbley git a pig's 'ead an' vill en wi' pins an' stuff 'en up yer chimbley as var as 'ee can."

A Year on Chesil Beach – A Sketchbook

by Jenny Hunt

My love of beachcombing began when I was 4 years old. At the time I was living in Kent. One day the family set off in a large black car to visit Brighton. The beach was a vast area of pebbles with wooden groynes running towards the sea. I noticed some of the pebbles had holes in them and I squinted at the view through these tiny portholes. My father told me these stones were lucky so I spent all day collecting a pile, intending to thread them on a string to make a necklace. Needless to say, the stones were far too heavy to hang around my neck, but the experience of collecting them stays with me.

I have always enjoyed writing and drawing. Aged 8 I won an Observer book of Wild Flowers for a drawing I entered in the Bexley Heath Horticultural Show. I became involved in botanical illustration later in life and exhibited

with the Society of Botanical Artists. In 2001 I achieved an MA in Creative Writing (with distinction) from Bath Spa University. Since then I have had poetry published in various anthologies and poetry magazines, as well as being successful in several poetry competitions.

In 2011 and 2013 I was runner up in the BBC Wildlife Nature Writing Competition. Then, in 2014, I was invited to become a Local Patch Reporter for the magazine, publishing a weekly nature blog. I did this for 2 years and enjoyed the challenge of finding something different to write each week, visiting many locations in West Dorset near my home. I found I was gravitating towards Chesil more and more, enjoying the diverse characteristics of this unique stretch of coastline. The beaches changed with the weather and the time of the year. It was always a delight to visit the coast, even in thunderstorms or icy cold days.

In 2017 I started reviewing my blog. Once published, a blog flies out into the ether and becomes an ephemeral thing. I decided I wanted to make something more permanent from the material I had written and resolved to create a book

A YEAR ON CHESIL BEACH, A Sketchbook by Jennifer Hunt is a limited edition, hand-finished spiral-bound book, with 16 full-page paintings and creative writing inspired by Chesil Beach, Dorset.

about the changing face of Chesil beach throughout the year. Starting with the pieces I had already had, I began sketching and re-writing. I kept going back to the beach, writing new material, taking photographs as an aide memoire and collecting shells and other material from the strandline to draw.

The book took on a life of its own and I became absorbed in the journey. I gave myself a deadline of mid-May 2018 to finish the book, in time for Dorset Art Weeks. I wanted the book to look just like the original sketchbook and spent some time choosing paper and cover boards etc with the help of my brilliant printers, Advantage Digital Print. Another printer in Dorchester, Epic, was enlisted for the binding which completed the sketchbook look.

I was surprised and pleased with the response to my book which has already been reprinted. A Year on Chesil Beach is on sale in Waterstones in Dorchester and Bridport, Dansel Art Gallery in Abbotsbury, the Gallery on the Square on Poundbury, Bridport Museum, Hive Beach Café and the Chesil Beach Centre. It is also available to order from www.archaeopteryx-imprint. co.uk, as is the calendar, just published, and which features the illustrations from the book.

Editor's note: - prevalent on Chesil Beach in all sizes, pebbles with holes through them are known as hag stones or holy stones and most fishing boats on Chesil Beach had one tied on them somewhere. They are said to protect you from witchcraft but are also seen as lucky stones. I dived for over 40 years off Chesil Beach and it can change into a very dangerous place within minutes so I made sure I had one tied on my aqualung and I survived each dive but as a stoker Petty Officer said to Earl Mountbatten when they both surfaced after HMS Kelly had been sunk 'Extraordinary how the scum always comes to the top, isn't it, sir?' either way, I have kept one in my pocket for good luck ever since. Jenny's book is an exquisite record of my favourite place.

Where the gulls cry

Judi Moore

Every spring, on the coast here,
herring gulls come in from the sea
and nest on our roofs and chimneys.

Throughout this annual enterprise
the gulls are noisy neighbours;
their joy, exhaustion and despair
displayed loudly, at all hours, by both genders,
and with infinite variety – something
parents everywhere may understand.

During spring and early summer
as well as their usual cries (which sound
like a crazed and overburdened donkey
sired by a banshee), the nesting gulls
honk like seals, complain like sullen
adolescents ('wha-aa-aat?'), express
their frustrations with the primal scream
of a solitary eagle patrolling the high sierra.
Their barnyard imitations are extraordinary too:
they cluck and croon like happy hens,
cock-a-doodle-do like roosters,
whinny like horses, moo like mournful cows,
bleat like sheep, bark like dogs, quack like ducks.
But even such a farmyard-full of sounds
is not the limit of their talents.

Picture: *courtesy*
Jenny Hunt

I have been woken in the early hours
by gulls screaming like teething babies,
yowling like fighting cats. They to-whit and to-whoo
like two owls at once. They wail like sirens,
squeal like a puppy in pain or a kitten shut in.
They hoot like distant trains, scream for help
like peacocks, whoop like refugee gibbons
from a distant rain forest. They creak
like a heavy gothic door swinging
on its oil-starved hinges
through a dark and stormy night.

This constant cacophony bounces off the walls
and alleys of the back-to-backs around me all day
and all night long. We get no other bird song.

Douglas V Duff
- Dorset Adventurer Extraordinaire!

Michael Ward

I've always been an avid reader. As a child, I was enthralled by boys' adventure stories. The Biggles books, by Captain W.E. Johns, were what we'd now term the market leader. But there were dozens of other authors whose books, by long defunct publishers, I devoured eagerly. Inevitably these authors were British: the values were very much God, king and country. G.A. Henty's books, such as 'With Clive in India' and 'With Wolfe in Canada' epitomised a spirit of benevolent imperialism. I took these books at face value; it never occurred to me to check when they were written. I didn't realise that I was reading them in the twilight of empire.

It also didn't occur to me to ponder the bona fides of the authors. Had they relevant experience? Did they know what they were writing about? Instead I fixated on plot. There was always a strong moral compass, an emphasis on doing the right thing, even under the most hazardous of circumstances. I'd never heard of the dictum that the only thing necessary for the triumph of evil is that good men do nothing. However my childhood heroes never did nothing. Instead they acted decisively – often with considerable courage. So, while values such as imperialism may have changed, I'd argue that early exposure to such a strong moral compass was beneficial.

As it happened though, some of the authors did have highly relevant experience and knew exactly what they were writing about.

W.E. Johns and Geo. Rochester had flown as combat pilots on the Western Front in World War I. Another of my favourite authors, the curiously named Douglas V. Duff, definitely inspired confidence. To this day, I remember a passage in one of Duff's books which really shook me, a glimpse into an adult world where outright evil existed.

I used to wonder about Duff. For instance, what did the V stand for – maybe it was Victor? And then childhood vanished; the decades whirled by. Many years later, in an upstairs room in Dorchester library, I chanced upon the most marvellous collection of Douglas V. Duff books. Was there a local connection, I wondered? Indeed there was. And there was a true-life story, more enthralling than anything I'd ever read in any of those boys' adventure books.

Douglas Valder Duff was born in Argentina in 1901. His father, Arthur Duff, was the British Consul. His godfather, Roger Casement, was a fellow Consul in the Congo and Brazil. In both  locations Casement exposed horrifying human rights abuses. In 1911 he was knighted for his work in Peru. In 1916 his knighthood was rescinded and he was hanged for an attempt to solicit German aid in the Irish uprising.

In 1906 Duff was sent to England and went to school at Bridport. In 1914 he began naval training and in 1916 he joined the Merchant Navy as his contribution to the war effort. In 1917 his ship, the Thracia, was torpedoed by a German U boat in the Bay of Biscay. The 15-year-old Duff was the sole survivor. The following year, another ship, the Flavia, was also torpedoed and Duff had to shoot several horses with his revolver to prevent them swamping the lifeboat. In a subsequent U boat attack, he suffered a broken leg. At the end of World War I, Duff helped to rescue White Russian refugees at the Black Sea. He was horrified to see former Russian noblewomen, rendered landless and destitute by the 1917 revolution, selling their bodies for food and shelter. For the rest of his life he would never talk about this experience, except to say that it was 'indescribable'.

When the Thracia was sunk and Duff was struggling in the sea, he vowed that if he survived he would dedicate the rest of his life to God. Accordingly, after World War I, he entered a monastery in Lincolnshire. Here he remained for almost two years. Sadly however, he discovered that closed communities can be havens of malpractice. In particular, the discipline was unacceptably harsh. Disillusioned, he left the monastery. Ironically his father disapproved of him joining the monastery and his mother disapproved of him leaving it!

Duff's next career change seems, to me at least, quite extraordinary. He joined the Royal Irish Constabulary Special Reserve, the feared Black and Tans, an infamous counter-insurgency force acting for the British government in the Irish war of independence of 1920/21. It's probably a safe bet that Duff was the only former monk in the Black and Tans! In Ireland, almost a hundred years later, the Black and Tans are still reviled for their brutality. Having said

that, in a guerrilla war, brutality is never the sole preserve of one side. Certainly loyalties were divided and emotions ran high. As we have seen, Duff's godfather, the eminent and famous Roger Casement, had been hanged, just a few years earlier, for his involvement. Although Duff's uncle Edward was the High Sheriff of Longford, his official position didn't prevent him from helping to hide members of the IRA. It was a terribly difficult time for many people caught up in the conflict.

DOUGLAS K. DUFF

My guess is that Duff must have been physically very tough indeed even to deal with his colleagues in the Tans, never mind the enemy. Having survived U boat attacks, he went on to survive IRA ambushes where often the only option was shooting your way out. One day, while walking the streets of Dublin off-duty (and therefore unarmed), Duff encountered a man whom he believed to be Michael Collins, the leader of his enemies. Collins was the most wanted man in Ireland, with a huge price on his head. Duff attempted to arrest the man, who indicated that he was indeed Collins. However he also pointed out that several seemingly innocent bystanders were members of his feared bodyguard. The unarmed Duff would be cut down in an instant. Why throw his life away needlessly?

For me, this encounter says so much about both Duff and Collins, the raw courage of the former vying with the humanity of the latter. A frustrated Duff, barely out of his teens, had no viable alternative but to let

Collins go and duly report the encounter to the intelligence officers at Dublin Castle.

In 1921 Michael Collins and Winston Churchill signed an Anglo-Irish peace treaty, partitioning Ireland into North and South. Sadly their hopes of avoiding further bloodshed were in vain. The civil war of 1922/23 was vicious. Former allies become deadly enemies. With supreme irony, enmity had transmuted into friendship between Collins and Churchill, who threw all of his energy into supporting the treaty. Both men knew full well that Collins would pay dearly for signing it. In 1922 he was assassinated.

The end of the war of independence put the Black and Tans out of work. In 1922 Duff and some of his former colleagues joined what became the Palestine Police Force. At the monastery he had railed against unnecessarily harsh discipline. On the sea voyage to Palestine he led a protest against poor pay and conditions.

Duff was stationed at Nazareth and Haifa, where he was in charge of patrol boats to catch tobacco and hashish smugglers. Echoing his experience at the Black Sea, he described 1923 Haifa as being like 'the Wild West'. Three years later he was promoted to inspector, in charge of law and order in Bethlehem and Jerusalem. In 1927 there was a severe earthquake, with many dead and injured. Duff helped to rescue the fortunate and retrieve the bodies of the unfortunate. In 1928 he was involved in the Western Wall controversy when he and his men were ordered to remove a screen which had been erected against the Wailing Wall. There was an enquiry and he was transferred to the command of Megiddo prison. Here he had only a single Jewish deputy and 45 Arab warders in charge of 500 inmates. In the 1929 Arab riots, Duff helped to protect the Jewish victims. After so many years of continual stress,

it may be that his immune system had become weakened. In 1927 he contracted malaria. Nevertheless the stress continued. Subsequently he became commander firstly of Acre prison and then the Tulkram district. Both were dens of lawlessness. In 1929 there was a riot at Acre prison while Tulkram was a hotbed of racial conflict and criminality.

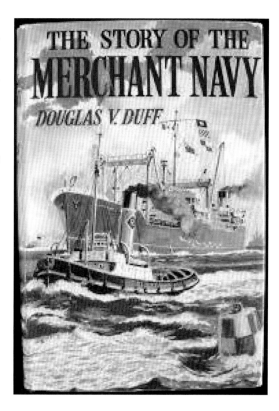

Following a recurrence of malaria, in 1932 Duff was forced to retire. He had hoped to obtain a position with the Jamaican police but clearly further sojourn in the tropics or the Middle East was undesirable. He married a lady named Janet Wallace, a nurse who had chased off an attack on her hospital in Nazareth will nothing more than a broom! Seemingly she was a kindred spirit. The newlyweds left Palestine, came back to England and set up home in Dorset. Two girls were born. Needing a second career, Duff became a journalist and prolific author. One of his interviewees was Haile Selassie, emperor of Ethiopia. 'Sword for Hire', the title of a 1934 Duff book, admirably summed up his early life, while clearly he was eminently qualified to write 'Palestine Unveiled' (1938). Intriguingly (well, for me anyway!) he updated two of G.A. Henty's books, "No Surrender!" and 'Redskin and Cowboy' (both 1939). I would imagine that Duff and Henty held similar views that the British Empire was a bastion of civilisation in an otherwise lawless world.

In World War II Duff joined the Royal Naval Volunteer Supplementary reserve, commanding a boat with the Dover Patrol. Subsequently he was appointed to the staff of Admiral Cunningham, Commander in Chief of the Mediterranean fleet. His experience of running patrol boats to intercept smugglers at Haifa probably stood him in good stead when he ran sailing schooners to break the blockade at Tobruk.

After the war, Duff returned to writing, specialising in adventure tales for young people. His backgrounds included the Middle East, South America and the sea. For continuity between books, he created heroes such as Bill Berenger and Adam MacAdam (whom I remember with affection). He also wrote under different pen names, such as Douglas Stanhope, Leslie Savage and Peter Wickloe. Back then, publishers had a nasty habit of paying a fixed sum for a book - usually not a lot - and many authors didn't benefit directly from sales. Making any kind of a living often required writing under many names, i.e. creating different brands.

In 1951 the popular television programme, 'What's My Line?' arrived in Britain. This was a game show which required celebrity panellists to question a contestant in order to determine his or her occupation. Duff, who seemed able to turn his hand to well-nigh anything, appeared regularly

on the programme. On one occasion the chairman (and presumably the audience) was startled when Duff suddenly broke into Arabic, in order to question one of the participants. Somehow I don't think you'd have wanted to be questioned by Duff if you'd got anything to hide!

Douglas V. Duff.

Duff continued writing and broadcasting throughout the 1950s, 1960s and 1970s. When he died, in 1978, he had written some 100 books. Effectively his life falls into two parts. From 1916 to 1932 he was, in one guise or another, a sword for hire, as he put it, acting for Britain in World War I and its aftermath. From 1932 to 1978 he was principally a writer, transposing his rich early experience into a plethora of adventure stories. He also wrote two autobiographies, 'May the Winds Blow' and the delightfully entitled, 'Bailing with a Teaspoon'.

What are we to make of Duff? I confess to being intrigued by him. His early life reads like Indiana Jones. Obviously he had a huge thirst for adventure. While I'm sure that it was only too easy to contract malaria in the Middle East, it seems to me no coincidence that Duff's health had broken down by the early 1930s. Effectively he had been on active service for a decade and a half, with very little respite. On many occasions he could easily have lost his life. Nowadays we have a much greater realisation that, even for the strongest of individuals, there's only so much that flesh and blood can bear.

Duff's photographs show a notably sturdy individual. In Palestine he was accused of brutality and it's rumoured that the expression 'to duff someone up' owes its origin to him. Certainly, in promoting law and order in Palestine, Duff must have saved a considerable number of lives from what we would now term ethnic cleansing. My own feeling is that Duff probably had a very strong moral compass indeed. His post World War I experience of the 'indescribable' horror of the disposed

Russian aristocrats by the Black Sea may have brought him to the conclusion that law and order must be preserved at pretty much any cost, otherwise civilisation is lost.

After the torpedoing of the Thracia, when Duff was struggling in the sea, he vowed to dedicate his life to God. Making good on that vow and entering a monastery is surely further evidence of high moral standards. Protesting at the bad treatment of others and having the resolve to leave the monastery indicates an unyielding determination to do the right thing, come what may.

I envisage Duff as a gruff, kindly figure, with a superb gift for communication, immeasurably interested in life. From someone who knew him: 'He was a fascinating man, in some ways a bit of an Ancient Mariner, full of wonderful yarns and a mine of information on the Middle East in particular…I was very fond of him and he was very kind to me.'

The Secret Garden

Fran Gardner

Nothing to prepare
for what lies within,
Set foot through the door
to the magic of Narnia.
An onslaught of colour,
shape and texture.
An eclectic mix of
colourful objet d'art.
Then for me sudden sight
of dark green wood, perfectly shaped.
Emotions rise as a lump
to the throat.
Real magic has begun
in the confines of
"The Secret Garden "
Creative inspiration runs riot
in diverse collections.
Exquisite shapes and forms of
rooms, grottos, statues and more.
So much to see and to
inspire creation of ones own,
Surrounded and cocooned by
trees and plants.
Enveloping shapes and the
safety of "green "
A masterpiece of creation,
man and nature combined.
Once is not enough !!

"The Secret Garden " and Serles House,
Wimborne. Open for the NGS Scheme.

Horrocks & Webb
Fine Jewellers

35b Salisbury Street, Blandford Forum, Dorset, DT11 7PX
01258 452618 sales@horrocksandwebb.co.uk /horrocksandwebb

OUBEE

*"Yippee!" ("Eureka!" is overworked these days). "Wow!" I shouted. I am always look-
ing for "Not a lotta people know that...." stories and realised I had stumbled on something new.*

Ian Andrews, Chairman of the Wessex Newfoundland Society

To go back a bit, I knew that a few of the native but now extinct Beothuk tribe (the original Red Indians) of Newfoundland had been brought to Britain and must have died over here, but previous appeals for information on where they were buried have produced no results – until now.

The story goes that the two well-known Lester brothers of Poole traded with Trinity in Newfoundland. Isaac stayed in Poole and organised crew, apprentice and worker recruitment and the supply of local produce (from cast iron to bricks and gravestones) to go out in ballast as well as the financial arrangements) while his brother Ben led the seasonal spring exodus in their ships and return in the autumn (their micro-filmed diaries can be read in the Poole Local History Centre). Settlement was discouraged in the early years of the 16th and 17th century, but in the 18th century heyday they needed a year-round agent who could look after their considerable assets "out of season". That lot fell to Thomas STONE.

He, in company with 2 others, in autumn 1791 had gone to Charles Brook in Notre Dame Bay, to wreak vengeance on a party of Beothucks who were believed to be responsible for the recent theft of their salmon traps, nets and other property. In a one sided affray that ensued, a Beothuk man was killed and a boy injured, a young girl called "Oubee" "captured as a fair prize". Two other women took flight and got away. "Oubee" was taken to Trinity and cared for "with care and humanity" by Thomas Strong and his wife..

While she was residing in Trinity, Capt. G.C. Pulling came to see her. Pulling was preparing a report on Beothuk-English relations and hoped that he would then be sent to the Beothuk on a peace mission. Being anxious to be able to communicate with them he asked Oubee for the Beothuk equivalent of 111 English words - the first to ever be recorded. There are no known descendants of the Beothuk Indians today as apart from armed attacks they had no resistance and were prone to easily succumb to European diseases.

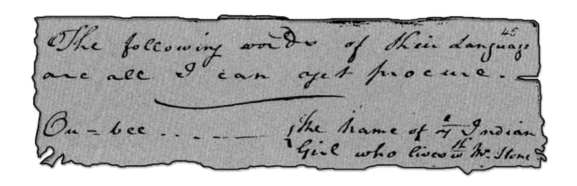

In 1792 Stone finally retired and returned to England with his family bringing "his little negro boy and Oubee with him". We know no more of the Negro boy, presumably from the slave settlements of West Indies, but they were exhibited on Poole Quay in a "penny-for-a-peep" show. It is believed that they lived in Howe Lodge (now demolished) later enlarged by Isaac Gulliver, the gentleman smuggler).

Isaac Gulliver hid smuggled goods in and around it.

Sadly Oubee died at a young age in 1795 and in the records of St Andrew's Church, Kinson, I found that in about 1795, Mr. Thomas Stone was paid twelve shillings and ten pence for expenses in connection with "Eomoy", presumably Oubee. As a non-Christian Oubee was buried in an

Howe Lodge, Kinson in the late 1800s.
Reverend Sharp, vicar of Kinson lived here for a time before buying Pelhams Park.

The twist in this tale is that I was responsible for researching for a grant for St Andrew's Church in Kinson from the Dorset Historic Churches Trust, as it had been unusable for about four years, although well known to tourists as the "Smuggler's Church" as

unmarked and unconsecrated plot in the large churchyard, with no headstone, but some sort of ceremony conducted by a clergyman. A letter written in 1797 stated that "Oubee" was "treated with great care and humanity by Mr and Mrs Stone."

The William Barnes Society

Brian Caddy and Devina Symes

The sun was shining on Sunday 8th October 2017 for the 10:30am, Morning Service at St Peter's Church, Dorchester, to commemorate the death of William Barnes. There was a good attendance from both the congregation and William Barnes Society members. The Service was officiated by the Revd. Claire McCelland and the Revd. Canon Richard Franklin preached the Sermon. Following the sermon, the society chairman, Brian Caddy, read a dialect poem Sleep did come wi' the Dew. The Service concluded with the choir processing to William Barnes's statue, singing Linden Lea. David Downton then laid a wreath at the foot of the statue, and Dave Burbidge read the first part of verse four from Culver Dell and the Squire.

Brian Caddy reading poetry

Two days later on Tuesday 10th October the Annual general Meeting was held where the officers were elected to serve the Society.* There being no changes from the previous year, John Blackmore entertained a packed room with his presentation of 'Music and Song.'

During his performance, he drew attention to the musicality of Barnes's verse and the beautiful but complex rhythms and structure that make the work distinctly 'Dorsetian'.

John's beautiful settings to some of Barnes's poems such as Blackmore Maidens, Blackmore by the Stour, and The Geate a-Vallen To were greatly enjoyed by all. He finished his performance on a personal note, with 'Gone to London' which he had written for his brother who had left the countryside for the bright lights of London.

The final event in 2017 was held at the Dorford centre on 12th December where a large number of members gathered for the Festive Celebration, Keepen up o' Christmas. Carols were led by Dave Burbidge, and Tim Laycock played some wonderful tunes including 'The Bells of St Mary'. Brenda Stevens played the viola and poems were read by various members of the society, making it a most enjoyable and happy occasion.

2018 has proved to be another very busy and successful year for The William Barnes Society; full of interesting and varied events which have taken society members to many parts of the county.

The year started with the first of the twelve outreach events which the society has performed in 2018, and was held in the Dorset County Museum in January, where some of the members were on hand to support Marion Tait, who is curator of the Barnes collection, as she took sixth form students from Rendcombe, College, Gloucestershire, to the Barnes gallery where they viewed the Barnes artefacts on display.

Members also performed and read Barnes' poetry as part of the William Barnes Educational Package, which was a great success ending with two of the students reading 'A Bit o Sly Coortin.' Another success was the second outreach event in January, which was held at Winterbourne Abbas, where selections of Barnes' poems were performed. Insert photo Brian Caddy and Devina Symes performing Barnes' eclogue 'A Bit O Sly Coortin'.

Victorian Fayre

On the 24th February we held our third Victorian Fayre in the Corn Exchange, Dorchester, which transported visitors back to the 19th century with a host of traditional skills being demonstrated. A more comprehensive account of this very successful event is covered in more detail within the pages of this book.
Insert Photo Victorian Fayre

Also in February a Barnes Supper was organised by The Ridgeway Singers and held at Portesham village hall, and proved to be a very enjoyable and happy evening.

For the March meeting, Dr Richard Bradbury gave a talk entitled, What's the point of William Barnes in the 21st century?, and, listening to this much researched subject we soon realised that there was a massive point in William Barnes today, and that things Barnes had written about and highlighted were as relevant today.

April saw some of the members travelling to Milborne Port. The society had been asked to go there and perform some of Barnes' poetry, along with some folk tunes and songs. After the programme finished many people from the audience spoke enthusiastically to members of the Barnes Society.

Another April outreach event was held at The Royal Oak in Cerne Abbas, and was part of the Giant Festival. The pub was packed, and after a delicious supper, poetry and songs were performed to a very appreciative audience; a very enjoyable and happy event for all who were present.

It was a sunny but chilly morning on the 22nd of April, as we made our way to St Peter's Church, Winterborne Came, for the Annual Service of Remembrance. The service was taken by Licensed Lay Reader, David Bowen, who led the congregation in Morning Prayer, which, as is tradition, was interspersed with Barnes poems. The delightful selection this year being 'May' read by Tim Laycock: 'Woakland Dell' read by Brian Caddy: 'Zunday' read by Dave Burbidge: 'The Direction Post' read by Barbara Whillock. The lessons were read by Jill Bryant and David Guy. Floral tributes were laid on the graves of William Barnes and his daughter, Laura, by the Chairman, Brian Caddy, and Vice Chairman, Devina Symes.

On a warm May evening (15th) members gathered at the Dorford Centre to listen to Phil Humphries give a talk on the history and music of the serpent, an ancient member of the brass family of musical instruments. During his talk, Phil, a native of Dorset, also touched on a few connections with the county and the poetry of William Barnes and Thomas Hardy.

Brian Caddy and Devina Symes performing Barnes' eclogue 'A Bit O Sly Coortin'

Phil's vast knowledge of the serpent, Dorset, Barnes and Hardy, gave the members an extremely enjoyable evening, and was well received by all who attended.

Our outreach event in June took us to Sherborne, where we had been invited for the second time, to take part in the Sherborne Literary Festival. We were made most welcome and served canapés prior to the performance, which was very well received by an appreciative audience, including Jenny Devitt from Abbey Radio, who interviewed some of the readers, afterwards, and so spreading the poetry and wisdom of William Barnes to a wider audience.

Following the success of last year's summer lunch at Cerne Abbas, it was decided to hold this year's summer lunch there again, with Mrs Joy Parsons providing another of her delicious lunches, and where the entertainment was provided by Virginia and Florence Astley who played beautiful and inspiring songs on the flute and harp.

The very hot weather in July saw some members of the Barnes Society performing at two of the Thomas Hardy Society Conference events: The first being on the afternoon of the 15th, the first day of the conference, where members read some of Barnes poetry at the Victorian Fair at Kingston Maurward: The second event was on the 19th, and was part of a Hardy/ Barnes walk, where Brian Caddy and Devina Symes read some Barnes poems in St Peter's Church at Winterborne Came, before Hardy Society members and visitors walked on to see the Rectory at Came, home to William Barnes for the last two decades of his life.

The month of August began with members of the society journeying to Sturminster Newton for a Dorset evening of words and music in aid of Sturminster Mill and Sturminster Museum.
It was a very warm evening and The Exchange was packed with a very receptive audience. Tim Laycock and John Blackmore were able to join in this very happy event, which made it all the more special.

One of the rare, very wet days of the summer, was on August 26th when members of the Barnes Society went to Oak Fayre at Stock Gaylard to perform some eclogues and poems

Poetry reading

in the church. This was the third year the society attended the event, and although, due to the torrential rain, there was a small audience for the first recital, numbers swelled immensely for the second performance, and we received a very warm reception. As summer merged into autumn the sunny days continued as we held our annual performance at Max Gate on the 15th September. The garden was almost full for this very happy event, as readers performed eclogues and poetry, which was interspersed with songs from JamPlease. Afterwards, tea and home-made cake and biscuits baked by Joy Parsons, were served, adding to this very enjoyable, Dorset Afternoon.

Another outreach event took place on 23rd September at Long Bredy, where a most delicious Harvest Lunch, organised by the local bell ringers, and in aid of funds for new bells, took place in the village hall. Members of the Barnes Society, Tim Laycock, Barbara Whillock, Angela Laycock and Dave Burbidge provided the entertainment with poetry and songs, which were in keeping with the harvest theme, and much appreciated by all who attended.

At the time of going to press the society look forward to a Harvest Supper at Broadmayne village hall on Michaelmas day, the 29th September, which will be the final event in a most varied and enjoyable year for society members and devotees of William Barnes.

* Officers of The Barnes Society 2017 – 2018:

Chairman	–	Brian Caddy:
Vice Chairman	–	Devina Symes
Secretary	–	Marion Tait
Treasurer	–	Keith Hooper
Publicity Officer	–	Peter Metcalfe: Auditor – Vacant
Website Officer	–	Mark North
Newsletter Editor	–	Dr. Aland Chedzoy

Committee: The Officers plus,
Jill Bryant, David Downton, Rod Drew,
Helen Gibson, David Guy and Audrey Loukes.

Dorchester Moving Back To The Future

David Forester

Hearing on 'Breakfast in Dorset' that the market may well be moving back to the car park in Charles Street, from its current situation in Weymouth Avenue, the memories of Dorchester Markets came flooding back to me. My first thoughts were that it was returning home, bringing with it some very happy childhood memories, recorded in my book Fordington Remembered, published by Roving Press. Let's take a trip down memory lane.

Dorchester being a market town, during the holiday periods markets were a great form of entertainment for local children. The Wednesday Market was held in Weymouth Avenue as it is now. However it was then a cattle market. On sale were cows, calves, beef animals and pigs, these were all sold in the auction ring. This now has stalls which are used to sell farm produced meat, sausages and eggs.

The cows could not always be moved to the buyer's farm until the next day, therefore they often required milking by hand in the stall where they stood, by men willing to milk the cows for some free milk. Indeed men arrived carrying a bucket, living in hope! This milk, often a real life saver was often carried a long way home to feed some very hungry children and to be shared with grateful neighbours.

In the undercover part of the market there were also cages, these contained live hens, cockerels, rabbits, ferrets etc. These were a great source of entertainment for us, of

Dorchester Market, *courtesy K. Gould*

course. I once put my finger through the wire into the ferret cage to try and stroke it, the ferret sank its teeth into my finger right down to the bone and wouldn't let go. I was rescued by a man saying "I told you not to put your fingers in the cage!" Another lesson learnt the hard way!

All the dead chicken, rabbits etc. were hung over rails in another part of the covered area. Also undercover were all the eggs, duck, chicken and goose. The local carrier had a big part to play in market day transporting people and produce. Quite often these eggs, chickens and ducks, both alive or killed and plucked, were collected from different cottages by a carrier on his way to town, This produce was then sold off and on the way back home the cash for the produce would be dropped off, lots of trust involved in an operation like that.

Photo courtesy of Dorchester Museum

The other Dorchester market was held on a Saturday, this was based in Charles Street in the area which is now a car park. This market as I remember consisted more of beef animals, calves and pigs. Market days were always very busy days in town when all the people from surrounding villages came to town for the day. For many it was the only

outing of the week, and with holidays being out of the question, market days were looked forward to with great expectation. The pubs were especially busy on these days, farmers struck many a deal in them, probably somewhat affected by the drink.

You will notice I have not mentioned sheep at the market; this is due to the fact that sheep fairs were held as separate occasions, either at Poundbury or on Fair Field in Weymouth Avenue.

Some days before, a great number of pens would be made using hurdles. These were panels made with split woven hazel strips. Sheep would be driven along roads from as far away as Blandford, Sherborne and Bridport. These would be rested in fields overnight around Dorchester; this would bring in a little much needed income for local farmers. The next morning they would be driven into town for the Sheep Fair, great excitement! Just imagine trying to do this today with modern day traffic.

Sheep Fair, Weymouth Avenue, *courtesy Dorset County Museum*

The 'Battle' at Bridport

Jack Sweet

Set in the chancel floor of the Parish Church of St Mary the Virgin at Bradford Abbas, is an echo of a conflict which had a terrible effect on hundreds of families and the populations of Somerset, Devon and Dorset. The memorial is dedicated to the memory of William Harvey who died of wounds received in the service of King James II at Bridport on the second of July 1685.

William Harvey, an officer in the Dorset Militia, was mortally wounded in a sharp skirmish between the Militia and the Duke of Monmouth's rebels in Bridport on the night of 13/14 June 1685 and died back at home in Bradford Abbas on 2 July.

King Charles II had no legitimate heir and on his death in February 1685 the crown passed to his brother James II. However, James Scott, 1st Duke of Monmouth and Charles II's illegitimate son, immediately challenged his uncle's succession and on 11th June 1685 began his bid for the throne when he landed unopposed on the beach at Lyme Regis with a tiny invasion force of 83 professional soldiers and a quantity of arms and ammunition. Following a successful progress through the West Country in 1680, the Duke was extremely popular and hundreds of men and youths came flocking to his green standard bearing the motto 'Fear nothing but God.' Soon after landing, James, Duke of Monmouth issued a proclamation asserting his right to the succession.

The re-action to Monmouth's 'invasion' was swift and within days the militias of Devon, Dorset and Somerset were mustered and moved to contain the rebels until the Royal Army could take the field.

By 13th June, the Dorset Militia had occupied Bridport and were threatening Monmouth's eastern flank. With his rebel army now numbering several thousand, the Duke felt strong enough to launched an attack on the militia and secure his right flank. On the night of 13th June under the command of Colonel Samuel Venner, Monmouth's principal military adviser and onetime professional soldier, 400 infantry supported by 40 cavalry commanded by Lord Grey, moved on Bridport but as they neared the town a report was received that the Dorset Militia numbered some 1200 foot and 100 cavalry, thus outnumbering them three to one. Undaunted the rebels pressed on and arrived on the western outskirts just before dawn on the 14th.

Bridport consisted of a long street running west to east with a stone bridge over a stream at each end and a cross street half way along. The militia was encamped just beyond the east bridge, a guard positioned in the centre with the cavalry, and an outpost at the west bridge. A number of officers had taken up quarters in the Bull Inn – the site of the present inn of the same name.

The militia commander, not anticipating an attack had sent out no patrols or outposts beyond the west bridge and the rebel vanguard of 40 musketeers under

Lieutenant Mitchell, one of the professional soldiers accompanying the Duke, approached unchallenged in the dawn mist. Taking the outpost by surprise the rebels swarmed over the bridge and sent the militiamen packing in full flight back into the town. The vanguard now supported by a company of 100 musketeers led by Captain Thompson, another professional, pushed on up the main street where they found the militia guard formed up to meet them, but a rebel volley sent them in full retreat back to the camp at the east bridge.

The main body of Monmouth's infantry and cavalry now entered Bridport and after placing a rearguard at the west bridge and an outpost to cover against a flank attack from the cross street running to the south, Colonel Venner began drawing up his command to advance against the militia at the east bridge. Venner's second in command, Major Nathaniel Wade was organizing a company to act as a reserve, and Lord Grey was drawing up his cavalry. Suddenly the windows of the Bull Inn were thrown open and shots were fired at the rebels who quickly recovering from the surprise stormed the inn. Charging into the Bull, Colonel Venner was shot in the stomach by a militia lieutenant, Edward Coker, and returning the fire shot Coker dead. In the short fight which followed, another militia officer, Wadham Strangways was shot dead and three others wounded, one of whom, William Harvey of Bradford Abbas would return home to die. A number of militia officers were captured and the inn secured.

With the flight of the town guard, morale began to falter in the militia camp but finally the officers managed to persuade their men to stand and fight from behind a barricade thrown across the road. With Major Nathanial Wade taking command, Monmouth's men advanced up to the barricade and fired a volley which was returned. Two rebels died in the exchange but the noise and flashes of fire caused Grey's inexperienced cavalry to bolt and gallop back to Lyme shouting that Major Wade was dead, the infantry cut off and all was lost.

To stand in a firing line at some 50 paces from the opponent takes all the courage of regular infantry, and when the opponent is behind cover, it takes exceptional bravery, but Monmouth's men were not hardened regulars; and also when your cavalry support disappears in haste, well what follows? The rebel infantry panicked and broke off the attack, some threw down their weapons and decamped and if the reserve had not come up, probably most would have run away. After some persuasion, a new rebel line was formed and preparations were made to re-launch the assault on the barricade.
However, the wounded Colonel Venner's nerve failed and he ordered Wade to withdraw from Bridport. After painfully mounting his horse he rode back to Lyme Regis leaving his second in command to retreat as best he could.

Unlike Samuel Venner, Nathaniel Wade was not a professional soldier, he was a lawyer, but he proved to be the equal of any professional in the way he disengaged, regrouped his men, and retired in order to the west bridge. He prepared for the counter attack but although the militia advanced back into Bridport, they remained prudently out of musket shot shouting insults at the rebels. After some half an hour of this shouting match, the rebels withdrew in good order back to Lyme Regis taking with them about a dozen prisoners and some 30 captured horses.

Twenty six years-old, Edward Coker, from Mappowder, was buried the following day at Bridport in the churchyard of St Mary's Church, and is remembered on a brass memorial tablet in the Church.

The Duke of Monmouth and his rebel army marched out from Lyme Regis the following day and on to bloody defeat some three weeks later on a misty night at Sedgemoor, and to his execution for treason. The Battle of Sedgemoor and wrath of King James II and the Bloody Assizes under the hated Judge Jeffries which followed, would leave several thousand West Countrymen dead or transported to the plantations of the West Indies, but could it all have been so different if the Monmouth rebels had chased the Dorset Militia from the barricade at Bridport?

Dorset - Our Joy and our Pride

Devina Symes

Entwined in Dorset's greenery
It paints such pretty scenery
As it sparkles so very clear.

We must think how we use it,
Try never to abuse it,
For 'tis so precious, my dear!

You sure can never make it,
Neither can you fake it,
Now that really is true.

Without a word of lie,
If we lost it, we would die,
'Tis our survival you!

Within this lovely county,
We're surrounded by the bounty,
Of the Frome, Stour and Bride.

Yes, water is God given,
And helps us continue living
In Dorset - our joy, and our pride!

Dippy Visits Dorchester

John Travell

In November 2017, to considerable media publicity, and great excitement locally, the plaster cast of a diplodocus skeleton which had been on display at the Natural History Museum in London since 1905, arrived at the County Museum in Dorchester, at the start of a nationwide tour. The fact that Dorchester, the smallest county town in England, had been given the privilege of being the very first place to receive this rare and important exhibit, was greatly to the credit of the Museum's Director, Dr. Jon Murden, and all his staff and helpers who had established the Museum's growing reputation as an outstanding institution. This had previously been endorsed by the British Museum, which a few years ago, allowed Dorchester to be the first Museum in the country to exhibit its touring Pharaoh Exhibition, which included extremely valuable and rare ancient Egyptian artefacts which the British Museum had ever allowed to be seen before outside its own galleries.

The media interest continued to grow as television crews came and filmed the careful reconstruction of the huge skeleton which filled the whole of the Victorian Hall of the museum which had been emptied of every other artefact to make room for it. Although it was a tight fit, the Hall proved to be an ideal place to display the dinosaur, and the Museum staff had skilfully planned the route for visitors to take as they came to view the creature. A live television link was set up with BBC breakfast and the national lunchtime news as well as BBC South, Sky News and ITV, as well as BBC and local radio channels, all reported on the dinosaur's progress. A greatly enlarged army of 201 volunteers was recruited and trained to direct and control the expected crowds, who were steered up the main staircase and into the Hall and then round the gallery, which was at head-height of the beast. This proved very popular, especially among the children, who were excited to have selfies taken of themselves with the animal's large and fierce-some face. Then they were guided down to the floor level, where they could look up to experience the size of the whole animal, before leading through into an area where the children were encouraged to draw pictures and make their own models, and then, through the enlarged shop, where there were knitted dinosaurs among many souvenirs to tempt them: Dippy hats were especially popular and nearly 10,000 of them could be seen on

Courtesy Dorset County Museum

the heads of small children and some of their parents all round the town during Dippy's stay.

The television companies were there and queues formed early on Saturday, 10 February 2018, the day the Exhibition was opened, and the event was in all the national press and main news channels. The Times newspaper's chief cartoonist, to make a political point, drew a large, accurate picture of Dippy with the bones of the skeleton spelling out the word 'BREXIT" in heavy black lettering. The Museum had formed a partnership with Brewery Square several months before the event began, and the Square contributed to the town tourist trail by creating life-size green diplodocus footprints as a 'way finder' from Dorchester South Station to the Museum. Dorchester BID gave a grant of £5,000 to provide 80 Dippy on Tour green flags to decorate High West Street. During the school holidays the BID Ambassadors were in the Dorchester car parks to show visitors the way to the Museum, and also at the Museum to help direct visitors around the town, and so extend their visit to Dorchester.

Visitor numbers rapidly passed the most optimistic estimates anticipated before the dinosaur's arrival: over 50, 000 people turning up in the first four weeks – equal to the number of visitors the Museum usually welcomed during a whole year. Booking had begun by the website well before the opening, but there were far more walk-in visitors than expected, with families arriving in the town from a wide area, especially during the school holidays.

Businesses all benefited from the event as customer numbers increased in cafes and shops as visitors sought somewhere to eat and spent time enjoying and exploring the town. Waterstones sold dinosaur books and held a dinosaur craft morning which brought families into the shop, and Brewery Square put on an Andy Dina Raps Show over the Easter weekend which attracted some 8,000 people to the Square. The Tourist

Courtesy Dorset County Museum

Information Centre was kept busy with people seeking information and 'saw lots of very excited children and experienced the general excitement and sense of community pride that Dippy on Tour brought with it.' As well as the main event in Dorchester, the Jurassic Coast Trust organised a creative outreach programme with a replica Dippy skull which also proved hugely popular as it toured to some fifty events across the region which stretched over 95 miles from Salisbury to Exeter and reached over 20,00 people.

When the exhibition finally closed, the Museum had recorded receiving 153,189 visitors, well over three times what had been hoped for before the event began. Of these, 8,433 were members of schools and children's groups. The Museum had made special arrangements with these, although it had failed to anticipate the demand for lunch and toilets. An urgent appeal to the Town Council helped solve the problem by opening the Corn Exchange next door for the schools to assemble in before making their visit. The Jurassic Coast Trust invited 25 children from the Julia's House Children's Hospice and their families to a private evening in the Museum. Thanking their hosts, Maria Carroll of Julia's House wrote. 'WOW! Thank you for making our families and friends feel like VIPs when we met Dippy, we had the Museum to ourselves and were made to feel really special. They all loved taking selfies, making hats and learning dinosaur facts.' There were 49 paid for school sessions, and 35 free and unguided school visits, together with 41 other pre-school groups, adult learning groups and special educational needs schools. Hannah Trevorrow for the Dorchester Area Schools Partnership of 17 schools wrote a 'Dippy in Dorchester' song which was first performed at the opening event in the Museum. From March to April she visited eight first schools and taught the song to about 1,500 children. Then, in May, 250 children sang the song at the closing event in the Museum.

The Museum had remained open for other visitors to see the rest of the collections, and these had also increased in number during the three months Dippy was there. Dippy's last day was Monday, 7 May, a Bank Holiday, with people still queuing to see it. The skeleton was then deconstructed and re-packed and taken off to the next venue on its national tour, which was to the big metropolitan city of Birmingham, with its far larger population. It has been estimated that if Birmingham manages to attract – in percentage terms of its population - as many as Dorchester achieved, then it would need to have received at least two million visitors to its Museum.

The impact of this outstanding event on Dorchester and the county was considerable, uplifting and wholly beneficial. During the three months of the exhibition the visitors spent around £2,25million, which, after deductions for purchases and indirect taxes meant that the town benefited from £1.1million to the local economy. The Museum has produced a review of the whole remarkable event, and the effect it has had on the whole town and community, which says that 'as well as the huge social and cultural impact acquired through family and school visits, the Dippy on Tour exhibition generated immeasurable goodwill in the town and many businesses will have benefitted through the promotion and marketing of not just Dippy but also the associated events.' This was an enjoyable and very memorable time for the town and county which lifted the spirits gave thousands of people and especially the children, an exciting and very happy time to remember and look back on with pleasure in later years.

Dorset's Exciting Route

Kay Ennals MBE

Follow the route that takes you to
    Dorset's Jurassic ground,
Where Purbeck rock and limestone lay
    in stunning scenery all the way--
Here, where historic fossils were found!

As you wander along where the seagull soars
    you are treading the path of the dinosaurs,
How they must have rampaged and roared
    In their fearsome struggles and brawls -
fighting and biting with teeth like swords!

With dinosaurs gone - who lived no more -
    during those millions of years before -
Nature decided that beauty should form
    along this very special shore -
Such as Dancing Ledge, Lulworth, and Durdle Door!

Make your way to Kimmeridge Bay
    Where the beach is flat and low lying,
or perhaps go on to Chesil's Fleet -
    Where a beautiful, sparkling, lazy lagoon
is relaxing - yet wholly reviving - a treat!

There's much to remember -
    more to discover -
        Which place did you love the most?
           You will find it for sure -
              along the Jurassic coast!!

Underwater Filming at Night

Colin Garrett

As the summer sun slowly starts disappearing below the horizon, locals and tourists stroll along the promenade at Chesil Cove (from The Cove House Inn to Quiddles Cafe) trying to capture an image of the distant golden orb on various electronic devices. Their photos then being shared to family and friends on various social media sites, depicting the perfect end to a long and warm June day.

Chesil Beach Sunset *Photo by Selwyn Williams*

Their day is slowly coming to a sun burnt close, for me, partner Sarah and good friend Alex however, ours is only just beginning.

It takes a lot of dedication to go scuba diving at night in the height of British Summer. The sun doesn't set until around 9.20pm, and after a full day at work, the idea of waiting for darkness to fall before slipping beneath the waves of Chesil Cove may seem like madness to some. For us though, this is the best time to go diving and seek out the many animals that either visit or reside here.

The underwater topography at Chesil Cove is a mixture of everything from bare pebbles, kelp covered rocks, sandy patches and endless bits of wreckage; a rusty reminder to us of how many vessels have fallen foul here over the years, so many in fact that the cove was at one time known locally as 'Deadman's Bay'.

In light of the many human casualties however, this varied seabed offers the perfect location for many species of wildlife.

The sheer diversity of marine life that can be found at this location is quite astonishing. Several species of shark (small spotted cat sharks, bull huss, smoothhounds); skates and rays (undulates, blondes, spotted, small-eyed); crustaceans (common lobster, squat lobster, edible, spider and velvet swimming Crabs). Numerous species of fish (ballan wrasse, john dory, gurnard, cod, bib, mackerel, bream, blennies, eels, angler fish and many more beside) and sponges, sea squirts, nudibranch, the list goes on and on.

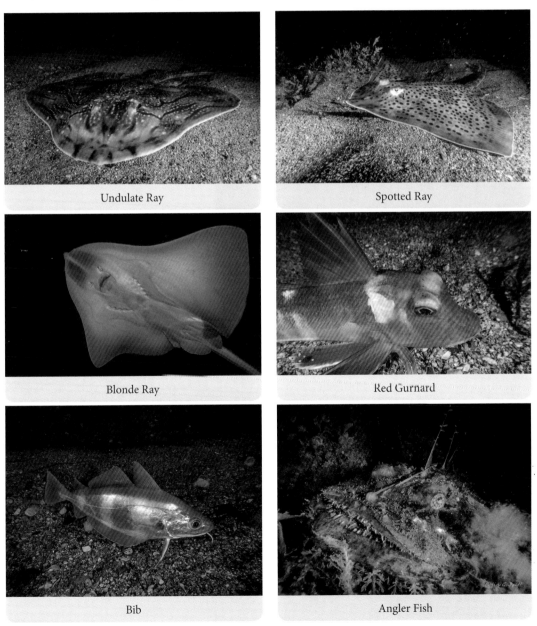

Undulate Ray

Spotted Ray

Blonde Ray

Red Gurnard

Bib

Angler Fish

Kitting up with cylinders, regulators and other diving essentials, the three of us, frequently take the short walk down the world famous pebble beach before slowly descending into the water and lighting up the inky blackness with our torches and video lights. Then after a brief check underwater to ensure all our equipment is functioning correctly, we begin the gentle swim out to sea with the only sounds being that of the bubbles exhaled from our regulators.

Around a depth of 6-8 metres at the base of the pebbles we pass the skeletal remains of the Greek vessel 'Preveza.' A subtle reminder of how powerful the oceans truly are. Her demise however, now offers shelter for crabs, small fish and occasionally lobsters. Beyond this the sea floor begins to change to large rocks and weed, this is the realm of ballan

John Dory

wrasse. Always found slowly moving around the cracks and crevices looking for food.

Continuing seaward around 12 metres depth, the seabed changes again to fine sand and for us, this is where we really start to enjoy our dive. This habitat offers a chance to finding and filming the most 'regal' looking fish in British waters, the John Dory.

Under the video lights, these beautiful fish are almost 'gold' looking, with a blue coloured eye that is simply mesmerizing.

Other species soon start to reveal themselves; red mullet are seen probing the sand with their barbels. Juvenile conger eels (known by fisherman as 'straps') stalk the rippled sand in search for prey. Lobsters patrol the sea bed in search for food, like blue armoured vehicles. Pollock wait patiently mid water. Cuttlefish, the masters of camouflage, hover just above the sandy bottom and in recent years they have been joined by the octopus.

Conger Eel

Lobster

It is humbling at times to be underwater in the darkness observing all these beautiful animals, creatures that are in perfect balance with themselves without human interference. All predators, yet all prey.

Changing direction from West to North, we drop down a reef to a depth of 16 metres. Here is where we often find the skates and rays, and this particular nights dive was no exception, with four species (undulate, spotted, blonde and small-eyed) all being found. Watching and filming these graceful

Cuttlefish

fish swim effortlessly around is one of my favourite pastimes but all too soon our air supplies dwindle and it is time to head back to shore and the sometimes strenuous walk back up the beach.

Octopus

Once out of the water and back at the car, the first thing I notice is noise; vehicles, sirens, wind, people. It is staggering how noisy the world above the waves is and I suppose that's why I dive and make underwater films in my spare time, simply to relax.

Over the years I have been humbled by some lovely comments by people far and wide who were at first surprised to learn what life can be found just off of our beaches here in Dorset, many thinking that these colourful and varied animals could only be seen abroad. But also saddened too, for some are people, through no fault of their own (health, age, finance etc), will only get the opportunity to see this world through our lenses. Their comments are still kind but I wish they could see it and touch it too, because I believe when someone truly touches the underwater world and its creatures, then and only then will they truly serve to protect it.

At this time in history and for the planet's future, that is needed more than ever.

All underwater photos – Colin Garrett

Hume Swaine

Grandson Robin Swaine

Hume's parents were Robert and Frances and he was born at 8.45pm on Friday 11 April 1856 at 27 Grove Place, Brompton, London. Hume was the first of twins born prematurely, it is said as a result of his mother's fall from a horse (his grandfathers were horse dealers and stable keepers and his father a horse dealer's clerk). Because they were at risk, the twins were baptised at birth and later formally christened on Tuesday 13 December 1859 in Holy Trinity Church, Brompton when they were 3 1/2 years old. The origin of the use of the name "Hume" in the family was in 1781 (celebrating a family friend) and it has been used five times to date. Hume's godparents were Capt James Wells and Mrs Frances Choppin. In spite of their bad start, the twins, Hume and his sister

Fanny survived to old age. Hume died on the 25th May 1938, aged 82, and was buried in the family grave in the Brompton Cemetery.

Hume, when aged 41, married Jane Jones aged 25 at St Pancras Register Office

Tilly Whim Caves

Durdle Door Rock

disapproved of Hume's marriage which might explain the couple's later move to Swanage and their comparative lack of riches in early marriage.

Hume, an eccentric, latterly earned money as an engraver and painter often of scenes along the South Coast: in the census return of 1881 he is an "artist of wood", in 1891 an "artist sculptor" and in 1910 a "Draughtsman on Block". In London Hume quoted the Pelham Street address for professional purposes and his "The Artist's Rambles round about Swanage" dated 1893, had it on the cover. Hume describes himself as a "draughtsman and engineer". Many of his original drawings, paintings, and engraved copper blocks remain with the family. The blocks were used to illustrate his guide books. There is evidence that similar guide books in the "Swaine Series" were produced incorporating scenes of Anglesey and Pembrokeshire. He

in 1898. The couple had known one another for at least 7 years for the 1891 census shows the twins, Hume and Fanny, living at 39 Pelham St with Jane Jones making her first appearance as a domestic servant aged 17; the twin's parents were away in Surrey at the time of the census. The marriage certificate shows Hume to be a "general engraver" and his father, Robert H. W. Swaine as of 'independent means'. There do seem to be some unusual features to Hume's wedding for it was by licence, in a register office in spite of the fact that he was the only son of a father anxious to maintain appearances and who thought himself quite wellborn; probably Robert felt that Hume was marrying beneath himself, Hume and Jane's marriage certificate shows them both living at the same address, 32 Pratt St, NW1 yet his address on his Weymouth guide of the same year is given as Pelham St, South Kensington possibly for professional reasons.

Hume and Jane had three children: Robert Cecil Bishop born 7.6.1900, John Evelyn born 26.6.06 and Mary born 14.3.08.

On the birth certificate of their first child Cecil, their address is given as 21 Trafalgar Square. They lived at no fewer than 4 London addresses including 39 Pelham St which features in his guide books. It is believed the Swaine family in general strongly

Studland Church

was also a designer and produced a comprehensive book of bicycles for the early Rudge/Humber cycle company.

Hume and Jane moved to Swanage in 1900 along with Hume's sister, Fanny. They lived at "Buona Vista" Newton Road then later moving to "Roughdown Villas", Salisbury Road and finally, in 1924, to "Cerne Abbas", 5 Stafford Road.

Hume spent a good deal of time away engaged in his business often travelling aboard the paddle steamers from Swanage Pier while Jane took in lodgers. His large wood-built workshop was in the back garden where he made the copper plates and engraved and pained. Hume seems to have been of moderate means and not have inherited any great wealth from the family maybe because of their disapproval. His grandmother, Anna Maria, died in 1870 when he was 14 leaving him £300 to be given to him when he reached 21; she had written this will on 16 April 1866 five days after Hume's 10th birthday (he was her first grandson carrying the Swaine surname) and she directed which investments had to be made and that the income be used for his education. It seems that Hume and his father, Robert were favoured by Anna Maria at this time.

The Village Inn, Studland

Hume's wife Jane, the daughter of William Jones, was born 3.5.1872 (according to her death cert) and died 29.12.1970 aged 98. Jane's age had been a matter of some conjecture because of a belief that she was very nearly 100 when she died and that she as falsified her age at marriage in order to appear older but the evidence seems fairly clear i.e. 17years in 1891, 25 at marriage July 1898 and 29 yrs in 1901 census. According to her death certificate and census returns she was born in Beaumaris, Anglesey and the family lived at some time Betws-y-Coed which is only some 18 miles away on the mainland. She was the daughter of a master Mariner who, with the name of William Jones, originating in Wales with the unknown date of birth and uncertain birthplace. It was decided not to investigate!

The information provided is the result of tireless research and is taken from "The Parsons & Swaines" A selective Family History from their origins to the early 21st Century by Dr Mike Parsons, grandson of Hume and Jane Swaine.

AN ARTIST'S RAMBLES ROUND ABOUT SWANAGE Originally published by Hume Swaine in 1893 Reprinted by his grandson Robin Swaine in 1989 and the current edition published in 2018.

Old Harry and His Wife,
The Pinnacle and Turf Rick Rocks

The Hangman Inn

Albert Douglas Gillen

Young farmers back from college tasks
Swilling ale from polished casks
The wounded soldier home from war
Showing everyone his scar

        The guarded Masons' room above
        Charity and brotherly love
        The drooling Squire, red in face
        The barmaid's bodice, undone lace

At tavern door the hunters meet
Impatient hounds, the fox to beat
Parsnip Polly on the floor
The barmaid serving her no more

        The handsome stranger, devil-may-care
        Finds it hard, not to stare
        At the mysterious lady, with French escort
        Who disembarked at Weymouth Port

The Landlord gross, of florid face
Dancing on the table
Made dancers of the human race
As the hangman, Martin Stable

        He'd loved to watch the dance of death
        Legs kicking in the air
        The tongue protruding from the head
        The eyes with bloodshot stare

His grisly business he'd enjoyed
With halter, blindfold, tiers
The courts to keep him full employed
Was all that he'd desired

        To measure men was his delight
        And good at calculation
        He'd check their health, their weight, their height
        Prepare them for damnation

Highwaymen, robbers of the mail
Were hung by Martin proud
His trusty halter never failed
To entertain the crowd

        Retirement as a hangman bold
        He'd taken this old coach – house
        Changed the name in letters gold
        From the renowned "Roach and Grouse"

Dorset and the Vikings

By Hilary Townsend

Viking invaders came here to the once deeply wooded Blackmore Vale in North Dorset and had the upper hand here until King Alfred, King of Wessex, rallied his troops for the decisive battle of Edington in Wiltshire in 878. Alfred was a clever tactician who, realising the value of big trees and dense greenery, drew his men from all around and especially near Pen Selwood. Then he stealthily advanced through the night to surprise the Vikings and besiege them in a fortress at Edington.

King Alfred had roused his troops by sending out groups at night to throw clods of earth and stones at the men's doors and W. S. Swayne, a nineteenth century curate at Stalbridge, told how the custom of clod throwing at front doors was still practised in Stalbridge on Panshard Night (Shrove Tuesday) – until Sir Robert Peel's new Police Act became law in 1829.

Alfred carried the day after a bloody battle at Slaughter Gate Farm, Gillingham

Viking mass grave uncovered at the Ridgeway, Weymouth. Courtesy of Wessex Archaeology

and peace was finally made at a place still called Peasmarsh. The King had defeated the Viking Commander Guthorm but realised that Guthorm's army was depleted – large numbers of his warriors were settling down on estates they had seized. So the king did not defeat the Vikings in a modern sense. Magnus Magnusson, the Viking scholar, maintains that Alfred was a realist who accepted the Viking presence in his Kingdom as a fact of life.

My father's family were always thought to have farmed in the Blackmore Vale, so could a Viking warrior have taken a wife from among my forebears? I first went to Norway in 1951 and, with the high cheekbones, fair skin and blue eyes often found in Norway, I must have looked such a typical fjordside village resident that I was often asked for directions by passing motorists.

Since then, I have travelled from Bergen to Finse in the depths of winter, skied in Geilo, explored the Jotenheim and Hardanger in early summer, loved the Lofoten Islands, delighted in the magic of the Midnight Sun in Hammerfest and watched fascinated as a local bus drove slowly past groups of grazing reindeer on the way to the North Cape.

I've listened to stories of the Norwegian Resistances during the war until the hairs on the back of my neck began to rise, joined in endless patriotic songs, risen to my feet with the crowd for the Bergener anthem, travelled the long arm of the fjord to Fjaerland wondering if I'd come to the end of the world, and seen the house in Fjaerland where Walter Mondale came on a visit to his place of birth. He was delighted to see his relations, discussed farming with them and was quite unspoiled by his fame as a USA statesman. On all my visits I have a feeling of coming home.

When I return, I walk in the woods at Pen Selwood where King Alfred might have glimpsed the helmets of the Viking warriors through the trees over a thousand years ago. And at Christmas 2016 my family gave me my DNA profile as a Christmas present. It proved that I am two per cent Finnish and twenty five per cent Norwegian.

War in the Middle East 1917-1918

Greg Schofield

After the disaster of Kut-el-Amara and the debacle of Gallipoli, the war against the Ottoman Empire in the Middle East went on to the back burner. The influence of the 'Westerners', officers who believed the war could only be won on the Western Front, meant that the British effort was concentrated in France and Belgium. However, the Turks were formidable enemies, and the threat they posed to to the Suez Canal and communication with India and the rest of the British Empire meant they could not be ignored.

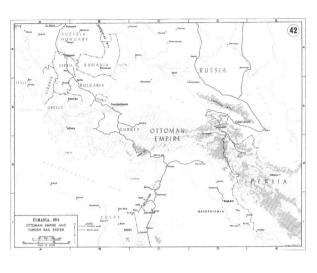

There were two main theatres of war in the Middle East; Palestine and Mesopotamia. Both were equally important and bitterly fought.

Palestine:

The campaigns here, led by General Allenby, are better known because of the activities of T.E. Lawrence (Lawrence of Arabia), and the Australian Light Horse regiments, but of course, there was a considerable British involvement as well as other elements of the British Empire. These were harsh conditions in which to fight, and for many there were strange departures; for example, the Royal Dorset Yeomanry were converted from horses to camels.

The main objectives were to drive the Turks out of Palestine, capture Jerusalem and link up with the Mesopotamian campaign.

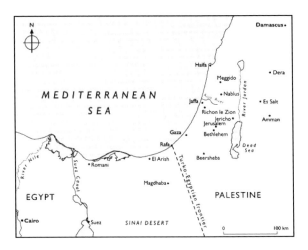

1916 and early 1917 was spent in a number of minor actions which secured the Sinai peninsula in preparation for an attack on the main Turkish defensive line between Gaza and Beersheba.

The following Weymouth men were killed:-

- BROWN Richard F.   Lance Corporal,   5th Connaught Rangers.
  Died 7th October, 1917.
  Lived 'Old Borough Arms', Chickerell Road, Weymouth.

- DOWNER Sydney   Private 1st/5th Welsh Regiment. Died 26th March, 1917, aged 23., Son of Albert and Helen Downer.
  Lived 19, Argyle Road, Weymouth.

Beersheba was captured on 31st October, 1917 and after further hard fighting which led to the collapse of the Gaza Beersheba line of defences, the British army was able to advance on the Judean Hills and Jaffa; Jerusalem being captured 0n 9th December, 1917.

The following Weymouth men were killed:-

- BETTS Edward   Private in 2nd/4th Dorsetshire Regt, Killed 22nd November, 1917, aged 39. Appointed a dispatch rider on a motor bike due to him being rather older than his comrades. Wounded and transferred to hospital, which was then blown up by enemy action. An assistant schoolmaster at Holy Trinity School, Weymouth. He volunteered for service to take the place of another teacher who had heavier family responsibilities. Left a wife, Maud, and one child.
  Lived at 17, Newberry Terrace, Weymouth.

- BUGLER Harold George   Private in Machine Gun Corps. Killed in action 13th November, 1917. Aged 24. Only son of Mr G. Bugler.
  Lived at 'Rodwell Garage', Weymouth

- COLLINS A.

  Private 16th Devonshire Regiment, killed 3rd December 1917.

- HOCKLEY S. W. J.

  Private 24th Royal Welsh Fusiliers. Died 27th December, 1917.

- KEELEY Ernest Joseph. R.

  Private 1st Dorset Yeomanry (Queen's Own). Wounded and reported missing. Declared dead 21st November, 1917.
  Member of Weymouth Conservative Club.

- LEGG William James

  Private in 2nd/4th Dorsetshire Regiment. Died 27th October,1917, aged 23.
  Lived 11, High Street, Weymouth.

- STRANGE William Walter Carter

  Private 1st Dorset Yeomanry (Queen's Own). Reported missing 28th November, 1917. Confirmed killed in action May 1919. Member of Dorset T.A. and joined the army in 1915. Sent to Egypt December 1916. Member of the Church Lad's Brigade. Worked as Clerk for Eldridge Pope (Weymouth). Married to Bessie Strange. Lived 51, Oakley Place, Weymouth

- SWANNIE Frederick

  Private in 2nd/4th Dorsetshire Regiment. Died 30th December, 1917.

- TARRANT Frederick Harold Edward

  Private 1st Dorset Yeomanry (Queen's Own). Killed in action 28th November, 1917, aged 21. Son of Frederick and Mary Tarrant.
  Lived 4, Cove Street, Weymouth.

Early 1918 was spent in actions in the Judean Hills and the Jordan Valley, and the capture of Jericho. The final major battle took place at Megiddo on 19th September, 1918, when in a brilliant action the Turkish Army was thoroughly defeated and virtually ceased to exist.

The following Weymouth men were killed:-

- COOMBES B.

  Private 1st Dorset Yeomanry (Queen's Own). Died 14th October, 1918, aged 21. Son of George and Sarah Coombes of Buckland Newton.
  Lived 2, Mulberry Terrace, School Street, Weymouth.

- DRAKE Arthur James

  Private 2nd Dorsetshire Regiment. Killed in action 19th September 1918, aged 22. Son of Sarah and James Drake.
  Lived at 78, Newstead Road, Weymouth.

- HOLLAND George William

  Private 2nd Dorsetshire Regiment. Died 22nd November, 1918, aged 34.

- PITMAN G. E.

Private 2nd/14th London Regiment (London Scottish). Killed in action 1st May, 1918.
Lived Cromwell Road, Weymouth.

- RIMMER J.

Sergeant Royal Engineers. Died 16th Octber, 1918, aged 37. Husband of Rose Rimmer.
Lived at 4, Victoria Street, Weymouth.

Mesopotamia:

General Maude conducted a brilliant campaign up the Tigris River which began on the 9th December, 1916. In a series of manoevures, the Turkish forces were outflanked and forced to retreat and Kut-Al-Amara was recaptured. The advance continued and on 11th March, 1917, Baghdad was captured, at which point the British advance was halted due to overstretched supply lines.

The following Weymouth men were killed:-

- EDMONDS Alfred George

Private, (Acting Lance Corporal) 2nd Dorsetshire Regiment. Died 5th March, 1917,aged 26. Reported wounded and missing in the Jesbit Haumrie Hills 50 miles north of Baghdad 25-03-1917. Confirmed died of wounds May 1919. Son of Francis & John Edmonds. Lived 3, Hartford Terrace, Gloucester Street, Weymouth.

- FIDLER Harry

Private, 2nd Dorsetshire Regiment. Died 25th March, 1917.

- NICKSON Frederick Edward

Sergeant 1st/4th Hampshire Regiment. Died 24th February, 1917, aged 22.
Lived Khartoum Road, Weymouth.

- LE MESURIER Arthur C. Edward

2nd Lieutenant, 6th Gurka Rifles. Died 9th March, 1917, aged 21. Son of May and Haviland Le Mesurier.

- PALMER Frank Seymour

Private, 2nd Dorsetshire Regiment. Killed in action 31st December, 1916, aged 36. Son of John & Mary Palmer.
Lived 70, Newstead Road, Weymouth.

• REAH Ralph W. Corporal 5th Dorsetshire Regiment.
Died 24th September, 1917, aged 31. Husband of
Ethel Reah.
Lived at 52, Ranelagh Road, Weymouth.

Early 1918 saw a number of minor actions against a disorganised and weakened Turkish army, until 23rd October 1918, when a sudden advance was launched. It advanced 75 miles in two days, and at the Battle of Sharqat defeated and captured the Turkish 6th Army, ending operations in this area.

The following Weymouth man was killed:-

• SCHOFIELD Alexander Traies Captain, Kent Cyclists Batallion. Died 10th
November, 1918, aged 26.
Son of Frank and Anne Schofield.

Editor's Note and Thanks

Thank you to all the contributors, to Chris Smith of Print Team (Dorset) Ltd for his expertise and extraordinary helpfulness, to Society of Dorset Men stalwarts Hayne Russell, Stuart Adam and especially to Peter Lush for his great help in proof reading many of the articles. Once again I think there is something for everybody in this Dorset Year Book about our beautiful county, its people, history, topography and flora & fauna, featuring real life stories, some Dorset fiction, poems and the news from our renowned Dorset Societies. I am also delighted that this second colour edition has some really stunning specialist photographs: - of the Jurassic coast taken from the sea by Steve Belasco, a myriad of the creatures under the sea by Colin Garrett and the stone mines at Portland by Mark Godden.

Due to other major commitments over the next two years this will be my third and last Year Book, at least for now, and I wish the new Editor all the best in what is a fulfilling job and I am sure they will get the same tremendous help I have had.

I have enjoyed reading each article as they come in and then seeing them illustrated in their final layout; the last two Year Books with colour available throughout. Although we are the Society of Dorset Men we have continually had some very fine female contributors to the Year Book and three who have sent in articles throughout are Kay Ennals MBE, Hilary Townsend and Devina Symes who celebrates 50 years of contributions in this issue. Having had the privilege of driving all around Dorset for my work, I personally love the farming and village stories illustrated by those old black and white photos, so evocative of those days, and Philip Knott has produced some more for this edition. We also commemorate the centenary of the end of the First World War with several Dorset related articles.

Please note all articles are printed in good faith and opinions expressed are solely those of the individual contributors and do not necessarily reflect the opinions of the editor or the Society of Dorset Men.

2nd Battalion Dorset Regiment in the Boer War 1899-1902

Roger Wyatt

The 2nd Battalion Dorset Regiment under Colonel Law embarked on the SS Simla at Southampton on 2nd November 1899 and reached Durban on 21st December via Queenstown, St Vincent, and Cape Town, where they immediately entrained for Estcourt to join the rest of the 5th Division under Maj. - General Coke as part of the 10th Brigade. The 5th had been sent after the Boer sieges at Kimberley, and Mafeking. Sir George White, had made an overambitious attempt to capture Boer guns, and got himself trapped in Ladysmith. When the Dorsets called at Cape Town they heard the alarming news of Magersfontein, the defeat at Stormberg and even worse, General Buller's defeat at Colenso, failing to cross the Tugela in his attempt to relieve Ladysmith.
At this point, Buller offered White the choice of fighting his way out or surrender, both of which White rejected.

So instead, Buller made steady but unsuccessful approaches, at first via Potgieter's Drift, then Trichardt's Drift, and General Warren, having been given command by Buller, made an attempt at Tabayama- all three were easily countered by the Boers who quickly moved into superior positions each time. Warren with Buller's agreement then shifted his attention to Spion Kop, using Coke's brigade and giving Coke general charge of Warren's right.

Originally the Dorsets and Middlesex were to have attacked Spion Kop but after reconnoitring that evening, January 22, Coke decided instead that General Woodgate's 11th Brigade should go in with 10th in support. So the Dorsets, having had a day in bivouac, began to climb to a ridge below the hill where they heard the cheers of the Lancashires taking the Kop. Unfortunately, what they thought was the crest of the Kop proved to be lower than the actual crest, moreover when the thick fog cleared at about 8am; their poorly sited shallow trenches in rocky ground were exposed to rifle fire from Tabyama and from the east and gunfire as well. The Boers now began reoccupying the crest as some Lancashires pushed forward to try to prevent this. At this critical moment at about 08:30 Woodgate was mortally wounded and thus the momentum swung away from our attack. The Dorsets started forward but were halted below the top and began passing water and ammunition to the top and helping the wounded as they started to flow increasingly down the hill. Colonel Thorneycroft and his Mounted Infantry (MI) came into the gallant defence together with the Middlesex.

Warren and Coke had little information, but Warren took a more favourable view and sent in the 2nd Scots at 15:00, Coke then ordered the Dorsets to follow then countermanded the order as the leading company reached the top, as It was overcrowded. Confusion reigned as Warren sent guns up the hill without telling Thorneycroft, who with his men now exhausted and, lacking communication, ordered an evacuation at 2200hrs.(He had apparently been put in charge earlier, but Coke didn't know). Colonel Law kept the Dorsets just below the crest expecting orders to reoccupy the hill until 04:45, when he ordered a retirement. Warren praised the Dorsets for having gathered up ammunition, tools and rifles as they descended and said Law was the only officer to obey his orders.

Botha immediately reoccupied the hill and a brief truce was arranged to bury the dead.

Buller, next, forced the Boers off a strong position at Vaal Krantz, but the Boers then frustrated him yet again by taking an even stronger position further back.

So having tried everything else, he decided switch to attack from the east and take first Cingolo, then Monte Christo and Hlangwane using his superiority in guns followed by infantry "hammering and squeezing out the Boers step by step, hill by hill" as the historian Thomas Pakenham later put it. The Dorsets were used to prevent a counterattack at Mission and Hussar Hills and again in support of Barton's Brigade taking Hlangwane (14th -17th February). On the 20th our troops could enfilade the Boer trenches facing Colenso. Overnight the Boers fled across the river leaving flour, ammunition and bibles.

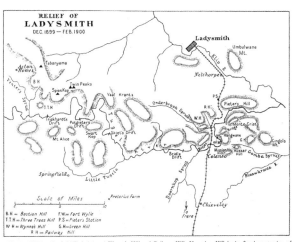

Terrace Hill (or Hart's Hill) is between Wynne's Hill and Railway Hill: Horseshoe Hill is the Southern portion of Wynne's Hill, Vertnek and Grobelaar Mountains are between the Tugela and the Onderbrook Spruit, about North of Bridle Drift.

Buller now crossed the Tugela 2 miles below the railway bridge near Colenso with the aim of advancing north taking Wynne's hill and Railway Hill. Botha however had once again rallied his men and developed effective defensive positions using the flat tops of kopjes and where the first crest was a false one.

The Dorsets, together with the Somersets, became involved in a fight at the Onderbrook Spruit which divided the two hills, and as they came under increasing fire, Coke decided to affect a difficult withdrawal under cover of darkness. The Dorsets were lucky to have only 1 killed and 9 wounded.

On the 22nd and 23rd February Buller took Wynne's Hill and Terrace Hill then completed the exercise by taking most of his guns back across the Tugela and on to Pieter's Hill making use of a creeping barrage. With the Boers pinned down by his newly sited artillery across the river Buller was able now to take Railway Hill more or less opposite, rendering the Boer defence unsustainable. Now Ladysmith could be freed. Colonel Law was mentioned in a dispatch for Tugela. Buller and Roberts (who had just taken Bloemfontein) could now concentrate on finishing off the Boers as they retreated towards Pretoria. Except that neither was ready to move. They both wanted to regroup after their exertions. Thus the Boers escaped. For the Dorsets there was an exhausting march after which the Divisional Ccommander called them "the best marching battalion he had seen".

The railway being out of action there was a shortage of supplies and a halt was called for the second division before the Boer position at Laing's Nek and the Fifth at Waschbank where a fresh draft of men and the Volunteer Company joined the Dorsets.

Buller now proposed to bypass the Laing's Nek position by crossing the Drakensberg at Botha's Pass. The Dorsets came up in support at Van Wyke's Hill, from where our guns could dominate the approaches to Botha's Pass. They were glad to leave however having spent a frosty night without blankets and grass and earth over their legs instead. Dorsets now led the advance towards Alleman's Nek where the

Boers had collected to impede our advance to Volkrust and Charlestown, Buller's next target.

Alleman's Nek is a pass across a branch off the Drakensberg, guarded by sharply sloping bluffs. By June 11th the Boers, had not had time to entrench this otherwise strong position. Our guns bombarded them for an hour from about 4000 yards, then the infantry, the 10th Brigade, attacked. The Dorsets with 4 companies, 2 of which were ordered to attack a conical hill which was in front of the main defence, and connected by a saddle; the supporting units on either side were slow to advance, but the Dorsets swept forward with fixed bayonets up the steep slope. The defenders retreated, some across the saddle, taking a pompom with them. Now heavy fire poured in from the front and the left to which our four companies replied including with some machine guns. Colonel Law having signalled this success, Buller ordered gunfire to bear on the Boers either side of the track. Meanwhile E Company tried to rush the saddle, 150yds, but were held by heavy fire. Law now ordered the supporting Dorset companies to advance round the south of the kopje, while F coy awaited development behind the northern spur of the kopje, until Law told them to fix bayonets and charge across the saddle. Though some fell as they came over the crest, the rest kept going across the saddle and up the steep slope beyond, E coy joining in as

they passed as well as some of the Volunteers. The Boers, about 200in number, now fled to their ponies. 12 Dorsets, men and NCOs, were killed or died of their wounds, 52 wounded, - modest losses.

A more vigorous pursuit might have allowed them to cut the railway north of Laing's Nek and thus intercept stores and a bigger haul of prisoners., but their success earned them plaudits and being the only battalion mentioned by Buller in his despatch on these operations. "A fine piece of work, grandly performed" was Cokes' verdict. Coke subsequently addressed them on the parade ground thanking them on Buller's behalf for their gallantry and determination,

The Dorsets were now ordered to guard the Volkrust-Zandspruit railway in what was to become the Guerrilla phase of the war.

Lord Roberts reached Pretoria on 5th June and won at Diamond Hill on 11th and 12th forcing the Boers away from the area of the capital enabling him almost to link with Buller using the Ladysmith- Standerton railway to connect with Johannesburg and Pretoria. Roberts then prepared to drive the Boers back on Koomati Poort by the end of September, thus to end the possibility of Boers keeping an army in the field. However, much to his disappointment, they would not surrender but instead took to guerrilla warfare, prolonging the war for nearly 2 years.

Now that the British had occupied all their main centres, with the Boers having no definite strategic targets to attack, it became more difficult to bring them to heel. They knew the ground far better than the British, who used inadequate maps and slow cumbersome convoys of ox-drawn wagons, all the while having to protect vulnerable railways which needed constant watchfulness. As the war developed, blockhouses linked by barbed wire fences were used to restrict Boer movement. This became monotonous; the only interest involved protecting convoys and escorting artillery, but not much fighting. Sometimes a company was asked to reconnoitre.

In mid- July Coke set the Dorsets to take Gras Kop, which they did very effectively. They were then sent to Ingogo, which was unappealing and unhealthy. Orders came in for the Dorsets to provide a company for the 5th Division Mounted Infantry (MI) – sent with Captains Butler (Adjutant), and Rowley and Lieutenant Hyslop. 70 men arrived on 27th September but this was offset by the Volunteers going home. There was even the occasional game of cricket with surrendered Boers taking part. Then the Dorsets joined a mobile column action making sweeps of territory to catch Boer units trying to escape the fences, often resulting in a haul of prisoners, cattle, sheep and wagons. Soon they were back to Kroonstad (September10th), a new draft of 80 men and a job at the Brandforth-Smaldeel railway with praise from Gen. Spense for their "efficiency, discipline and hard work". The Dorsets now had to hold 30 miles of line and 20 blockhouses with 600 men including the MI group formed from C Coy. The blockhouses were less than a mile apart connected by barbed wire each with 11 NCOs and men. The Dorsets spent 6 months, difficult and boring months, on this railway. With occasional attempts to get through the wire by Boers, usually beaten off to the Boers' loss

At this point the battalions detachment with the Fifth Division MI were involved in very heavy fighting in defeating a major attack on 2 outposts on

the border with Zululand, at Fort Prospect and Itala. Botha had intended an invasion of Natal to disrupt British operation by sucking in reinforcements from the Orange Free State, but these arrived more quickly than anticipated so he had to turn back and, as compensation attacked these two forts, mistakenly identified by Botha as poorly defended.

On 26th September 30 MI under Lieutenant Hyslop, who had come over from Fort Prospect with a convoy, were detained to help with an expected attack. Most of the Dorsets were at a post on the hill behind the fort which was overwhelmed in the small hours and were killed or captured, those taken being mostly wounded. In the fort below, the Boers' repeated attacks were repulsed with great determination despite being outnumbered 7:1. They rushed a trench but were driven off. As evening approached the tempo slackened and Boers withdrew in disappointment. Over 100 Boers were buried. The British losses, including prisoners were just over100. 5 Dorsets were killed. Hyslop and 6 men held one small trench tenaciously and at one point when the Boers had broken in, held them up while horses and ammunition were moved to safety. The Fifth Division Adjutant, Captain Butler, wounded in the shoulder, also distinguished himself. Lance Sergeant Wheeler was conspicuous for his gallantry.

Meanwhile at Fort Prospect the Boers, under Botha's respected Lieutenant Grobelaar, attacked at 4am approaching to within 20 yards of the perimeter under cover of the mist. However Captain Rowley had sited his defences well, the central keep using a machine gun to defend the trenches all around the fort as the mist lifted against the heavy and regular onslaughts of the Boers. The enemy withdrew after 12 hrs with 60 casualties to the garrison's 6, 1 Dorset private being killed. Capt Rowley was lucky to escape when a bullet went through his helmet, grazing his forehead. His bravery and effective leadership earned him a DSO, and CSM Young the DCM. It was Botha's severest defeat during the War and the Fifth Division received a special telegram of congratulation from Lord Kitchener.

March 1902 saw the battalion transferred to similar duties on the Delagoa Bay Line with the same monotony but with no battle casualties and only 6 from sickness.

The Peace was signed at Vereeniging on 31st May 1902. Orders were received for the battalion's return. Embarkation was on the SS German leaving Cape Town on the 24th September to disembark at Southampton on Oct 19th. They then returned to Portland, via Dorchester, receiving an enthusiastic welcome in both places.

With acknowledgements to the Keep Military Museum, Dorchester.

Determined Autumn

Kay Ennals MBE

I waited for the summer blooms
  to fade, with their perfumes and multiple hues,
I watched the grasses and arid ferns
  thrown into the fires to bum,
but, now, at last, I can invade -
    it's my time - I take my turn.

I make the hillsides drench with rain -
  and pavements shine like slate again!
My canopy I extend
  to spread with changing colours
    - gold, orange, and red.

I tell the winds to increase until raw -
  Lights fall dim to almost obscure---
Trees loose their branches -
  I've stripped to their core -
    I leave grey mists, and white crystals of hoar!

I mesmerise and fascinate---
  Autumn is me -
see what I create!
  This is my season -
    Winter can wait!

A Day in Dorchester

(Taken from Friends of the Congregational Library Newsletter – Autumn 2018)

John Thompson

The Friends' annual summer event was held in Dorchester on 2 June 2018. The sun shone as John Travell, vice President and organiser of the day, received Friends from the London train at the doors of the United Church, a dignified and beautiful presence in the town's main street and the surviving home of Dissent in a town once renowned for it. After coffee, a gathering of around forty were welcomed in turn by the mayor of Dorchester, dressed for summer but wearing his heavy chain of office, and Revd Stephen Woods, who was to be chairman for the day.

The morning lectures honoured two of Dorchester's well known Dissenters of earlier times. Revd David Cuckson spoke on William Benn and the Great Ejectment. Benn was rector of All Saints in the town and ejected, but not silenced, in 1662 by the Act of Uniformity. Known for his work among the poor and prisoners in the jail, he observed the spirit of the Five Mile Act by settling in a nearby village, but he continued to preach more widely in the county at risk of imprisonment and in Dorchester as well, before and after securing an Indulgence to teach there in 1672. He died in 1680 and is buried in All Saints churchyard (No-one asked if Tony Benn was a descendant. One can imagine some resemblance).

Mr Peter Mann, author of the history of the Dorchester United Church, and a former mayor of the town, then spoke on McClune Uffen. If Benn might be considered the earliest of Dorchester's Nonconformist ministers, McClune Uffen, who arrived in 1891, was prominently in his train. Through his preaching and outreach to other churches in the area, he led the revival and strengthening of the Congregationalist cause in the late nineteenth century heyday of Nonconformity. He stayed till 1911, "though sought by larger churches elsewhere". There are memorial windows to both men in the church, similarly designed, and facing one another on opposite sides of the church.

When we broke for lunch, the town crier of Dorchester arrived and took an eager party off to show them the main sights of the town. He too was dressed for summer but his voice told his office. When we reassembled, the afternoon was devoted to Thomas Hardy, Dorchester's best known son.

Revd AIan Argent, minister of Brixton Congregational Church and Research Fellow of Dr Williams' Library, spoke on Hardy's early years, in particular what he called his Congregational schooling. Hardy attended a National School, to which Nonconformists sent their children. His teacher was Isaac Last a deacon of the Congregational church. Hardy, called later by John Travell "an agnostic Anglican", retained a lasting respect for Last as great writers often do for the teachers who have influenced them. If progeny is any guide, Last was unusual: the school teacher's son became director of the Science Museum and his grandson head of an Oxford college. There are several references to Nonconformists in Hardy's novels. Dr Argent supplied a handout noting these and mentioned particularly those in "Far from the Madding Crowd" and "The Laodicean".
The last speaker was John Travell himself, but in his role as historian of the Society of Dorset Men and as a leading local commemorialist of all things Hardy. His title was the Casterbridge Congregationalists and his subject was the development from dramatic readings of Hardy's novels by members of the Dorchester Debating Society to the eventual formation of the Hardy Players. What was so remarkable, he said, giving illustrations, was that from the debating society's origins in the Congregational Church, (McClune Uffen in the chair), through to the formation of the Hardy Players and their fame and success, so many of the actors, men and women, amateurs all, were towns folk connected with that Church. Among the names was even one who went to Hollywood. *

After a light chapel tea, the sun still shining, we dispersed. Warm thanks were first expressed to our hosts, the United Church, the chairman Mr Woods, and Dr Travell, by the Friends' Chairman, Revd Jon Dean and the Congregational Librarian, Dr David Wykes.

A much fuller account of the remarkable story of The Casterbridge Congregationalists by Dr Travell appeared under that title in The Journal of the United Reformed History Society in the November 2009 issue and may be read by those who are not members of the History Society at the Library, 14 Gordon Square. (Full reference, Vol8, No 5, page 291).

Windswept Chesil Beach - *Hayne Russell*

"Come down to Dorset and visit this curiosity known as Chesil Beach. Fight your way up to the summit and stare out upon a waste of waters whipped to chaos by a westerly blow. Lean upon the wind, savour the salt upon your lips. There is nothing between you and the wild Atlantic."

Lost Dorset, The Villages & Countryside

In 1870 the General Post Office introduced a halfpenny stamp for postcards, later permitting the printing of an image on one

Bulbarrow

side, the writing and address on the other. Britain's High Street photographers wasted no time venturing out into the countryside in search of suitable subjects for picture postcards. By 1910 not far short of a billion were being handed over post office counters or pushed into pillar boxes. The halfpenny postcard was the equivalent of a modern text

Chetnole

message. Many were written in the morning, posted in the afternoon and delivered the following day – occasionally to someone in the same village. And they were delivered seven days a week, whatever the weather and

usually on foot. Bloxworth's 19th century postman, Frank Squire, is reckoned to have walked 165,000 miles during his 42 years of service.

I have long been fascinated by old photographs of Dorset. Indeed, my first book, A Dorset Camera 1855-1914, published in 1974, was an attempt to show Dorset from the first known photograph taken in the county to the outbreak of the First World

Chiswell

War. But the postcard, although originally a photograph, tells a very different story. For a start they were intended to be sold, usually in the village post office or nearest town, and were posed with some care. It is not difficult to imagine a gaggle of curious children gathering when the local photographer

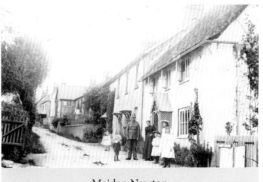

Maiden Newton

climbed down from his pony and trap and set up his tripod and plate camera in the middle of their village street. Many of those children, and their parents, what Thomas Hardy called the 'work folk', found their way into the finished postcards , putting a human

Portesham

face on what might otherwise have merely been a pleasant view of a village or row of cottages.

Choosing the 350 or so postcards in Lost Dorset was never going to be easy. It was not my intention to select only those of a place that is truly 'lost' – though many do. Nor have I included one of every village in Dorset: there are many for which no early postcard exists. What I have tried to do is choose those that give a sense of the way of life in rural Dorset in the late 19th and early 20th centuries – a period of upheaval and change as great as any in its history. There are postmen on their round, children playing outside now closed village schools – even a doctor and nurse attending a gypsy birth on Bulbarrow. Waggons, carts, and Dorset's first motorcars trundle country lanes that are now its main roads. Church, chapel and the rough and tumble of

electioneering were all suitable subjects for the photographer, as were Dorset's craftsmen – its thatchers, hurdlemakers, blacksmiths and wheelwrights. There are country fairs and meets of Dorset's four hunts. Both the Kaiser and Edward VII pose for the camera. One farmer stands amidst his pigs, another his cheeses. And the list could lengthen.

But I write this shortly before the centenary of the end of the First World War. Amongst the postcards is one of young volunteers for the Dorset Regiment lined up outside a Marnhull pub. Lost Dorset is a portrait of a way of life that existed when they left to fight – in India, the Middle East and on the Western Font – but like a fading photograph was already disappearing when the survivors finally came home.

LOST DORSET: The Villages and Countryside 1880-1920, by David Burnett, is a large format 200 page hardback, price £20, and is available in all bookshops throughout Dorset or direct from the publishers at www.dovecotepress.com

Puddletown

The War to End All Wars

by Graham Allard

It is hard to imagine that just 100 years ago this year 2018, that the war to end all wars was finally over. This horrific war having killed millions, and injured many more young men, was to eventually cease at last. This enabled the lucky ones who had survived the tragedies to return once more to their loved ones. The war had started in August 1914 and finally after four years an armistice was agreed and signed in a railway carriage at Compiegne at five o'clock in the morning on the eleventh of November 1918. The actual ceasefire took place at the agreed time of eleven o'clock. So at the eleventh hour of the eleventh day, of the eleventh month 1918 the guns fell silent.

Who were all these soldiers that were killed? Well we certainly do not know them all by name but one can easily find out their names today, for from the largest city to the smallest of hamlets each will have a war memorial of some sort showing the names of those young men who laid down their lives for us. Almost all families will have someone who was sadly killed or injured during this terrible war. I personally have two relatives in my family history who were killed in action during this war. One on my maternal side of the family was 14704 Private William Langmaid, 30th Coy; Machine Gun Corps who died aged 25 on 24 April 1918 and on my paternal side with a Dorset connection was 18656 Private Henry (Harry) William Wright, 1st Battalion of the Dorsetshire Regiment. He was killed on the 30th September 1918, just forty two days before the armistice was signed, whilst attacking Pontruet in France alongside the 46th (North Midland) Division. He and several other brave men of the 1st Dorset's were mowed down and killed by heavy fire from German machine guns, such a waste and such a sacrifice. Pte Harry Wright left a wife, Gertrude, and his son George Henry, who was only born in 1915 at Coryates near Portesham. Pte Wright is still remembered to this day however on the Weymouth War Memorial, he is the last, but certainly not least as the names are written alphabetically. It is most fitting in its way as it was Weymouth where he had enlisted out of duty for King and Country in 1914.

I looked for an appropriate verse to finish off this article as my small contribution to the anniversary of the war ending and I came across, The Soldier. This was the last sonnet that Rupert Chawner Brooke wrote in his series of war sonnets that dealt with the death and accomplishments of a soldier in WW1. What I had not realised though was that Brooke had actually written this last sonnet whilst being stationed at Blandford Camp, Dorset in 1914. He was accommodated at the time in Hood Lines and the address can be seen on the top of the paper on which he actually wrote his last sonnet.

Hood Battalion
2nd Naval Brigade
Blandford, Dorset

The Soldier

If I should die, think only this of me:
That there's some corner of a foreign field
That is for ever England. There shall be
In that rich earth a richer dust concealed;
A dust whom England bore,
shaped, made aware;
Gave, once, her flowers to love,
her ways to roam,
A body of England's,
breathing English air,
Washed by the rivers,
blest by suns of home.

And think, this heart,
all evil shed away,
A pulse in the eternal mind, no less
Gives somewhere back
the thoughts by England given;
Her sights and sounds;
dreams happy as her day;
And laughter,
learnt of friends and gentleness
In hearts at peace,
under an English heaven.

The life story of Rupert Chawner Brooke, as short as it was due to the war, dying at the age of only 27, is quite fascinating and I feel sure known to many of you. I will not therefore do a summary pen picture of his life. What I will say though is that he was at Blandford Camp Dorset in 1914, accommodated in Hood Lines as he had been commissioned into the Royal Navy Volunteer Reserve as a temporary Sub-Lieutenant. Blandford Camp at this time was the Royal Naval Division Headquarters and training camp. Incidentally the Royal Naval Division's Battalions and also the encampments within Blandford Camp were allocated the names of Nelson, Benbow, Drake, Anson, Hawke, Howe, Collingwood and Hood. Apart from taking part in the Royal Navy Divisions' Antwerp expedition. in October 1914, Sub-Lt Rupert Brooke sailed with the British Mediterranean Expeditionary Force on 28 February 1915 for Gallipoli. Sadly on the voyage he developed sepsis from a mosquito bite and was

transferred onto the French hospital ship Duguay-Trouin, which was moored in a bay off the Greek Island of Skyros. At 4.46 in the afternoon Rupert Brooke died. Insert photo Service Record. The ship had been ordered to sail, so his body was buried at 11.00 that night in a peaceful, fragrant olive grove on the Island of Skyros with a wooden cross. How apt his final sonnet, 'that there's some corner of a foreign field'. His grave still remains there today with a permanent memorial. The wooden cross is now with a collection of other memorials belonging to old Rugbeians at Rugby School, which he attended in his youth.

"They grow not old
As we that are left grow old.
Age shall not weary them
Nor the years condemn.
At the going down of the sun
And in the morning,
We will remember them."

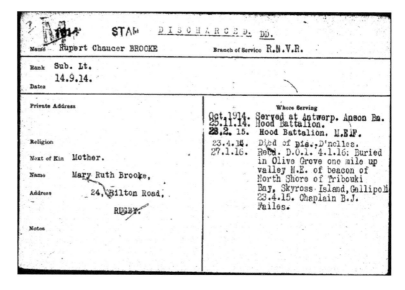

George Mills and Elsie Guy

Philip Knott

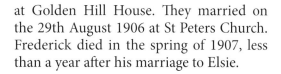

Research into the lives of the men from Stourton Caundle, who served in the armed forces during the two world wars, has revealed some poignant stories, none more so than that of Elsie Guy and George Mills. Elsie, born in 1886, was one of eight sisters. They were the daughters of James

at Golden Hill House. They married on the 29th August 1906 at St Peters Church. Frederick died in the spring of 1907, less than a year after his marriage to Elsie.

George, the son of Mr and Mrs John Mills, living at Felsham, near Bury St Edmunds in Suffolk, was born in 1883. George was a Bands-man in the 2nd Battalion the Suffolk Regiment, based at Stanhope Lines Aldershot at the time of his marriage to Elsie. The Suffolk Regiment formed part of the British Expeditionary Force, landing at Le Harve on the 17th of August 1914. The Regiment was soon in action at The Battle of Mons and the subsequent retreat, after suffering

and Amelia Guy, living at The Red House Brunsells Knapp Farm.

The wedding of Elsie Florence Guy and George Ernest Mills.
Back Row-Ethel Mills, Daisy Guy, George Mills (Bridegroom), Elsie Guy (Bride), William (Bill) Guy, May Guy (nee Mills) the brother of George and wife of William), Freda Guy and Beatrice Guy.
Front row- Amelia Guy, Doris Guy, Stella Guy, Olive Guy and James Guy

The wedding of Elsie Florence Guy and George Ernest Mills took place on August 16th 1913 at St Peters Church. Elsie was a widow having previously married Frederick Henry Cook a postman, born in 1886. Frederick was the elder brother of Frank Cook the local builder, who lived

heavy casualties at The Battle of Le Cateau on the 26th August 1914. At the Battle of Le Cateau the Regiment was almost totally decimated as a fighting unit, after over eight hours of incessant fighting. The 2nd Battalion was gradually outflanked but would still not surrender. Those remaining alive, and who failed to escape the German entrapment were taken captive, spending the next four years as prisoners of war and not returning home until Christmas Day 1918.

George was one the few from the battalion who survived this battle but was killed in action just 18 days later on the 13th September 1914, just over a year after his marriage to Elsie and less than four months after the birth of their daughter Yvonne, on the 22nd May 1914. His body was not recovered and he is commemorated on the La Ferte-Sous-Jouarre Memorial. The memorial commemorates nearly 4,000 officers and men of the British Expeditionary Force who died in August, September and the early part of October 1914 and who have no known grave.

It is impossible to imagine the heartache and despair the news of George's death must have caused Elsie, leaving her a widow for the second time just one year into a marriage, with a 3month old daughter who would never know her father. George is commemorated on the war memorial at Felsham, with the following citation in the Roll of Honour. Bandsman 5646, 2nd Battalion Suffolk Regiment who was killed in action on the 13th September 1914, aged 30. Born Felsham, enlisted Guernsey. Son of Mr. and Mrs. John Mills, of Felsham, Bury St. Edmund's; husband of Elsie Florence Mills, of The Red House, Waterloo, Stalbridge, Dorset. No known grave. Inside the church is a plaque unveiled on the 2nd January 1921 by his wife Elsie and daughter Yvonne.

Private William Guy, 5th Battalion Dorsetshire Regiment, brother of Elsie, and the only son of James and Amelia Guy, was born in Stourton Caundle in 1892. Bill had eight sisters. The family moved to a newly built house at Brunsells Knapp Farm in 1902. The 5th Battalion Dorsetshire Regiment was formed at Dorchester in the August of 1914 and Bill enlisted on the 26th August. The Battalion trained at Belton, Grantham, Lincolnshire prior to moving south in 1915. The battalion sailed from Liverpool on the 3rd July 1915, going via Mudros to land at Suvla Bay Gallipoli at 10.30pm on the 6th August 1915, under the cover of darkness, along with the Queens Own Dorset Yeomanry and the two Devon Yeomanry Regiments. Most of the troops were in action for the first time and in common with the other units learned the hard lessons of warfare at a terrible cost.

William received a gunshot wound to the leg at Suva bay on the following day. The following extract is from a letter to his family dated 13th August 1915 with no mention of the gunshot wound. "Just a postcard to let you know I am al-right up to the present. We have been in the firing line all week and are now come back from the frontline for a couple of days rest, but I think it is most likely that we will go up again tonight. We have had a rough time the Turks started banging at us before we landed but when we got ashore they didn't half run for about 4 miles. I expect you will have seen by the newspapers that we have done fairly well. Bill is still al-right on machine guns but twelve of them got knocked out on the first day".

William returned to England to receive treatment and convalesce from the leg injury as the result of the gunshot wounds sustained on the first day of the Suvla Bay landings. While recuperating in hospital he completed a silk work, featuring the regimental cap badge, with the flags of the allies, which is now on display, along with his medals, in the Dorsetshire Regiment's museum.

William Guy, with the surviving seven of his eight sisters, from left to right- Beatrice, Freda, Doris, William (Bill), Elsie, Daisy, Olive, Stella. Bill married May Mills in March 1916 at Hendon. May, born at Felsham Suffolk in 1890, was the sister of George Mills, who married Bill's sister Elsie in 1913.

Bill married May Mills, brother of George, in March 1916 at Hendon. William and May had one daughter Dorothy born December 1916 and three sons William (Jim) born in 1918, Vernon in 1922 and George in 1929. Following the death of May on the 4th May 1938, her elder sister Ethel, born in 1885 at Felsham, moved to Brunsells Knapp, as the housekeeper for William, his daughter and three sons. Ethel was a widow, having lost her husband in the war. William and Ethel married in 1938. William died on the 31st October 1957 at the age of 65. A number of Bill's grandchildren are still living in and around Stourton Caundle including Robert, son of George, who operates an agricultural contracting business based at Brunsells Knapp Farm.

County Dinner 2018

Hayne Russell

Members of the Society together with their wives, partners and guests gathered at the George Albert Hotel, Warden Hill, Evershot on Saturday 27th October for the annual County Dinner. The tradition of holding this dinner has now been maintained for some 114 years or so, firstly of course in London and from the 1960's in the County. However, although numbers attending sadly continue to decline, those who did attend this dinner were fulsome in their praise of the food, service and the speaker. Our President Lord Fellowes, together with Lady Emma, welcomed everyone on arrival. We were joined this year, once again, by the Lord Lieutenant, the High Sheriff and our guest speaker the Rt Hon Michael Gove MP. This year we were also pleased to welcome Dr Jon Murden Director of the County Museum to whom we presented our Dorset Award. The President, in making the award said that Dr Murden had been responsible for changing the face of the Dorset County Museum, He had brought both the highly successful Pharaoh exhibition and "Dippy the dinosaur" to the museum and secured funding of £11.4million which will enable the museum to expand and be transformed.. The Society believed that his contribution and achievements had been such that he was a worthy recipient of the award. In reply Dr Murden thanked the Society but paid tribute to his team of helpers at the museum, without whose support this could not have been achieved.

The President with his guests. *Photograph: Trevor B Matthews*

The Blue Vinny cheese was tasted and toasted by the President in the traditional manner and the following dialect message of loyalty to HM The Queen was read by member Noel Spreadbury and the reply by the President.

"Yer Majesty - Tis thick time agin' when we members o' The Zociety o' Darzet Men voregather ver our yerly veast at t' Jarge Albert 'Otel, down yer in Darzet. We d'zend yer majesty our 'artvelt greetins an' expression o' loyal zupport. May you be long spared t' reign auver us an' guide us t'peace an' prosperity" I d'bide yer Majesty's vaithvul zarvent Julian Fellowes The Lard Vellowes o' West Stafford, Prezident o' The Zociety o' Darzet Men.

Our guest speaker the Rt Hon Michael Gove MP as Minister for the Department of Environment, Food and Rural Affairs found no difficulty in resonating with the members, many if not all of whom, are connected with the land and sea in this rural county of Dorset. Further, he is a most able speaker who held his audience throughout. Against the backdrop of our Society flag, he took his theme from our motto "Who's a fear'd" which he illustrated with two (hopefully apocryphal) stories of Dorset men who were not feared to offer the truth to no lesser a personage than Lloyd George who years ago was campaigning on behalf of Freddy Guest, an ex President of the Society.

As a leading figure in the saga of Brexit, it was inevitable that he should touch on this subject but he did so with consummate ease and in a manner that, whilst acknowledging there were two sides to the argument, did not offend either of them, Finally, asking for questions from the floor he answered with ease and authority.

A very successful evening was brought to a close by the Chairman proposing the toast to the President who then thanked all for attending and wished them a safe journey home.

Winterborne Houghton's Witch - *Hayne Russell*
Incredibly just before WW2 a doctor in practise in the Blandford district reported that all the illness in the village of Winterborne Houghton was attributed by the inhabitants to a woman who lived there who just happened to be a seventh child of a seventh child and therefore was a witch!

Is this one of Dippy's friends on the Jurassic Coast?
Durdle Door. *Photograph by Steve Belasco*

IN MEMORIAM

The President and Members mourn the loss of the following worthy fellow Dorsets and tender their sincere sympathy to their relatives.

MICHAEL SPAVINS (West Lulworth)	Member	Dec 2017
ANDREW WEEKS (Swanage)	Life Member	23/11/17
GEORGE WILLEY (Swanage)	Member	Dec 2017
ADRIAN DOWNTON (Dorchester)	Member	24/12/17
DR GRAHAM ELMES (Wareham)	Member	24/12/17
ALAN COOPER BA FRSA (Wimborne St Giles) *(Regular contributor to the Year Book)*	Life Member	Dec 2017
REV NORMAN BEGGS (Dewlish)	Member	10/2/18
MICHEL HOOPER-IMMINS (Weymouth) *(Committee member and Newsletter Editor)*	Member	20/2/18
JOHN DENNIS (Swanage)	Member	10/1/18
DAVID FOYLE (Winterborne Houghton)	Vice President	2017
ROY GAINEY (Weymouth)	Member	21/1/18
ARTHUR SMITH (Bridport)	Member	9/1/18
DR JOHN CROSS (Poole)	Member	3/11/18
SIDNEY SAUNDERS-SYMES (Stalbridge)	Member	17/12/17
ROBERT CAREW (Winterborne Whitchurch)	Member	22/4/17
MAJ GEN C.SHORTIS CB CBE (Shaftesbury)	Life Member	2017
E (BOB) MANNING (Dorchester)	Member	10/7/18
PETER RIDLER (Bridport)	Member	June 2018
PHILIP JAMES (Dorchester)	Member	21/7/18
JOHN HARDING (Wimborne)	Life Member	3/6/18
D CURLING (Preston)	Member	12/6/18
DAVID ELLIOTT (Blandford)	Member	4/4/18
IAN BISHOP (Wimborne)	Member	31/10/15
JOHN GRANT (Dorchester)	Member	20/8/18
F LITTLE (Gillingham)	Member	2018

RULES OF THE SOCIETY

(Incorporating the alterations passed at the Special General Meeting of the Society
held on 23rd April, 2017)

NAME

1.   The name of the Society shall be "THE SOCIETY OF DORSET MEN."

OBJECTS

2.   The objects of the Society shall be:

To make and to renew personal friendships and associations, to promote good fellowship among Dorset men wherever they may reside, to foster love of County and pride in its history and traditions, and to assist by every means in its power, natives of Dorset who may stand in need of the influence and help of the Society.

MEMBERSHIP

3.   The Society shall consist of a President, Deputy Presidents and Honorary Deputy Presidents if desired, Life Members and Members.

QUALIFICATIONS

4.   Any person connected with the County of Dorset by birth, descent, marriage, property or past or present residence in the County, shall be eligible to be elected to membership.

MODE OF ELECTION AND TERMINATION OF MEMBERSHIP

5. (i)   The names of all candidates for election shall be submitted to the Committee, who shall have full power to deal with the same.

  (ii)   The Committee shall have power to remove from the list of Members the name of any Member whose subscription is in arrear for 12 months.

 (iii) The Committee may also at any time in their discretion terminate the membership of any person without furnishing reasons for their action, in which event a pro rata proportion of the subscription will be returned.

SUBSCRIPTIONS

6.   The Subscriptions to the Society shall be:

  (a)   Life Member - one payment £200.00

  (b)   Ordinary Member- per annum (payable on the 1st October) . . .£15.00
These subscriptions will apply whether the member is residing in the UK or overseas.

OFFICERS

7.   The Officers of the Society shall be:
        Chairman, Deputy Chairman, Honorary Treasurer, Honorary Editor,
        Honorary Secretary, Honorary Membership Secretary and Honorary
        Newsletter Editor and they, together with the President and Deputy
        Presidents, if desired, shall be elected at the Annual General Meeting each
        year.
        The Committee shall have the power to fill any vacancy arising during the
        year.

COMMITTEE

8. (i) The Society shall be governed by a Committee not exceeding twenty in
        number, to be elected from the Members at the Annual General Meeting.
        In addition, the Officers of the Society shall be ex-officio Members of the
        Committee. Seven shall form a quorum.
  (ii) The Committee may delegate any of their powers to a Sub-Committee.
 (iii) The Committee shall retire annually, but shall be eligible for re-election.
  (iv) Not less than twelve days before the Annual General Meeting the Honorary
        Secretary shall send to every Member a notice of the Meeting. The Notice
        shall also intimate to the Members that any two Members may nominate
        one or more Members for election as Officers or to the Committee, and that
        such nomination must be sent to the Honorary Secretary not less than four
        days before the Meeting.
   (v) The Committee shall have power to fill any vacancy arising during the year.

MEETINGS

9. (i) The Annual General Meeting will be held on a date to be decided by the
        Committee.
  (ii) The Committee may at any time convene a Special General Meeting and
        they shall do so within six weeks of the Honorary Secretary receiving a
        written requisition signed by not less than twenty Members. Members
        requiring such Meeting shall state in their requisition the subject or subjects
        to be discussed, and the resolution or resolutions to be submitted thereat.
        Notice of the date and place of all Special Meetings shall be sent by the
        Honorary Secretary to each Member twelve clear days prior to the date
        fixed for the holding of a Meeting, and such notice shall state the object or
        purpose for which such Meeting is convened.

BOOKS AND RECORDS TO BE KEPT

10.   Proper Books of Account, showing all receipts and expenditure, shall be
        kept by the Honorary Treasurer, and the Honorary Secretary shall record
        and keep Minutes of all Meetings of the Committee. The Membership
        Secretary shall record and maintain a list of members.

EXAMINATION OF ACCOUNTS

11.   At each Annual General Meeting two Examiners shall be elected to examine the Accounts of the Society for presentation to the members at the next Annual General Meeting.

ALTERATION OF RULES

12.   These Rules may be amended, altered, or varied by a majority of two-thirds of the Members voting at a Special General Meeting.

COMMITTEE CHAIRMAN:
STUART ADAM
Court Barton, West Bagber, Taunton, TA4 3EQ. Tel: (01823) 432076
Email: stu.adam@outlook.com

MEMBERS OF COMMITTEE:
D BEAZER, T CRABBE, S CREGAN, A HUTCHINGS,
A PROWSE, J ROUSELL, S WOODCOCK

OFFICERS:

Hon. Secretary: H. C. RUSSELL,
34 Brunel Drive, Preston, Weymouth, DT3 6NX. Tel: (01305) 833700
E-mail: hrussell@gotadsl.co.uk

Hon. Assistant and Membership Secretary: P. LUSH
25 Maumbury Square, Dorchester, DT1 1TY. Tel: (01305) 260039
E-mail: peterlush3@hotmail.com

Hon. Treasurer: I. MORTON
1 Wainwright Close, Preston, Weymouth, DT3 6NS. Tel: 01305 832722
E-mail: ianvalmorton@fsmail.net

Hon. Editor "The Dorset Year Book": S. WILLIAMS
41 Everest Road, Weymouth, DT4 0DQ. Tel 07805 884786
E-mail: selles.macuquina@btinternet.com

Hon. Newsletter Editor: J NEIMER
Rowan House, 26 Corfe Road, Stoborough, BH20 5AB Tel: 01929 552622
E.mail john@jandpneimer.plus.com

Society Archivist and Historian: REV. DR. J. TRAVELL
44 Cornwall Road, Dorchester, DT1 1RY. Tel: 01305 264681
E-mail: johntravell@outlook.com